Methods and Models
in Demography

Three fundamental precautions must be taken before proceding to the analysis and interpretation of demographic statistics. First, it is necessary to have a clear and precise understanding of the descriptive terms that are used. Second, the quality of the observed data should be ascertained . . . .. Third, in the case of data that have been derived by computation, the process should be studied critically.

(Spiegelman 1968: 6)

Methods and Models in Demography

Colin Newell

The Guilford Press
New York

Published in the USA and Canada by The Guilford Press,
A Division of Guilford Publications, Inc.,
72 Spring Street, New York, New York 10012

Library of Congress Catalog Call Number: 88-45079

ISBN 0-89862-783-4

Printed in Great Britain

Contents

List of tables

List of figures

'Exercise' and 'answer' tables

Acknowledgements

Many teachers, colleagues and friends will recognise, in this book, their own ideas, explanations and examples. I hope that they will accept my numerous unacknowledged plagiarisms as a compliment to the way they taught and advised me.

Special thanks are due to my wife, Marie-Louise, a fellow demographer, who helped with much of the calculating, revising, editing and proof-reading as well as providing many ideas, suggestions and, of course, support and encouragement. Thanks are also due to all the staff of the Centre for Population Studies at the London School of Hygiene and Tropical Medicine, especially Sandra Eldridge without whom the chapter on nuptiality would have been much the poorer.

The origins of this book were a set of lecture notes for a course on formal demography, given by me since 1981, for students attending the MSc Medical Demography course at the London School of Hygiene and Tropical Medicine. In 1983 these notes were turned into a typescript entitled 'A Manual of Formal Demography'. The Manual went through three editions in four years, and this book is effectively the fourth edition. It was written in a deliberately informal style, using the minimum of algebra, proofs and theory, with the aim of teaching formal demography as a set of practical, useful tools. This, together with the exercises, should, hopefully, make it possible to use the book as a self-teaching aid, as well as a conventional textbook.

I am grateful to the following for permission to reproduce copyright material: Academic Press for three tables from A.J. Coale and P. Demeny (1983) *Regional Model Life Tables and Stable Populations, Second Edition*; The Population Investigation Committee, London School of Economics for Table 1.4.1 of N.H. Carrier and J. Hobcraft (1973) *Demographic Estimation for Developing Societies*; the editor of *Population Index* for a table from A.J. Coale and T.J. Trussell (1974) in *Population Index* 40.

Colin Newell
July 1987

Part I

Basic formal demography

1 Introduction

Formal demography and population studies

The English edition of the excellent *Multilingual Demographic Dictionary* (van de Walle 1982) defines 'demography' as 'the scientific study of human populations, primarily with respect to their size, their structure and their development'. But all such definitions, whether as broad as this or narrower, produce many anomalies whereby some topics commonly thought of as part of demography are omitted, while many others, which normally fall within the realms of sociology, economics, statistics or whatever, are included. Moreover, it is an arid exercise since almost all of demography can be regarded, to a greater or lesser extent, as anthropology, medicine, geography or whatever, and all demographers also consider themselves to be partly anthropologists, doctors, geographers and so on, depending on their original training and interests. Indeed, it is exactly this strongly interdisciplinary nature of demography which makes it such an interesting, fertile and productive subject.

Therefore, rather than concentrating on its fringes and boundaries, consider its core. For some there is a theoretical central focus to the subject with 'Demographic Transition Theory' at its very heart. For many, though, there is a more practical central focus of demography, comprising a set of techniques by which data collected in censuses, surveys and vital registration systems about age, sex, births, deaths, migrations, marriages and so on are described, summarised and manipulated. These tools are collectively known as 'formal demography'. The subject is defined by the *Multilingual Demographic Dictionary* as 'the treatment of quantitative relations among demographic phenomena in abstraction from their association with other phenomena', particularly when applied to the size and structure of the population. This is contrasted with the broader term 'population studies' which 'also includes the treatment of relations between demographic events and social economic or other phenomena'.

Mainly in the interests of conciseness, this book only rarely, and then briefly, strays into the field of population studies. It should be regarded as no more than a tool-box containing the tools commonly employed by demographers and others in their 'scientific study of human populations'. Although it describes what these tools are, and how they are used, it says very little about the results they produce. That is the realm of population studies.

The main features of formal demography are thus that it is fundamentally descriptive or analytic rather than explanatory in nature, and that it is concerned with demographic phenomena in isolation, not with their interaction with economic, social and other phenomena. In other words, it tries to answer questions which begin 'What is . . .', rather than questions which begin 'Why . . .'. Note that many people who are not demographers ask these 'What is . . .' questions, and use the answers to them. They include, in particular, planners in government and service industries as well as academics. Perhaps the largest exercise which tries to answer some of these questions in nearly all countries of the world is the population census. This, together with the two other main sources of data used in demography, namely surveys and vital registration systems, comprise the subject-matter of Chapter 2.

The book is divided into two parts. The former, comprising Chapters 1 to 9, covers the topics conventionally found in introductory textbooks of demographic methods such as Barclays (1958), Spiegelman (1968), Pressat (1972), Shryock and Siegel (1976), Cox (1976) and Pollard, Yusuf and Pollard (1981). These topics are the basic measures used in the analysis of fertility, mortality, nuptiality and migration. Reference is made to these texts wherever more detailed or rigorous coverage, or a good alternative explanation, is available. More advanced texts such as Wunsch and Termote (1978) and Keyfitz (1968) are cited where appropriate. Some attempt is also made to note where nomenclature or notations differ, since this is a frequent cause of confusion.

The most frequently cited text is that of Shryock and Siegel (1976), which is large and quite comprehensive, despite being a condensed edition of the huge, two-volume work *The Methods and Materials of Demography*, published in 1971 by the United States Bureau of the Census. It has, during the last decade, become the standard reference work on formal demography, even supplanting Barclay's classic, but still useful, *Techniques of Population Analysis* (1958), which was for so long the bible of formal demographers, and which, remarkably, remains in print, unrevised, nearly thirty years after it was published.

The second part of the book, entitled 'Demographic Models' covers less well-trodden ground, except for Chapter 11 on Stable populations and Chapter 15 on projections. The application of models, especially model life tables, has become so frequent and widespread in demography in the past fifteen or twenty years that they now have to be included in any good demographer's 'tool-box'. The models described are those which are in common use for demographic estimation, and thus tend to describe the patterns of mortality and fertility in terms of age. Models used for more theoretical or explanatory purposes, such as Henry's panmitic components model of nuptiality (Henry 1972b), or the wide range of models of human fecundability, are not covered. Nor is there any mention of models of the migration process.

The remainder of this chapter begins with a very brief discussion of the historical background to formal demography. There follows an introduction to some of the very basic concepts and measures used in formal demography, covering rates, ratios and proportions; and types of demographic data. Then there is a discussion of the 'Basic Demographic Equation' and some problems of defining a population. Lastly, there is a short consideration of Demographic Transition Theory which emphasises particularly the strong interrelationships between mortality, fertility, migration and population structure.

Historical background to formal demography

Prior to the late nineteenth century, the development of what is now known as formal demography is essentially the story of the evolution of the life table as a means of analysing and presenting mortality data. This process was driven largely by the commercial interests of the actuarial profession. Before 1900 the topics of fertility, nuptiality, migration and age structure were rarely studied with any degree of mathematical sophistication, though one famous exception is Euler's invention in 1760 of the concept of the Stable population. Euler's remarkable achievement occurred some 150 years before Lotka, who is generally regarded as the father of Stable Population Theory, published his first paper. The original paper is reproduced by Smith and Keyfitz (1977) in their invaluable collection of, and commentary on, dozens of important historical papers tracing the development of mathematical demography.

The earliest tables which can be said to bear any resemblance to modern life tables date back to Roman times, but the first real demographic work was that of John Graunt, whose analysis, in 1662, of London's 'Bills of Mortality' included the production of a life table of sorts, though the rather obscure method of calculation, discussed at length by Glass (1950), is very different, to say the least, from that described in Chapter 6. The other important development in the late seventeenth century includes that of Edmund Halley (1693), Astronomer Royal of comet fame. He calculated, for the city of Breslau (now Wroclaw in Polish Silesia), the first life table based upon actual numbers of deaths by age.

There were few important developments in the eighteenth century, but in the early nineteenth Milne (1815) is generally credited with formalising the conventional calculation and presentation of the life table as we know it today. Thus, by 1841, when William Farr, the famous Victorian Registrar-General of England, started producing the decennial series of English life tables, which continue to the present, the life table was recognisably similar to its present form. By 1900 the distinctive notation used for life tables today had become established.

After 1900 the major developments in formal demography are first attributable to Alfred Lotka, who in three papers totalling just thirteen pages (Lotka 1907; Lotka 1922; Sharpe and Lotka 1911), developed the mathematics of a Stable population, showing how a closed population tends, if the schedules of age-specific mortality and fertility remain constant, to develop along a predictable path to a final, fixed age-structure. Later, in 1925, Lotka, with Louis Dublin (Dublin and Lotka 1925), incorporated the concepts of 'intrinsic' (or 'true') rates into the theory.

In the field of fertility analysis, the Total Fertility and Net Reproduction Rates, which had been developed by German demographers in the late nineteenth century, became widely used largely through the work of Kuczynski (1935). Cohort analysis of fertility data only really became widely used after the Second World War, especially in American fertility surveys, the classic first application there being by Whelpton (1954).

Another post-war development is that of Hajnal's Singulate Mean Age at Marriage (Hajnal 1953). This is noteworthy as the first of many demographic 'indirect' techniques whereby information on one topic (here proportions single by age) is used to estimate another (here the mean age at first marriage).

The first widely used demographic models (if Lotka's Stable population is excluded) were the model life tables published by the United Nations (1955, 1956) and described on pages 131–4 below. These were followed by the 'Princeton regional model life tables' of Coale and Demeny (1966), whose continued importance and usefulness is attested by the publication of a second, extended edition in 1983. For a description of these models, see Chapter 12 below. The mortality models were followed, also from Coale and his Princeton colleagues, by somewhat similar models of nuptiality and marital fertility (Coale 1971; Coale and McNeil 1972; Coale and Trussell 1974). Along parallel but quite different lines, Brass and his colleagues in London were developing their 'relational' models of mortality (Brass 1971) and fertility (Brass 1981), whereby age-patterns of fertility or mortality are related, via mathematical transformations, to a standard pattern. These are described in Chapters 13 and 14 below.

By the 1980s the main areas of advance in formal demography are in the areas of model building, much of it made possible by the ever-increasing power and sophistication of computing and related statistical and database tools. An excellent example of this is the multi-regional demographic modelling of Rogers (1975) and others which uses accounting techniques within a framework of matrix algebra.

Demographic measures

Nearly all demographic data take the form of frequencies of either qualitative or discrete (i.e. counted) quantitative variables. Only rarely are continuous (i.e. measured) quantitative variables used. The statistics used to manipulate such data are rates, ratios and proportions. They thus constitute the most basic tools of formal demography. Essentially, they enable comparison by eliminating differences due to population size.

A *ratio* is simply any number divided by any other number. An example is the Sex Ratio — the number of males per 100 females (see p. 27)

A _proportion_ is a special type of ratio in which the numerator is included in the denominator. That is, it has the form:

$$\text{Proportion} = \frac{x}{x + y}.$$

For example, the proportion of the population that is female is the number of females divided by the total number of males and females together. Note that a proportion can only range from 0.0 to 1.0. It is, though, very common to express proportions as percentages simply by multiplying by 100, in which case the range of possible values is from 0 per cent to 100 per cent. At school a proportion was often called a 'fraction'. In algebraic notation, a proportion is conventionally denoted by p.

The term _rate_ is used very loosely in demography (as elsewhere) and this can cause confusion. Strictly, the numerator of a rate is a number of events, such as births or deaths, occurring during a period of time. The denominator is the number of 'person-years of exposure to risk' experienced by the population during the period under consideration. The crucial point is that some time period has to be specified.

In demography rates are most frequently calculated for periods of one year. This means that the total number of person-years of exposure to risk can usually be approximated by the population at mid-year. To understand this, consider the calculation of an annual death rate. Each person surviving for the whole year will contribute one year to the total number of years of exposure to risk, while those dying during the year will contribute only a fraction of a year. This fraction will be, on average, half a year if people die evenly throughout the year. The total number of years of exposure to risk arrived at by adding these fractions to the total contributed by those who survived is the same as taking the average population total during the year and letting each person in that average contribute a whole year of exposure. And, since the average population can normally be approximated very closely by the population total at mid-year, the mid-year population can, under most circumstances, be used for calculating annual rates. This is why government statistical services produce annual population estimates relating to the middle of each year, rather than the beginning or end.

It should be reiterated that many measures which are commonly called 'rates' in demography are strictly ratios, proportions or more complex indices. For example, the 'Literacy Rate' is just the proportion of the population that is literate while the 'Crude Birth Rate' is really a ratio since it includes in its denominator the old, children and males, none of whom are at risk of giving birth. The Total Fertility Rates (see p. 41) is more complex than a normal rate.

The Basic Demographic Equation

This is one of the most fundamental relationships in formal demography. It can be written as:

$$P_{t+1} = P_t + B - D + IN - OUT.$$

In words, the population of an area at time $t + 1$ is just the population at time t plus the number of births between t and $t + 1$, less the number of deaths, plus the number of migrants entering the area, less the number leaving. The difference between the numbers of births and deaths gives the 'natural increase', while the difference between the numbers of migrants in and out gives the 'net migration'. Thus the equation can be written as:

Population change = Natural increase + Net migration.

In some parts of the world, population change is dominated by the rate of natural increase, in others net migration is more important, and in some they are of roughly equal importance.

Sometimes the Basic Demographic Equation is called the 'Balancing Equation', yet it is a characteristic of the equation that it never balances exactly. Taking the population at one census and adding to it the natural increase and net migration that occurs during the inter-censal period will never give exactly the population recorded at the next census. The extent to which the figures differ is known as the 'Error of Closure'. Its magnitude is a sensitive indicator of the consistency of demographic data and of the quality of data collection. The inconsistencies may be due to differences in definitions of the populations being used, or to errors and omissions. The measurement of births, deaths, migrants and population size is a very imprecise and error-prone process, even in highly developed societies.

The equation can also be expressed in terms of rates, by dividing each element by the mid-year population (MYP). Then the rate of population change is just

$$\frac{P_{t+1} - P_t}{MYP} = \frac{B}{MYP} - \frac{D}{MYP} + \frac{In}{MYP} - \frac{Out}{MYP}.$$

The difference between the Birth Rate and Death Rate is the Rate of Natural Increase, and the difference between the In-and Out-Migration Rates is the Net Migration Rate so the equation can also be written as:

Growth Rate = Rate of Natural Increase + Net Migration Rate.

These are in fact all *crude* rates. They are defined more formally and discussed further in Chapters 4 and 6.

Types of demographic data

The raw materials of demography are data collected in censuses, surveys, registration systems and elsewhere. They can be presented in a wide variety of ways, but divide into two fundamentally different forms. First, there are the data collected in population censuses or census-like surveys. A census produces a record of *individuals* at a particular instant in time. It yields a static, cross-sectional snapshot of the population *stock*, its size and structure, as it was on census night. Comparisons within or between censuses usually involve either absolute numbers or, frequently, the calculation of proportions.

Second, there are the data usually collected by registration systems. The data produced are a record of *events* during a particular time interval, usually a year. They are essentially dynamic in nature, because they give information on *flows* over time. Because the number of births, deaths, moves or whatever, occurring during a period are affected by the numbers 'at risk' of having a birth, dying, moving or whatever, it is common to calculate rates. This enables comparison of levels of mortality, fertility, mobility or whatever, rather than just births, deaths or moves.

The different ways of collecting demographic data are considered in more detail in the next chapter.

The definition of 'population'

The term 'population' is used in different senses in demography and in statistics. In demography the term relates to the number of people in a given area, while in statistical usage, particularly when talking about sampling, it means the universe of units under consideration, which may be people, light bulbs, rats or whatever. The demographic usage is thus very similar to normal English usage.

However, the phrase used in the previous paragraph — 'number of people in a given area' — is vague in several ways and a definition of 'population' for demographic purposes has to be much more precise. There actually exist numerous ways of defining a population, mainly depending on whether one includes or excludes groups such as visitors, seamen, armed forces, diplomats, institutional populations, those temporarily away or those missed by the census.

Broadly, though, there are just two types of population counts — *de facto* and *de jure*. The former is the population actually present at some moment — the population 'in fact' there. The latter is a vaguer term. It means the population who belong to the area, or have a right to live there through citizenship, legal residence or whatever. In order to try to obtain some comparability between nations, the United Nations recommends that each country should produce, from its census, a population total which excludes foreign military and diplomatic staff currently in the country, but includes its own armed forces, merchant seamen and diplomats who are currently abroad.

In the United Kingdom several different population definitions are used. In the Census it is usual to publish some tables, particularly early results, on the basis of the 'Enumerated Population', while most tabulations are based on the population of 'usual residents' where visitors, students, armed forces, diplomats, travellers, and seamen are included, excluded or moved to their 'usual residence' as asked for in a specific, extra question in the census.

Mid-year population estimates for England and Wales used to be made for three different population definitions — 'total', 'civilian' and 'home' — but since 1981 only the last is used. The 'home' population includes all those who are usually resident in England and Wales, allocating armed forces to the area in which they are stationed and students to their term-time address. This is the definition to use when calculating vital rates as it is the population at risk of experiencing the events. (For more details, see OPCS 1983.)

In the United States there are also three definitions in use. The 'resident' population is used in census reports, and for the calculation of vital rates. It comprises the residents of the fifty states and the District of Columbia. It thereby excludes the populations of Puerto Rico, Guam, the US Virgin Islands and so on, and also American citizens living overseas, both military and civilian. Including all these groups with the resident population produces the 'total population including armed forces overseas'. Excluding US Armed Forces based in the US from the resident population yields the third definition, the 'civilian population'.

Demographic Transition Theory

Although a study of the demographic transition is not part of formal demography, it is nevertheless useful to discuss it briefly here, first because it helps to set the scene for the following chapters, and second because it emphasises the strong interrelationships between population structure, fertility, mortality and migration, which lie at the heart of formal demography as defined earlier.

The so-called Theory of the Demographic Transition was first described in the 1940s. Since then it has been attacked, modified, added to and rewritten many times until now there is no single, clear, generally accepted view of precisely what it comprises. The classical description of the theory, as set out by Notestein (1945), Blacker (1947) and others, is roughly as follows. There are a series of stages during which a population moves from a situation where both mortality and fertility are high, to a position where both mortality and fertility are low. Both before and after the transition population growth is very slow. In between, during the transition, population growth is very rapid, essentially because the decline in mortality tends to occur before the decline in fertility.

The theory can be disputed on several grounds, both of a theoretical and a descriptive nature. It has been criticised because it is unclear whether it is purely descriptive or whether it also includes statements about the actual causes of the transition. The early writers about the theory differ in the emphasis they place on causal factors. Because it is formulated at a very general level, it is very difficult to generate from it hypotheses which can be tested or refuted convincingly, a requirement for any scientific theory. It has also been criticised by Coale (1973) and others, on descriptive grounds. In particular, they have shown that in many parts of Europe the decline in fertility occurred either before, or simultaneously with, the decline in mortality. The best-known example of this is France, where fertility fell to a low level very early on, before any substantial decline in mortality.

Despite these criticisms, Demographic Transition Theory remains at the heart of demography as an academic discipline, perhaps partly because of the lack of anything better to replace it. As a result, it has had a very great influence on the way the subject has developed. One particularly detrimental influence is that it has led demographers to consider the subject of migration as not being a part of demography. Yet for most practical purposes, especially population estimates and projections, and for explaining both current and historical trends in population growth and development, migration is an essential ingredient. One only has to consider the growth of the United States or Australia during the nineteenth century, the current population of London, the depopulated rural areas of Ireland or the rapid growth of urban areas in developing countries, to realise the crucial impact of migration.

Zelinsky (1971, 1979) has shown that it is possible to consider migration as undergoing a series of transitional stages in a way which forces attention onto the relationships between migration, mortality, fertility and population structure. At its crudest, the 'Hypothesis of the Mobility Transition', as Zelinsky calls it, states that migration increases as development and modernisation proceeds. In the initial pre-transitional phase there is little migration. People have short horizons, transport is difficult, and most people live and die close to where they were born. With the onset of modernisation, changes in agricultural and industrial production, improved transport and communications, and the growth of a market economy, horizons widen and longer-distance migration increases. This second stage is one of rapid urbanisation and of large-scale international migrations. In the past these international flows were mainly from Europe to the Americas and Australia, while today they tend to be from developing countries towards the Gulf, Europe and other developed countries.

The third stage sees a decline in both urbanisation and the rate of rural depopulation. International migration also becomes harder and less attractive. But many more short-distance moves occur both within and between cities, often to suburban and semi-rural areas for housing reasons and for occupational and social mobility. Eventually, a new steady state evolves where there is much movement but little net population redistribution.

This transition view of migration shares the same drawbacks as the demographic transition view of fertility and mortality in that it is formulated at a very general level, does not necessarily reflect reality very closely and is based on Western experience, which is of doubtful relevance to the Third World today, but the approach at least has the advantages that it encourages a dynamic view of migration and forces consideration of migration as well as mortality and fertility in the determination of the structure and development of populations.

2 Data Collection

It might at first be thought inappropriate to include a chapter on data collection in a book on demographic methods. However, some understanding of the way data are collected, and the errors and biases they are likely to contain is an essential prerequisite to understanding why they are analysed and interpreted in the ways described in subsequent chapters. This is essentially because the range of data which can be collected, and the way it is done, strongly influences, often in subtle but crucial ways, the ways in which they can be analysed, most usually by severely restricting the range of possibilities. The requirements of demographic (and statistical) techniques also affect the way in which data are collected, but that is not of primary interest here.

This chapter therefore focuses mainly on the principles and methodology of data collection. The more practical, organisational aspects are of lesser interest and so are not covered in any comprehensive or systematic way. The first section sets the scene by briefly considering the purposes of data collection generally and the economic, political and social milieux within which it takes place. This is followed by sections on census taking, on vital registration systems and on various types of demographic sample surveys. Finally, there is a short guide to international data sources.

The purposes of data collection

Very few data indeed are collected primarily for demographic purposes. Most are in fact produced for, or as a by-product of, administrative exercises carried out by, or under the control of, governments or international agencies. Consequently the demographer normally has relatively little control over the precise way in which demographic data are collected, aggregated and presented. Instead, he has to make do with what there is.

The chief administrative exercises which produce data suitable for demographic analysis are vital registration systems, censuses, migration controls, public-health campaigns, population control programmes and special surveys. Vital registration systems and migration controls exist primarily for legal purposes — the production of birth and death certificates, passports, identification cards, work permits, residence qualifications and citizenship. Censuses exist mainly to aid planning, especially the provision of basic services such as power, water and roads, but also other facilities. Most democratic countries' population distribution, as determined by the census, also determines the level of electoral representation and possibly also the pattern of resource allocation from central government. Many government interventions in the fields of health and welfare produce demographic data, usually as part of an evaluation programme. For example, a well-run family planning programme will have carried out surveys of fertility levels and contraceptive use both before and after the campaign so as to make possible a reasonably objective assessment of its impact.

Another source of demographic data, often produced more or less independently of the administrative system, are surveys (or possibly other types of investigations) which are designed with more strongly research-oriented objectives in mind. They are usually designed either to assess the impact of existing policies, to aid the planning of those yet to be implemented, or to influence governmental or other agencies. The pure advancement of knowledge generally, or demography in particular, is most often a secondary objective. Consequently, they commonly look at the impact of economic, social and environmental factors, or governmental policies on levels and patterns of health, fertility, migration and so on.

Thus demographic data are generated mainly by the activities of central governments and their agencies or by international organisations. The quantity and quality of data that emerge depends partly upon the wealth of these organisa-tions, as well as their objectives. But it also depends very much on social attitudes towards data collection, a consideration which has grown rapidly in importance in recent years as public awareness of the quantity of personal infor-mation held by governmental and other agencies rises and the ease with which computers, through record linkage and data transfer over networks, can extract and combine such data. The greater liberalism of many societies is being balanced by a greater reluctance to answer 'personal' questions so that in many developed countries there is strong public feeling against large data-gathering exercises such as the census.

So far the discussion has been mainly concerned with the situation in developed countries. The same problems of expense, complexity and necessity of sophisticated organisation exist in developing countries, but they are multiplied many times so that a large exercise such as a census is often only financially feasible if it is largely funded by, say, the UN Fund for Population Activities. There are, however, on top of these, additional problems which are more specific to poor countries. For example, questions may not be understood because they are phrased in an inappropriate, Western cultural frame where concepts as well as language are different. Respondents, particularly the illiterate, may not know the answers to simple questions, especially those which involve dates or measurements. There may be severe problems of political, racial or religious instability or other cultural problems which make data collec-tion particularly difficult and error prone.

Overall, therefore, the data used in demographic analysis is often very far from perfect, restricted by economic stringency, by public suspicion (or at least indifference), by the origins of such data in a bureaucracy set up for some other purpose, by ignorance and by many other economic, legal, social and cultural factors.

Censuses

A census is the largest single data-gathering exercise carried out in a country. It involves the setting up of a large administrative body which has not only to carry out the actual data collection but also the formulation of the questionnaire, the planning and organisation of the whole exercise, the processing of the completed questionnaires, and tabulation and publication of the results. Such a process is spread over several years and at its peak, on census day, may employ many thousands of people. It is therefore a very costly exercise, involving great administrative effort and disruption. Under such circumstances it is understandable that the need to hold a census at all is often brought into question. Indeed, it is difficult to justify a census in strict economic terms. The advantages to a country are often very long term and hard to pin down as they are spread over such a wide range of activities, not only within central and local government but also in private industry and services, in research organisations and elsewhere. Many censuses are consequently held partly for prestige reasons, because it is felt that the country needs one, in the same way as it 'needs' a national airline. The encouragement and sponsorship of international organisations, especially the United Nations, is also very important.

The United Nations recommends that censuses should be held at least at ten-yearly intervals, preferably in years ending in 0 or 1. The object is, first, to obtain information at regular intervals to facilitate comparisons over time and, second, to try to synchronise census taking so as to improve comparability between countries. The recommendation is adhered to in a large and increasing number of countries, but some hold quinquennial censuses (Japan, Turkey and Korea, for example), and in others it is less regular. Within the year the most suitable time to hold a census depends very much on local factors such as rainy seasons, labour availability, migration and holiday periods. Consequently, there are no international recommendations.

The chief characteristics of a census, which differentiate it from a survey, are first that it is a complete recording of the entire population within a geographically well-defined area. It does not involve sampling. Second, each person must be enumerated separately. Third, it must have a legal basis making it compulsory to be included and to provide the information requested. It cannot be a voluntary exercise. Finally, it must relate to a single point in time, not a period, even though the enumeration itself may be spread over days or even weeks.

A crucial consideration in the design of a census is whether it is to be completed by enumerators, or by respondents themselves. The choice affects not only the design of the forms but also the number and type of questions that can be asked, the number of enumerators required and the level and type of training necessary. In countries where illiteracy is widespread, enumerator completion is unavoidable, but in developed countries there is a real choice. In the United States respondents complete the census themselves, mailing back the completed forms, while in Britain the responsibility is shared, with the householder filling in the questionnaire, which is checked by the enumerator when it is collected.

Some censuses are very simple indeed, containing no more than a few simple factual questions. Others are more complex, extending to almost any level of detail. In Western countries recent censuses have often tended to become shorter than before, partly in response to the increasing unwillingness of the public to fill in large forms and complex questions. But while it is universally accepted amongst census takers that a census should ask only what it is necessary to know, and not what one would like to know, there is much disagreement about what is really necessary and what is not. The usual minimum selection of questions is name, age, sex, relationship to head of household, marital status, race/religion/ethnic group, education, occupation, employment status, migration, housing and amenities. Additionally, in countries where vital registration is poor or non-existent (a category which covers most developing countries), there are normally questions on the number of children ever borne and how many are still alive. There may also be questions on widowhood and whether one's parents are alive or dead. The responses to these 'indirect' questions are extremely important in demography as they can be used to produce estimates of fertility and mortality and thereby make up for the absence of registration data.

The quality of responses and thus extent of errors is, in general, less where questionnaires are kept short and questions simple and factual. One way of squeezing more questions in without burdening respondents excessively is to use sampling, whereby not everyone answers all questions. This, however, leads to greater administrative complexity, which is undesirable, so the extra questions are often relegated instead to a post-enumeration survey held soon after the census itself.

A large part of the organisation and design of the census is concerned with the minimisation of errors. But errors in census taking are inevitably very great, especially in underdeveloped countries, and are all the more serious because they are frequently grossly underestimated, especially by those responsible for the conduct of the census! The errors fall into two main categories. One is incomplete coverage. (Overcounting is rare, though not unheard of.) An undercount may arise because whole areas are simply missed, or because certain subgroups are hard to cover completely. Such groups include the homeless, nomads, infants, students, vagrants, seamen and those living in institutions. Errors of coverage can be increased greatly if an incomplete or out-of-date frame (list of addresses, or possibly villages) is used, but new, accurate frames are difficult, time-consuming and expensive to produce, often involving mapping and laborious fieldwork.

The other source of error is of quality rather than quantity. Response errors may be accidental and due to such things as the enumerator recording the answer given to him wrongly, the respondent misunderstanding the question, not knowing the answer or the question being inappropriate in that cultural context. Questions on employment and industry often fall into this last category in developing countries because differentiation between, say, housework and 'real' work or gardening and farming become difficult. Alternatively, response errors may be deliberate. The respondent may choose, for reasons of pride, shame, fear or possibly even sheer mischievousness, to give the wrong answer. For example, a prospective army conscript may lie about his age, an unmarried mother may omit to mention her child, the houseproud may overstate the size of their house and the amenities they have, or divorced people may declare themselves to be single.

Once the census has been taken, the task of processing the results begins. This stage will, if the census has been organised properly, already have been tested using the results of the preliminary pilot survey used to aid training and test the questionnaire. Processing involves checking and coding of questionnaires, keying the responses into the computer and producing the tabulations. The coding of responses to questions such as industry, occupation, birthplace and migration (such as previous address) is a very time-consuming activity and can introduce substantial errors and biases if not carried out carefully and checked meticulously. Data-entry is another stage where errors can be made, though double-entry and automatic verification procedures should minimise these.

Note, however, that even the most fastidious checking of questionnaires will not by any means uncover all errors. Errors of coverage, especially, will be missed. These are normally assessed by means of a post-enumeration survey. The idea is that a small, high-quality survey should be conducted among a small sample of the population, using the best interviewers, ideally independently of the census. The results are compared with those of the census and the extent of the differences give some idea of the extent of error in the census results.

If the census has been properly run and well-financed, then hopefully the final tabulations will be published within a reasonable time after the enumeration. Two years is probably a realistic target, though frequently complete publication of all volumes takes longer, up to five or six years. Long delays are bad because they mean that when the results become available to the users they are already out-of-date and therefore of much less use than if they have been available earlier. Having results which are accurate but out-of-date is only a slightly more attractive proposition than having data which are timely but full of errors.

In conclusion, the ability to carry out a census from inception to final publication stretches even the best administrative organisations. It is easy to make a mess of things, but even the best-run censuses will inevitably contain a myriad of errors and biases. The intelligent census user must be constantly and acutely aware of this, and should, if possible, ensure that the results and conclusions drawn from census data are robust against likely or known errors. That usually means *keep it simple*!

Vital registration

In almost all developed countries vital registration systems provide the main source of information on births, marriages and deaths, and sometimes also on migration. In developing countries, however, such systems are either non-existent or, more frequently, seriously incomplete, and are sometimes not even exploited for demographic purposes. The explanation of this last comment is that the objectives of a registration system are essentially administrative and legal, not demographic. Demographic data are merely a by-product, extremely useful to demographers, planners and others, but not, in themselves of sufficient importance to justify the administrative effort and cost involved in setting up and maintaining a registration system.

Because registration is carried out mainly for administrative purposes, only a few, simple questions are usually asked. They cover items such as the date of the event, age, sex, marital status, occupation, cause in the case of a death, and possibly something about previous similar events in the case of a birth or marriage.

The earliest registers were almost all set up and maintained by religious authorities. In France they began in the fourteenth century; in England and Wales, in the established Church of England, in 1538; while in the United States they started during the seventeenth century. But while ecclesiastical registers provided immensely valuable data, their usefulness is reduced by the fact that they record baptisms instead of births, and burials instead of deaths, and also that they are restricted to those who attend church. Such limitations do not, of course, apply to civil registration systems, and these were instituted in most European countries during the nineteenth century. England and Wales was fairly typical in that civil registration there began in 1838, but it wasn't until the 1870s that it covered all, or nearly all, events.

Vital registration systems are fully effective in only a few countries. This is for many reasons. At the most basic level, if the need for individuals to register is not there, then few will bother, even if there is a legal requirement to do so. In most developing countries there is still little need to possess a birth or marriage certificate, unlike in developed countries, where proof of age, birthplace, marital status, parentage and so on is essential to obtain all kinds of services and rights, and documents such as identity cards, driving licences or passports.

But even if there is a strong perceived benefit to be gained from registering, so that 100 per cent of events are in fact registered, that does not imply that the demographic tabulations produced by the system are also 100 per cent complete. For that to occur requires an unusually good administrative structure reaching right down to the local level where the registrations are actually made. A poor structure, or a poorly motivated, poorly paid, overstretched administrative system, will lead to errors and omissions which can be surprisingly large. The process of collecting the data from possibly many thousands of registrars from all over a country, and then processing them to produce the final tabulations is something few countries can honestly claim to be able to do with great accuracy.

The combined impact of non-registration and incomplete aggregation is that the demographic data produced by most registration systems are seriously deficient. Many fail to capture even half the events which occur. Moreover, the omissions are not randomly distributed but tend to be concentrated amongst certain groups. For example, infant deaths are notoriously badly covered, as are the births of those who die when they are still very young. Registration also tends to be better in urban than rural areas, and is often sex-biased, especially in communities where the status of women is low.

The information gathered in a vital registration system is thus likely to be poorer than in a census, and the underlying causes are such that improvement is generally difficult, expensive and slow. However, that does not mean that registration systems should not be set up or maintained in developing countries. One has to start with poor ones, and moreover, there are techniques which can detect and estimate the extent of errors in registration data from its structure, and thus correct or at least improve it.

Sample surveys

The sample surveys used in demography take a variety of forms, but the common feature is that they involve taking a sample of the population. The advantage of sampling is that it reduces the effort required, and hence cost, compared with a complete census-type enumeration, but the price is the introduction of sampling error. If the sampling is carried out randomly from a suitable 'frame' this error can be measured and is generally much less than non-sampling errors, as long as a reasonably large sample is used.

Sample surveys are important sources of demographic data largely because of the aforementioned problems of census and registration data — the impossibility of asking many or complex questions and, especially in developing countries, the poor quality of the data they produce. The advantages of sample surveys, apart from cheapness, are that they can be organised and executed relatively quickly, that they can gather much more detail than a census, including attitudinal information, and that interviewers can be intensively trained. Their main disadvantages are almost all consequences of the introduction of sampling error. This means that large numbers are required to yield accurate results and that comparisons between sub-groups or small geographic areas are severely limited.

The principles of sampling are well covered in numerous textbooks, such as Cochran (1977) or Moser and Kalton (1971) and so will not be considered here, except to say that in most general-purpose demographic surveys the unit of observation is the household, not the individual, and that cluster sampling (of, say, whole villages, streets or blocks) is common to reduce cost and especially administrative complexity.

Several distinct types of demographic sample survey are used. First, there are census-type enquiries, which may actually replace a full census or, more commonly, will supplement one by asking a wider range of questions of a sample of the enumerated population. Such a survey is often combined with a post-enumeration survey. Surveys designed to investigate some particular topics such as contraceptive use, female employment and childbearing, or the causes and consequences of migration, also fall into this category.

Second, there are retrospective surveys, so-called because they ask questions about events which happened in the past. In developing countries they are primarily designed to gather information which a registration system would normally provide. The standard retrospective questions used by demographers, roughly in order of importance, are:

1. Total children borne alive.
2. Numbers living at home, away and dead. (Used to check (1) and to estimate child mortality.)
3. Time since last birth. (Used mainly to determine births during the last year.)
4. Whether the mother is alive.
5. Whether the father is alive.
6. Whether the first spouse is alive.

There exist widely used and sophisticated 'indirect' techniques which use the answers to these specific questions to produce estimates of mortality and fertility levels, both current and, by using the data from older respondents, in the past. For details see United Nations (1983). The general idea is that these are simple yet specific questions which can be answered accurately by almost everyone. More ambitious retrospective surveys will additionally ask women to provide a detailed maternity history containing dates of and outcomes of all their pregnancies. Such questions can, of course, also be used in censuses, and should be.

Several other less frequently used types of survey also exist. One is the serial or prospective survey which, ideally, involves first carrying out a normal census-type survey, which acts as a baseline, followed by repeated visits to check for and record subsequent events. The length of interval between visits varies. Short intervals improve accuracy but increase cost. Typically, the interval will be three to four months, maintained for two or three years. The main problems are the difficulties of recontact, the very large population which has to be covered if sufficient events are to be recorded, and the cost and other difficulties of maintaining such a system for so long. They can, however, be used successfully in conjunction with, say, health interventions such as vaccination campaigns or newly set up primary health-care systems.

Another variation, now largely fallen from favour, is the dual-record survey. This involves running two statistically independent surveys covering the same population, and matching the results. Some events will be caught in both surveys, some in just one and some in neither. This last, unknown component can be estimated from the extent of overlap using statistical formulae devised by Chandrasekar and Deming (1949). The disadvantages of this method are, first, the impossibility of running two surveys which are truly independent and, second, the difficulties involved in the matching process on which the method crucially depends.

Conclusion

The three main sources of demographic data described above are not in any way alternatives, even though one can often be used to make up for the absence of, or deficiencies in, another. A census is more or less essential to provide a baseline without which a registration system or sample survey is much less useful. Sample surveys can, in developed countries, investigate specific topics in depth, putting flesh on the bones provided by census and vital registration. In developing countries, especially through use of retrospective questions, they can make up for the absence of a vital registration system and hence provide data on population flows.

The data produced by the different sources above vary not only in the extent and type of errors they contain but also in more fundamental ways. Censuses and census-type surveys generally produce information on population stocks at a moment in time, while vital registration systems produce information on flows, counts of events occurring over time. The latter can also be obtained indirectly through retrospective questions in surveys and censuses or by prospective surveys. Both kinds of data are widely used, frequently in combination, in demographic analysis, as will be seen in the following chapters.

3 Age and sex structure

The close two-way relationship which exists between the structure of a population and the numbers of births, deaths and moves occurring in it is one of the major themes which runs through the whole of formal demography. It is also absolutely crucial to an understanding of both the dynamics of population change, and the age and sex composition of a population at any single point in time. A brief discussion of it therefore provides the starting point for this chapter.

This is followed by a description of the measurement of age and of age misreporting. Then the various ways of describing age and sex distributions using population pyramids, the Sex Ratio and Dependency Ratios are considered. A full discussion of the determinants of age structure, and of the effect of age and sex structure on measures of fertility, mortality and migration, must await the more detailed description of those measures in later chapters, but a general introduction is included here.

The interdependence of structure and vital events

Births, deaths and moves do not occur equally to people of all ages and both sexes. Instead, they tend to be concentrated among, for example, the old, the very young or women of childbearing ages. Consequently, the numbers of births, deaths and moves occurring in a population at any particular time are determined not only by its overall size and the levels of fertility, mortality and migration but also by its age and sex structure. A prime objective of formal demography is to develop measures which eliminate the effects of population size and age structure so as to produce 'pure' measures of fertility, mortality and migration.

But the structure of a population is also entirely determined by, and provides to some extent a record of, past fertility, mortality and migration. For example, high fertility during one period will produce, a generation later, a comparatively large number of women of childbearing age, and consequently a comparatively large number of births. Or perhaps heavy emigration, or mortality caused by war, will tend to deplete the numbers of young male adults in a population, and this will still be reflected, perhaps fifty years later, as a relatively small number of elderly men.

The age and sex composition of a population is thus both determined by, and is a powerful determinant of, the numbers of births, deaths and moves occurring in that population.

The measurement of age

If you ask someone how old they are, they might reply that they are 25. This means that they have already had their twenty-fifth birthday but not yet their twenty-sixth. They are giving what demographers call their 'age last birthday'. It is in fact a very unusual measurement.

The conventional way of measuring heights, weights, distances, areas, volumes and so on is to round figures up or down to the nearest whole number. Thus a distance described as being '25 metres' really means 'somewhere between 24.5 and 25.5 metres'. Age, however, is perhaps unique in that it is always rounded *down*, so that an age given as '25 years' really means 'somewhere between 25.0 and 26.0 years'.

To avoid confusion, the terms 'exact age' or '*n*th birthday' are sometimes used in demography to distinguish it from 'age last birthday'. But often it is not explicitly stated whether a given age refers to the exact age or to age last birthday. It is normally only the context which implies one or the other. For example, the age groups in Table 3.2 are ages last birthday so that '0–4' includes everyone up to exact age 5. On the other hand, phrases involving cumulation, such as 'the proportion dying by age 5', refer to an exact age.

Age misreporting

Distortions in age distributions may be real and caused by past changes in the levels or patterns of mortality, fertility and migration, or they may be due to errors. The errors may be caused either by some individuals being omitted from the survey when they should have been included, or by some individuals' ages being wrongly reported.

A great problem for formal demography, frequently prohibiting the use of conventional techniques, is that people often simply do not know their age, or if they do, may choose not to tell the truth. This is not normally a problem in developed, literate societies, but in many parts of the world questions on age, asked in censuses and surveys, will frequently yield very implausible age distributions. Figure 3.2, showing the uncorrected 1974 Bangladesh age structure, is a good example of this.

Age misreporting can take two basic forms: 'heaping' and 'shifting'. With age heaping, or 'digit preference' as it is often called, too many people report ages ending with 0 or 5 while relatively few give ages ending in 9, 1, 4 or 6. This is apparent in Figure 3.2a, where one can also see a preference for ages ending in 2 and 8. The precise pattern of digit preference varies considerably between societies, and between ages, and of course depends on whether age was asked directly or was computed from a reported date of birth. (For a more detailed discussion, see Carrier and Hobcraft (1973: 2–5).

Age shifting is a more serious problem than age heaping, largely because it is harder to detect and adjust for. Typically, older people tend to exaggerate their ages, particularly in societies where age confers status. Young men may understate or overstate their age to avoid military service. Young mothers may exaggerate their age, while older, unmarried women may understate theirs. This last is especially common in populations where many people do not know their age so that interviewers have to make estimates themselves. It is often difficult to decide whether a particular distortion in an age distribution is real or whether it is due to age shifting or to complete omission.

Numerous techniques exist, both to estimate the extent to which ages are misreported and to 'correct' age distributions. Techniques for adjusting or smoothing ages are often complex and will not be discussed here. For details see Shryock and Siegel (1976, Appendix C) or Carrier and Hobcraft (1973, Ch. 3). Here only one simple measure of age heaping, known as 'Whipple's Index', will be described.

Whipple's Index is a measure of preference for ages ending in 0 and 5. Only the ages 23 to 62 are used because outside of this range shifting and other problems often tend to confuse the normal pattern of heaping. The Index is calculated simply by expressing the population reporting ages ending with 0 and 5 as a percentage of the total population aged between 23 and 62, and then multiplying by five. The range of the Index is then from 100, indicating no preference for 0 and 5, up to 500, indicating that only 0 and 5 were reported.

The Whipple's Index for Bangladesh, 1974, is:

$$\frac{\text{Pop. } 25, 30 \ldots 60}{\text{Pop. } 23 - 62} \times 100 \times 5$$

$$= \frac{15,911,386}{25,175,563} \times 100 \times 5$$

$$= 316.0.$$

The United Nations have published the scale shown in Table 3.1 for estimating the reliability of the data. The Bangladesh data are thus, according to this classification, extremely rough. Clearly, though, Whipple's Index is itself a very crude measure. In particular, it only takes into consideration the terminal digits 0 and 5, and it excludes ages outside the range 23 to 62.

There do exist numerous other more complex measures of age heaping. 'Myers' Blended Index' is the most widely known of these. It is substantially more complex to calculate than Whipple's Index but does yield an index of preference for each terminal digit as well as an overall measure. (For details, see Shryock and Siegel 1976: 116–18.)

In general, the best that these indices of heaping can do is to indicate in a broad way the quality of age reporting in a population. Usually, a more detailed impression can be obtained by drawing a population pyramid.

Table 3.1 UN score for estimating reliability of age data

Quality	Whipple's Index
Highly accurate	Under 105
Fairly accurate	105–10
Approximate	110–25
Rough	125–75
Very rough	Over 175

Population pyramids

Population pyramids are an elegant and useful way of graphically presenting an age/sex distribution. Some examples are shown in Figures 3.1 and 3.2. A pyramid essentially comprises two ordinary histograms placed on their sides and back to back. The rules for drawing pyramids are generally the same as those for producing histograms, given in most introductory statistics texts, but there are certain conventions and special features which should be noted.

First, pyramids are always drawn showing the male population on the left hand side and the female population on the right. The young are always at the bottom and the old at the top. It is conventional to use either single-year or five-year age groups, though other groupings are possible.

Second, the last, open-ended age group is normally omitted entirely from the pyramid because it is impossible to draw truthfully.

Third, the bottom scale can be graduated as either absolute numbers or percentages. The shape of the pyramid is not affected at all by this, but it is essential that the percentages are calculated using, as a base, the total population of both sexes combined. If the percentages are calculated separately for males and females, then the pyramid will present a false picture. It will not reflect the different numbers of males and females in the population because the areas on either side of the pyramid will be exactly equal. Even Keyfitz and Flieger (1971: 24) sometimes get this wrong.

Fourth, the choice of scales affects greatly the final shape of the pyramid. For example, stretching the age scale and squashing the horizontal one will inevitably produce a tall, thin pyramid. In Figure 3.1 two pyramids are shown which are identical except that in the lower one the horizontal scale is halved. The impressions they convey are substantially different. Choice of scales are particularly critical if comparisons between pyramids are to be made. Ideally, the scales should be identical for each pyramid, but this is often impossible because the population totals are very different. In such circumstances, if the horizontal scales are different, then the age scales should also be different by the same proportion. However, if the actual size of the pyramid is not of importance, then a percentage pyramid is satisfactory.

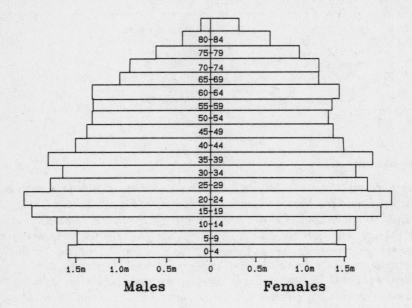

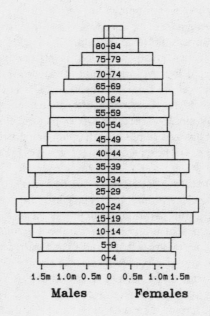

Figure 3.1 Population pyramids: England and Wales, 1985

Normally, two pyramids should be drawn, one showing single years of age and the other five-year age groups, because they tend to reveal different features of the age and sex structure. Figure 3.2 shows both pyramids for Bangladesh, 1974. A single-year pyramid is essential for looking at the pattern of age heaping, and shows well, for example, the undercutting of the pyramid at young ages, but it is too detailed for many purposes. A five-year pyramid displays better the broad pattern of the age structure, perhaps revealing signs of age shifting. A young age structure, such as in Bangladesh, will produce a roughly triangular pyramid with a broad base, while an old age structure, such as England and Wales, 1981, will produce a more rectangular pyramid with a relatively narrow base (see Figure 3.1b).

The Sex Ratio

The overall Sex Ratio is simply the ratio of males to females in the population. It is normally expressed as the number of males per 100 females. That is:

$$\text{Sex Ratio} = \frac{\text{Males}}{\text{Females}} \times 100.$$

In some countries, though, particularly India, it is conventional to express the ratio the other way round, as the number of females per 100 males. Here the former convention, recommended by the United Nations, is used.

The overall Sex Ratio is entirely determined by

1. The Sex Ratio at Birth.
2. Sex differences in mortality.
3. Differential migration.

Each will be discussed in turn.

The Sex Ratio at Birth is just the number of male births per 100 female births. It is normally around 105, that is 105 boys are born for every 100 girls, but it does vary somewhat between populations and sub-groups. For example, in England and Wales in 1985 there were 336,835 male and 319,582 female births, so the Sex Ratio at Birth was

$$\frac{336,835}{319,582} \times 100$$

$$= 105.4.$$

Interestingly, in England and Wales the Ratio seems to have been slowly increasing for a long time. It was 103.5 in 1900. Note that if the Sex Ratio at

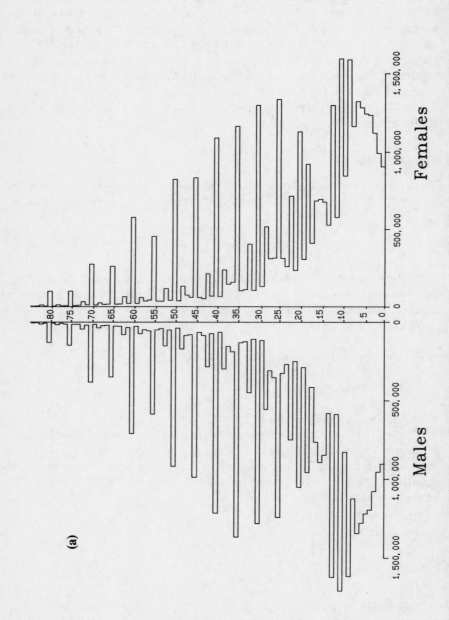

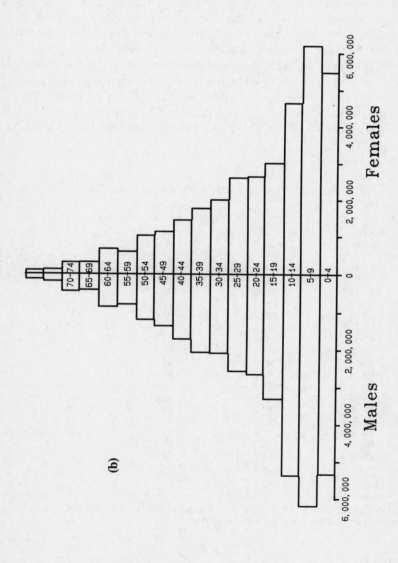

Figure 3.2 Population pyramids: Bangladesh, 1974

Birth is 105, then, of every 205 births, on average 100 are female. In other words, the proportion who are female is thus 100/205 = 0.488.

Sex differences in mortality and migration cause the Sex Ratio to vary between ages. In most parts of the world, female mortality is lower than male mortality at all ages. Women live longer, on average, than men. Thus the Sex Ratio tends to decline with age. The figures for the United States, 1985, shown in the first column of Table 3.2, show that at very old ages there are several times as many females than males. The figure of 39.9 for those aged 85 and over implies that there are 2.5 times as many females as males in that group.

In India, however, and many other high-mortality countries in South and East Asia, female mortality tends to be higher than male mortality, probably due to worse malnutrition among young females and the risks of maternity. Consequently, the pattern of Sex Ratios by age is very different from that in the United States. The last column of Table 3.2 gives, as an example, the figures for India, 1971.

Table 3.2 Sex ratios by age: United States, 1985; England and Wales, 1921; India, 1971

Age group	United States, 1985	England and Wales, 1921	India, 1971
0 –4	104.9	102.5	107
5 –9	104.8	100.8	106
10–14	105.8	100.8	106
15–19	103.7	97.3	106
20–24	100.3	85.0	107
25–29	100.2	82.7	107
30–34	99.3	84.3	109
35–39	97.5	86.5	111
40–44	96.1	88.7	112
45–49	95.1	93.4	111
50–54	93.3	93.1	110
55–59	90.3	92.0	109
60–64	87.4	88.3	108
65–69	82.2	83.7	107
70–74	73.8	74.5	104 (70+)
75–79	63.5	67.7	
80–84	53.0	59.4	
85+	39.9	48.7	
All ages	94.8	91.2	107 .5

Sources: United States, from U.S. Bureau of the Census (1986); England and Wales, from 1921 Census Report; India, from Cassen and Dyson (1976).

The Sex Ratios for England and Wales, 1921, are included in Table 3.2 because they show clearly the effect of the high mortality among young adult males during the First World War. The figures for the 25–29 and 30–34 age groups in particular are very low. Patterns similar to this can also be caused by heavy migration. Many large-scale migration streams contain a disproportionate number of young adult males. This will produce low Sex Ratios at these ages in the area of origin and high ratios in the area of destination.

Dependency Ratios

One frequently used index summarising an age distribution is known as the Dependency Ratio. Strictly, this is the ratio of economically active to economically inactive persons in a population, but often, because of lack of data or difficulties in defining economic activity in many countries, a ratio of age groups is used instead. Then the ratio is just

$$\text{Dependency Ratio} = \frac{\text{Children} + \text{Elderly}}{\text{Working ages}} \times 100.$$

The precise ages used depend very much on the population being studied, but for, say, England and Wales the most appropriate are probably school leaving age (16) and retirement ages (60 for women, 65 for men). Thus, for England and Wales, where there were, in 1985, an estimated 10,251,300 children, 30,571,500 adults and 9,098,700 elderly the ratio was:

$$\frac{10,251,300 + 9,098,700}{30,571,500} \times 100$$

$$= 63.3.$$

However, a much more easily interpreted measure of dependency, which uses the same data and gives exactly the same amount of information, is just the proportion of the total population in the working ages. For England and Wales, 1985, using the same age groups, this is:

$$\frac{30,571,500}{30,571,500 + 10,251,300 + 9,098,700} \times 100$$

$$= 61.2 \text{ per cent.}$$

Ratios using only children, or only the elderly in the numerator, are also sometimes calculated.

The determinants of age structure

At the start of this chapter it was pointed out that any age and sex distribution is entirely determined by the levels of mortality, fertility and migration occurring in the past. But these three factors affect an age distribution in different ways and to different extents.

A change in the level of fertility will, at first, affect just the youngest age groups. Only over many years will it work through to affect older ages. A decline in fertility initially has the effect of narrowing the base of the pyramid as the number of births falls. If the fall is rapid, the effect can be quite dramatic. It may produce a pattern similar to that which can be seen in the two Bangladesh pyramids in Figure 3.2. They show substantial undercutting at young ages, which could be caused by a sharp decline in fertility, but, in this case, is probably mainly due to the omission of young children or exaggeration of their ages.

Variation in the level of infant mortality tends to produce an effect very similar to that caused by a change in fertility, affecting first the youngest ages and only gradually working through to the whole age range.

A change in adult mortality has, however, generally, a much less dramatic impact on the shape of an age distribution than either fertility or infant mortality changes. This is largely because it is not concentrated in one age group but is spread over all adult ages. Mortality is also inherently less variable than fertility, at least in developed countries. In developing countries high mortality due to famines, epidemics or wars which affect particular age groups disproportionately can, however, have a big impact which is noticeable in the age structure for many years.

Migration can cause big distortions in age distributions because it is normally concentrated among young adults, and is sometimes also sex selective. Areas from which substantial numbers have emigrated will, in extreme cases, have top-heavy pyramids with an unusually high proportion of the population in older age groups, few young adults and, consequently, few children. Conversely, areas where substantial numbers of immigrants have settled will have a young age structure, with many children and very few elderly.

Overall, therefore, an age distribution is best regarded as being determined primarily by fertility, and modified, to a greater or lesser extent, by mortality and migration. This observation is not intuitively obvious but is of great importance. It is perhaps more clearly seen if each age group is considered separately. The numbers in, say, the 70–74 age group is determined (if migration is ignored) by the numbers born 70–75 years ago, depleted by mortality.

The impact of age and sex structure on vital events

Having briefly considered the impact of vital events on age/sex distributions, this section turns to look at the opposite relationship.

Clearly, if a high proportion of a population is in the age groups which are at greatest risk of giving birth, dying or moving, then the numbers of these events occurring will be higher than if there are small numbers in these age groups. As has already been said, much of formal demography is devoted to trying to control for this effect of age structure and thereby to measure the underlying levels of fertility, mortality and migration.

This observation has important consequences for population dynamics. If, for example, at some time a large number of births occur in a population, due either to high fertility or to there being many women in the prime childbearing ages, then there will inevitably be a large number of births between twenty and thirty years later when the original births begin producing children of their own. Then there will be another peak another generation later, and so on, like echoes.

The implication for future population growth of this simple observation is of enormous importance. The populations of most developing countries currently contain a very high proportion of young children, and these will begin child-bearing during the next twenty or so years. Thus, even if an extraordinarily rapid decline in fertility does occur in these countries in the near future, there will nevertheless still be large numbers of births occurring. This is simply because there are very large numbers of potential parents entering the child-bearing ages. The populations will thus continue to grow in size. This 'demographic momentum' explains why demographers can state with absolute confidence that the populations of most developing countries will continue to grow rapidly for many years to come, irrespective of future levels and trends in fertility, mortality or migration.

Exercises

1. The age/sex structure of the Caribbean island of Dominica, derived from the 1981 census, is shown in Table 3E.1. Draw an age pyramid of these data. What are the main features of the pyramid and what may have caused them?

2. The 1969 census of Rhodesia, held on 1 April, asked respondents for their year of birth rather than their age. The data that were collected are given in Table 3E.2. Represent these data graphically by means of an *age* pyramid. Are there any advantages in asking for year of birth instead of, or as well as, age in a census, survey or registration system?

Table 3E.1 Age and sex structure of Dominica, 1981

Age group	Males	Females
0	756	727
1 –4	3 446	3 267
5 –9	5 277	4 850
10–14	5 595	5 488
15–19	4 779	4 611
20–24	3 722	3 286
25–29	2 521	2 190
30–34	1 764	1 755
35–39	1 404	1 416
40–44	1 133	1 328
45–49	1 058	1 292
50–54	1 051	1 311
55–59	950	1 097
60–64	959	1 190
65–69	850	962
70–74	611	872
75–79	383	584
80+	340	689
Not stated	155	126
Total	36 754	37 041

Table 3E.2 Population by year of birth, census of Rhodesia, 1969

Year of birth	Population Males	Females	Total
1969	34 460	36 750	71 210
1968	104 020	111 510	215 530
1967	90 790	94 870	185 660
1966	82 830	87 770	170 600
1965	83 220	83 970	167 190

4 Period fertility

In demographic usage the term 'fertility' relates to the number of live births a woman has actually had. Fertile thus means roughly the opposite of childless. It means that a woman is, or was, a mother. The physiological ability to bear children, on the other hand, is known as 'fecundity'. Fecund is thus the opposite of sterile. The words 'fertile' and 'fecund' are therefore used by demographers the other way round from the general public. To confuse matters further, in French, Italian, Spanish and related languages the demographic meanings of 'fecund' and 'fertile' are reversed: 'fertility' becomes 'fécondité' in French, while 'fecund' becomes 'fèrtile'. However, 'natalité' is frequently used in French as a synonym of 'fécondité' (see van de Walle 1982, para. 623).

It is thought that the maximum number of children an average woman can theoretically produce is about fifteen if she starts childbearing as soon as possible after menarche, which occurs around ages 12–14 (younger in developed countries than in developing ones), and continues until menopause in her middle or late forties. Of course, no population ever reaches that maximum, and there is great variability between women. Some women are, for various reasons, unable to bear any children, while, according to the *Guinness Book of Records*, the greatest number ever officially recorded is sixty-nine by a woman living near Moscow during the eighteenth century (sixteen pairs of twins, seven sets of triplets and four sets of quadruplets). The highest recorded average for any population is about ten births per woman among the Hutterites (see p. 45).

Populations in which no deliberate attempt is made to limit the number of births, such as the Hutterites, are said to experience 'natural fertility'. This very important and widely used concept was first identified and named by Louis Henry (1961, 1972a). Such fertility is essentially a biological phenomenon, and its level varies between populations mainly according to social customs such as varying average ages at marriage and differing breast-feeding and weaning practices. In other words, there is no fertility-limiting behaviour which is in any way dependent upon the number of children already born.

The last frequently used concept that will be mentioned here is that of 'fecundability'. This relates to the physiological ability to conceive, and is the statistical probability of conceiving per menstrual cycle. It is particularly important in the statistical modelling of the process of family building, and in estimation of the effectiveness of family planning programmes.

Period and cohort analysis

There are, broadly, two ways of approaching the study of fertility: period and cohort. The essential quality of period fertility analysis is that it looks at fertility cross-sectionally, that is at births occurring during a specified period of time, normally one year. Cohort analysis, on the other hand, looks at fertility longitudinally, that is at all births occurring to a specific group of women, normally all those born or married during a particular year. One is looking over time, at their reproductive history.

Period analysis is generally simpler than cohort analysis and is more frequently used. Thus it will be considered first. Cohort analysis is covered in Chapter 5. In this chapter a series of measures of period fertility are defined and discussed. They are ordered roughly according to their complexity and data requirements, starting with the simplest, the Child/Woman Ratio.

The Child/Woman Ratio

This can be defined as:

$$\text{C/W Ratio} = \frac{\text{Children aged 0–4}}{\text{Women aged 15–44}}.$$

From Table 4.1 the C/W Ratio for Bangladesh, 1974 is:

$$\text{C/W Ratio} = \frac{7{,}457 + 7{,}192}{3{,}777 + 3{,}101 + 2{,}636 + 2{,}161 + 1{,}793 + 1{,}484}$$

$$= \frac{14{,}649}{14{,}952}$$

$$= 0.9797.$$

For England and Wales, 1985, the comparable figure is 0.2927. There is, however, no strict rule about the age ranges used. Sometimes only children aged 0 are included in the numerator, while the denominator may sometimes be women aged 15–49. Using the latter reduces the England and Wales 1985 figure to 0.2591.

The usefulness of the ratio arises from the fact that it requires only information on the age and sex structure of the population. No data on births are needed at all. This makes it particularly useful when using census data. Obviously, it is an extremely crude measure, but, broadly, if fertility is high, the Child/Woman Ratio will be high, while if fertility is low, the ratio will be low. It is, however, quite sensitive to reporting errors and to the level of infant mortality, so it is dangerous to use the ratio to compare populations with

Table 4.1 Age and sex structure of Bangladesh, 1974

Age group	Males (000s)	Females (000s)
0–4	7457	7192
5–9	5820	5625
10–14	4730	4533
15–19	4017	3777
20–24	3362	3101
25–29	2891	2636
30–34	2391	2161
35–39	1983	1793
40–44	1635	1484
45–49	1343	1222
50–54	1066	974
55–59	858	784
60–64	658	601
65–69	487	440
70–74	339	304
75+	399	334

Source: ODM (1977)

substantially different levels of infant and child mortality, or where under-reporting of young children is a problem.

Crude Birth Rate

This is the simplest and most frequently used measure of fertility. It is defined as:

$$CBR = \frac{\text{Births in year}}{\text{Population at mid-year}} \times 1,000.$$

It is always expressed per 1,000 population. The reason it is a 'crude' rate is that it includes all ages and both sexes in the denominator. No attempt is made to relate the births to the women at risk of having those births. Because of this it is strictly not a measure of fertility at all. Nor, indeed, according to the definitions given in Chapter 1, is it a true rate. Strictly, it is just a ratio.

Taking Bangladesh, 1974, as the first example, there were an estimated 3,689,000 births in a total population of 76,398,000. The CBR was thus:

$$\frac{3,689,000}{76,398,000} \times 1,000$$

$$= 48.3.$$

This is a high figure, close to the maximum that one is likely to observe in normal populations. Towards the other end of the spectrum, in England and Wales, 1985, there were 656,417 births and the estimated mid-year population was 49,923,500. The CBR was thus:

$$\frac{656,417}{49,923,500} \times 1,000$$

$$= 13.1.$$

The range of values the CBR can take in normal populations is thus from about 10 up to around 50. A major problem with it is that it is affected greatly by the composition of the population as regards age, sex and other characteristics. Thus it can mislead if used for comparing different populations, or the same population at widely different times, because they may vary greatly in their composition. There are, though, three reasons why it is a useful measure. First, it is very easy to understand. Second, it requires few data and is easy to calculate. All that is required are the total number of births and the total population. Third, it is possible to subtract the Crude Death Rate from the CBR to get the Crude Rate of Natural Increase, which, along with the Crude Net Migration Rate (see Ch. 9), determines the population growth rate.

General Fertility Rate

The definition of the General Fertility Rate is:

$$GFR = \frac{\text{Births during year}}{\text{Women 15–44 or 49 at mid-year}} \times 1,000.$$

This is a fertility rate rather than a birth rate because it expresses the births relative to the number of women of reproductive age. Sometimes the denominator includes women aged 45–49, sometimes it doesn't. This is important because comparing a 15–44 GFR with a 15–49 GFR will be misleading. To illustrate just how misleading it can be, consider the following GFRs for the United States, 1985:

1. United States, 1985, ages 15–44:

$$GFR = \frac{3,750,000}{56,755,000} \times 1,000$$

$$= 66.1.$$

2. United States, 1985, ages 15–49:

$$\text{GFR} = \frac{3,750,000}{62,724,000} \times 1,000$$

$$= 57.8.$$

The difference is more than 8 points or 13 per cent. As another example, Bangladesh, 1974, illustrates the magnitude of GFR one obtains from a high fertility population:

Bangladesh, 1974, ages 15–44:

$$\text{GFR} = \frac{3,689,000}{14,952,000} \times 1,000$$

$$= 246.7.$$

Thus the range of possible values is roughly from 50 to 300. Note that more data are required to calculate the GFR than the CBR — one has to know the age composition of the female population between ages 15 and 50, not just the overall population size.

The main advantage of the GFR over the CBR is that it substantially controls for age and sex structure by relating the births to roughly the women at risk of having them. But it does not control entirely for age structure since there may be substantial variations between populations within the reproductive age range. For example, in one there may be a relatively large number of girls aged 15–19, while in another there may be only a few, and because births are not spread evenly over the reproductive age range, comparisons using the GFR can be misleading. To overcome this it is necessary to move to a substantially more sophisticated level and consider fertility rates for each age group.

Age-Specific Fertility Rates

The usual definition of these is:

$$\text{ASFR} = \frac{\text{Births in year to women aged } x}{\text{Women aged } x \text{ at mid-year}}. \quad \times 1000$$

Often, though, ASFRs are expressed per 1,000. Normally, seven are calculated, one for each five-year age group 15–19, 20–24 . . . 45–49, as in Table 4.2, but single-year rates are also common.

Note there is a big jump in data requirements over the measures

Table 4.2 Age-Specific Fertility Rates: Bangladesh, 1974

Age group	Women	Births	ASFR per 1,000
15–19	3 777 000	756 900	200.4
20–24	3 101 000	1 046 000	337.3
25–29	2 636 000	819 500	310.9
30–34	2 161 000	565 100	261.5
35–39	1 793 000	353 200	197.0
40–44	1 484 000	141 600	95.4
45–49	1 222 000	16 500	13.5

Source: OMD (1977)

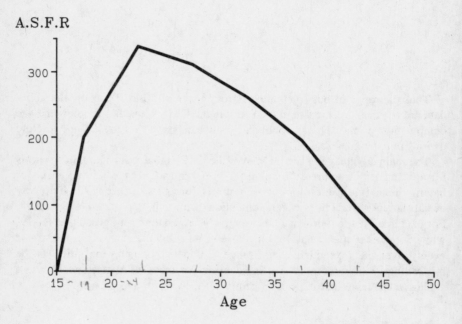

Figure 4.1 Age-Specific Fertility Rates: Bangladesh, 1974

considered so far. It is necessary to have births classified by age of mother. Often such data are not available, or not reliable. Even in England and Wales the age of the mother has only been collected at birth registration since 1938. ASFRs can be graphed, as in Figure 4.1, and tend to show regular features — a rapid rise to a peak in the early or mid-twenties and a gradual decline to very low levels after age 40. These regularities make ASFRs amenable to mathematical modelling. Currently, the only widely used models of fertility by age are those of Coale and Trussell (1974), and Brass (1981). These are introduced in Chapter 14.

It is conventional to include any births occurring to girls aged under 15 in the 15–19 age group, on the grounds that their ages are probably being understated. Similarly, births to women over 49 are usually added into the 45–49 group. The effect of this is always negligible since there are so few births at these ages. Note that the GFR is just an ASFR covering the age group 15–44 or 49.

The great inconvenience of ASFRs is that they are not a single number but a set of at least seven. This makes comparisons complex and tedious, but fortunately it is possible to overcome this by using the Total Fertility Rate.

Total Fertility Rate

Occasionally, this is called a Total Period Fertility Rate (TPFR), particularly in publications of the Office of Population Censuses and Surveys (OPCS) in England and Wales. It is probably the measure of fertility that is most widely used by demographers. It is calculated very simply just by adding up the ASFRs. However, two problems complicate matters a little. First, each ASFR usually relates to five years. It can be thought of as the average of the rates for each of the five years. Thus it is necessary to multiply the five-year rate by five. Second, the TFR is almost always expressed per one woman, whereas ASFRs are often expressed per 1,000. If that is the case, then it is necessary to divide by 1,000. The formula is thus:

$$\text{TFR} = \frac{\text{Sum of ASFRs} \times 5}{1,000}$$

It should be mentioned, however, that in some standard demography texts, including Shryock and Siegel (1976: 287), the TFR is defined as a rate per 1,000 women rather than per woman. This is not conventional now, but is still used in official US statistical publications.

Using the figures from Table 4.2, the TFR for Bangladesh, 1974 is:

$$= \frac{(200.4 + 337.3 + 310.9 + 261.5 + 197.0 + 95.4 + 13.5) \times 5}{1,000}$$

$$= 7.08.$$

Note that if single-year ASFRs are being used, then there is no need to multiply by five. The five is used only because the age intervals are five years long. Also, it of course makes no difference whether you multiply the ASFRs by five and then add them, or the other way around, except that it is easier to add them up first.

Finally, it is perfectly acceptable to include ASFRs for the age groups 10–14 or 50–54, or to omit the 45–49 one. They are always so small that they make very little difference to the final figure.

The great value of the TFR is that it is a single-figure measure that is independent of age structure. The GFR only partially controls for age structure, and the CBR doesn't do so at all. One problem, however, is that it requires a lot of data — births by age of mother and women by age group — and these are usually only available where there are high-quality registration and census systems. Another problem is its interpretion. Formally, the TFR can be thought of as the number of children a woman would have *if* (1) she survived to age 50 and (2) throughout her reproductive life she experienced exactly the ASFRs for the year in question.

To understand this better, consider a group of women in Bangladesh aged 15. Each year while they are 15–19 they have an ASFR of 200.4, then 337.3 while they are 20–24 . . . and 13.5 when 45–49. Then, if they all survive to age 50, they will have had, on average, 7.08 children each.

ASFRs, and the concept of a 'synthetic cohort' which is being used in this interpretation of the TFR, are considered further in Chapter 5.

Specific Fertility Rates

Ordinary Age-Specific Fertility Rates (ASFRs) are calculated by dividing the births occurring to women aged x by the total number of women aged x. However, it is also possible to define fertility rates that are specific to many other things, almost always in conjunction with age. The most common is by marital status.

Consider first the General Fertility Rate (GFR). It is really just an ASFR for the age group 15–44 or 15–49. Recall that the GFR is a better measure of fertility than the CBR because it relates the births more closely to the people at risk of having those births. Now, because in most societies births occur predominantly to married women, clearly it would be useful to have a measure similar to the GFR but which uses married women rather than all women in the denominator. There are in fact two in common use. One is the General Marital Fertility Rate (GMFR), defined as:

$$GMFR = \frac{All\ births}{Married\ women\ 15\text{--}44\ or\ 49} \times 1,000.$$

The other is the General Legitimate Fertility Rate (GLFR):

$$GLFR = \frac{Legitimate\ births}{Married\ women\ 15\text{--}44\ or\ 49} \times 1,000.$$

For completeness it is also convenient here to define the General Illegitimate Fertility Rate (GIFR):

$$\text{GIFR} = \frac{\text{Illegitimate births}}{\text{Single, widowed, divorced women 15–44 or 49}} \times 1,000.$$

The problem with these measures is that they do not have well-established names. For example, the GLFR is often called the 'General Marital Fertility Rate', while Woods (1979: 107) just calls it the 'Marital Fertility Rate'. Both because of this, and because the age range used in the denominators can vary, it is essential when using these measures to state precisely the formula being used, not just its name. The names used here are those given by Shryock and Siegel (1976: 281).

In societies where illegitimacy is negligible, such as India and Bangladesh, the GMFR and GLFR are identical. Normally, though, it is preferable to use only legitimate births in the numerator, since it is only those which married women are at risk of bearing.

Now, to generalise the above from GFRs, ASFRs which also control for marriage by using only legitimate births in the numerator and married women in the denominator are called Marital ASFRs or sometimes 'Age-Specific Marital Fertility Rates'. Both these names are widely used. Table 4.3 shows figures for the United States, 1984, as an example.

Table 4.3 Marital Age-Specific Fertility Rates: United States, 1984

Age group	Legitimate births	Married women	MASFRs
15–19	208 578	608 000	343.0
20–24	862 386	4 576 000	188.5
25–29	1 028 755	7 855 000	131.0
30–34	599 235	8 403 000	71.3
35–39	174 839	7 838 000	22.3
40–44	23 148	6 496 000	3.6
45–49	955	5 559 000	0.2

Just as it is possible to sum ASFRs to produce a Total Fertility Rate (TFR), so it is also possible to sum MASFRs to produce what is often called a 'Total Marital Fertility Rate' (TMFR). Just as with the TFR it is necessary to multiply by 5 if using five-year age groups, and to divide by 1,000 if the MASFRs being used are expressed per 1,000 women. However, there are problems with the interpretation of the TMFR which make it less attractive than the TFR as a measure of period fertility.

First, the interpretation of the TFR mentioned above is the number of children a woman will bear *if* she survives to age 50 and *if* she experiences the given ASFRs. Now, for a TMFR these 'ifs' still apply, but there are two additional ones. These are that the woman is married by age 15, and that she stays married at least until age 50. So, if, say, a TMFR is 10.0, it only means that a woman will have, on average, ten children if it is assumed that:

1. She married before age 15.
2. She survives until age 50.
3. She remains married until age 50.
4. She experiences exactly the MASFRs used.

The TMFR is little used in demography for two main reasons. First, and more importantly, there is the problem that the MASFR for the 15–19 age group is almost always extremely high, in large part because it is inflated greatly by premarital conceptions. Even though only a very small number of women aged 15–19 is usually married, their high MASFR is nevertheless given exactly the same weight in the TMFR as each of the other age groups and therefore has an excessively large impact on the overall rate. The second problem is the difficulty in the interpretation of the measure. In particular, the first of the four assumptions that have to be made, that of marriage before age 15, is quite unrepresentative of the average woman's experience in any normal population.

These problems can be reduced substantially by calculating a TMFR which simply leaves out the 15–19 MASFR altogether, and this is often done, particularly in historical demography, where the measure is used extensively. But because it is so easy to misinterpret, it is often better not to use the TMFR at all, but instead to calculate a rate which is similar but in which the age groups are weighted using the proportion married. Another alternative might be to control for marriage using some form of standarisation of the TFR (see Shryock and Siegel 1976: 288), though that produces a measure of overall rather than just marital fertility.

ASFRs can be calculated that are specific to many other characteristics, such as birth order (i.e. *n*th pregnancy), religion, residence or education (see Shryock and Siegel 1976, Ch. 16). The important thing is to ensure always that the population in the denominator includes all those at risk of producing the births in the numerator and excludes those not at risk. And, as always, it is also important to explain precisely the measures used and the source of the data.

Coale's Indices

In the late 1960s Ansley Coale, then Director of the Office of Population Research at Princeton University, set up a large-scale study of the decline of fertility in Europe during the nineteenth and twentieth centuries. It is known as

'The Princeton European Fertility Study'. The data available for such a study essentially comprise the total population broken down by age and sex, and the annual total number of births. The population figures, including age structure, were available from censuses, while the births were derived from registration data, mainly parish records of baptisms.

Such data made it possible to calculate GFRs, but not TFRs, because the births were not broken down by age of mother. GFRs were, however, inadequate because they did not fully control for age, and because they did not use the information available on the age structure of the population between ages 15 and 50.

Coale thus developed three measures or indices of fertility — one for overall fertility, one for marital fertility and one for illegitimate fertility. These are memorably named:

$$I_f = \text{overall fertility}$$
$$I_g = \text{marital fertility}$$
$$I_h = \text{illegitimate fertility.}$$

Essentially, these indices are just indirectly standardised ratios. They express the level of fertility as a proportion of the fertility a population would have had if it had experienced the highest fertility pattern on record. Thus Coale is firstly asking how many births the population would have had if their fertility had been the highest ever recorded? Then he asks how close to that maximum the population actually got? For a more general discussion of standardisation, both direct and indirect, see Chapter 6, pages 66–7 below.

The group of people with the highest reliably recorded fertility are the Hutterites. They are a small Christian religious group living in north-central United States and southern Canada. Their religion encourages them to have as large families as possible. They tend not to marry unusually early, but once they do they produce children very rapidly. They breast-feed for a relatively short period and practise no form of contraception. The very highest Hutterite fertility was achieved during the decade 1921–30. The Marital ASFRs they attained are given in Table 4.4.

These rates are expressed per one woman. The rate for the 15–19 age group was in fact invented in an arbitrary way because the real figure of 0.700 was considered to be too high and unrepresentative, and would have had an excessively large effect on the final rates.

The calculations required to compute Coale's Indices comprise first applying the standard Hutterite rates to the observed population in order to get an 'expected' number of births, and second expressing the actual observed number of births as a proportion of the number expected. This is done for I_f in Table 4.5. The total number of births in the United States in 1984 was 3,659,176.

Table 4.4 Hutterite marital ASFRs, 1921–30

Age group	MASFR
15–19	0.300
20–24	0.550
25–29	0.502
30–34	0.447
35–39	0.406
40–44	0.222
45–49	0.061

Table 4.5 Coale's I_f: United States, 1984

Age group	Total females	Hutterite standard	Expected births
15–19	9 189 000	0.300	2 756 700
20–24	10 620 000	0.550	5 841 000
25–29	10 603 000	0.502	5 322 706
30–34	9 694 000	0.447	4 333 218
35–39	8 477 000	0.406	3 441 662
40–44	6 868 000	0.222	1 524 696
45–49	5 829 000	0.061	355 569
			23 575 551

Thus:

$$I_f = \frac{3,659,176}{23,575,551}$$

$$= 0.155.$$

So in 1984 women in the United States produced 15.5 per cent of the births they would have had if they had experienced the fertility rates that were achieved by married Hutterite women during 1921–30.

Now, for I_g, the index of marital fertility, the same procedure is repeated, but using married women only, and legitimate rather than total births. This is done in Table 4.6. The total number of legitimate births in the United States in 1984 was 2,897,896. Thus:

$$I_g = \frac{2,897,896}{15,361,990}$$

$$= 0.189.$$

Table 4.6 Coale's I_g: United States, 1984

Age group	Married females	Hutterite standard	Expected births
15–19	608000	0.300	182400
20–24	4576000	0.550	2516800
25–29	7855000	0.502	3943210
30–34	8403000	0.447	3756141
35–39	7838000	0.406	3182228
40–44	6496000	0.222	1442112
45–49	5559000	0.061	339099
			15361990

I_h, the index of illegitimate fertility, can be calculated by subtraction of the legitimate from the total observed and expected births as follows:

$$\text{Obs. illegitimate} = \text{Obs. total} - \text{Obs. legitimate}$$
$$= 3,659,176 - 2,897,896$$
$$= 761,280$$

$$\text{Exp. illegitimate} = \text{Exp. total} - \text{Exp. legitimate}$$
$$= 23,575,551 - 15,361,990$$
$$= 8,213,561.$$

Then $I_h = $ Obs./Exp. as before:

$$= \frac{761,280}{8,213,561}$$

$$= 0.093.$$

Now, Coale also defined a fourth index which he called I_m. This is not a measure of fertility but an index of marriage. It is calculated quite differently from the other three indices. It is simply a weighted average of the proportions married of women aged 15–19, 20–24 . . . 45–49 where the weights are the Hutterite ASFRs. The calculations are most easily done using the statistical functions of a calculator, but are shown in full in Table 4.7.

To calculate a weighted average one first multiplies the values, labelled (a) in Table 4.7 by the weights, labelled (b). Then one sums the resulting products and divides by the sum of the weights. Here the sum of the products is 1.6599 and the sum of the weights is 2.488, so the weighted mean, I_m, is 1.6599/2.488 = 0.667.

Table 4.7 Coale's I_m: United States, 1984

Age group	Total females	Married females	Proportion married (a)	Hutterite standard (b)	(a) × (b)
15–19	9 189 000	608 000	0.0662	0.300	0.0199
20–24	10 620 000	4 576 000	0.4309	0.550	0.2370
25–29	10 603 000	7 855 000	0.7408	0.502	0.3719
30–34	9 694 000	8 403 000	0.8668	0.447	0.3875
35–39	8 477 000	7 838 000	0.9246	0.406	0.3754
40–44	6 868 000	6 496 000	0.9458	0.222	0.2100
45–49	5 829 000	5 559 000	0.9537	0.061	0.0582
				2.488	1.6599

A useful short-cut is that I_m can also be calculated as the ratio of the expected births that would occur to married and to all women if they experienced the standard Hutterite fertility rates. These figures have already been calculated for I_f and I_g so, for the United States, 1984 we have:

$$\text{Expected births to married women} = 15,361,990.$$

$$\text{Expected births to all women} = 23,575,551.$$

Thus:

$$I_m = \frac{15,361,990}{23,575,551}$$

$$= 0.652 \text{ as before, except for rounding error.}$$

There is a relationship between all four indices which can be written as:

$$I_f = I_g I_m + I_h(1 - I_m)$$

If illegitimacy is negligible or non-existent, then the second part of the right hand side becomes zero since $I_h = 0$ so the equation simplifies to:

$$I_f = I_g I_m$$

It is important to realise that the calculation of the indices is just straight-forward Indirect Standarisation (see Ch. 6). The standard rates are the Hutterite MASFRs, and the index population is, in the example above, the United States, 1984. The indices I_f, I_g and I_h are equivalent to 'Standardised Mortality Ratios'

(SMRs). Indeed, in many cases it would be preferable to use a different standard than the Hutterite one. For example, if one was comparing the fertility levels of the regions of a country, then the most appropriate standard would be the national rates.

Summary

This chapter has introduced a number of measures of period fertility ranging from the Child/Woman Ratio through the CBR, GFR, Coale's Indices and ASFRs to the TFR. The decision about which of these should be used on any particular occasion is often difficult. The best advice is that it should always be based, first, on which measures can be calculated given the data available and, second, on the purposes for which it is to be used. No one measure is best for all purposes and all occasions.

Some further measures of period fertility, the Gross and Net Reproduction Rates, are described in Chapter 9, but the next chapter turns to consider cohort rather than period fertility measures.

Exercises

1. Tables 4E.1 and 4E.2 are taken from the 1975 Statistical Abstract of the Seychelles. Using the data they contain, calculate:

(a) The Child/Woman Ratio.
(b) The Crude Birth Rate.
(c) The General Fertility Rate.
(d) Age-Specific Fertility Rates.
(e) The Total Fertility Rate.

Under what circumstances would it be preferable to use the CBR rather than the TFR?

2. Table 4E.3 gives the data needed to calculate Coale's Indices for Bangladesh, 1974. Before calculating them, try to guess roughly what results you should obtain. The estimated total number of births in Bangladesh in 1974 was 3,689,000 and there was a negligible amount of illegitimacy. When would it be particularly appropriate to use Coale's Indices in preference to any of the other measures of period fertility? What assumptions are you making when using the indices to compare fertility levels between different areas or over time?

3. Table 4E.4 shows an age distribution of married women, derived from a census of a parish in southern Germany, dating from the late eighteenth century. Inspection of the baptismal records of the parish for the year in question produced an estimate of 208 legitimate births. What does this information enable you to say about fertility in the parish?

Table 4E.1 Estimated mid-year population, Seychelles, 1975

Age group	Total	Males	Females
0 –4	8 460	4 331	4 129
5 –9	8 131	4 071	4 060
10–14	7 941	3 996	3 945
15–19	6 516	3 426	3 090
20–24	4 210	2 324	1 886
25–29	3 248	1 768	1 480
30–34	2 804	1 489	1 315
35–39	2 606	1 212	1 394
40–44	2 824	1 389	1 435
45–49	2 323	1 144	1 179
50–54	2 160	1 041	1 119
55–59	1 764	871	895
60–64	1 668	754	914
65–69	1 248	569	679
70–74	1 118	472	646
75+	993	318	675
Total	58 014	29 175	28 839

Table 4E.2 Registered births by age group and parity of mothers, Seychelles, 1975

Age group of mothers	1	2	3	4	5	6	7	8	9	10	11	12	13	14	15+	Total
<15	1															1
15–19	287	101	23	2				1								414
20–24	195	124	96	50	17	9	1	1								493
25–29	54	72	66	50	44	32	18	3	1			1				341
30–34	25	27	24	35	39	39	43	20	11	10	1	2	1			277
35–39	5	3	14	9	23	23	35	21	24	15	8	6	2	3	3	194
40–44	2	3	1	1	7	4	8	12	6	11	11	5	2	2		75
45–49				2	1			2		4		1				10
50+										1						1
Total	569	330	224	149	131	107	105	60	42	41	20	15	5	5	3	1806

Table 4E.3 Data for calculating Coale's Indices for Bangladesh, 1974

Age group of women	Hutterite standard	Estimated population (000s)	
		All females	Married females
15–19	0.300	3 777	2 432
20–24	0.550	3 101	2 828
25–29	0.502	2 636	2 494
30–34	0.447	2 161	2 012
35–39	0.406	1 793	1 606
40–44	0.222	1 484	1 211
45–49	0.061	1 222	892

Source: ODM (1977)

Table 4E.4 Age distribution of married women, south German parish

Age group	Married women
20–24	109
25–29	110
30–34	87
35–39	77
40–44	64
45–49	49

5 Cohort fertility

The exact relationship between cohort and period fertility is difficult to grasp, especially since it is rarely possible to look at both using the same data source. This chapter therefore begins with a broad discussion of their relationship, and introduces some of the simpler ways of presenting and manipulating birth and marriage cohort data. This is followed by a description of the concept of a 'Synthetic cohort', one of the main sources of confusion between cohort and period modes of analysis. Lastly, there is a brief introduction to Parity Progression Ratios and an overview of birth interval analysis. One longer and quite readable discussion of cohort measures of fertility is by Campbell (1983, Ch. 2).

Cohort and period fertility analysis

The essential feature of cohort analysis is that it considers the experience of one group of people over time, usually all those born or marrying during a particular time interval. This is in contrast to period analysis, introduced in the previous chapter, in which events occurring during a particular time period are studied.

A cohort approach to fertility is a comparatively new idea, having become widely used only in the last twenty years or so. It is used mainly for explaining fertility levels and trends, rather than forecasting, and is consequently normally of more interest to academic researchers than to administrators and planners.

There are three big problems associated with cohort analysis. The first is that it requires data in the form of a fairly long, consistent time series, and such data are rare, even in highly developed societies. The second is the problem known technically as 'censoring' — that one does not know what will happen in the future so the later experience of young or more recent cohorts is unknown. The third is that it seems to be rather difficult to think about cohorts. Our minds are so used to thinking in a cross-sectional way that it is hard to think in any other way.

Consider the array of ASFRs in Table 5.1. By looking at successive columns one can compare how fertility varies by age, period by period. By looking at successive rows one can compare how fertility varies by period, age by age. However, the women who were aged 15–19 in 1940 will be 20–24 in 1945, 25–29 in 1950, and so on. They are the birth cohort of 1920–4. Thus by considering diagonals of the table one can compare the fertility of different birth cohorts. One can therefore regard each ASFR as being associated with a particular age group, a particular time period and a particular birth cohort, and each ASFR will

Table 5.1 ASFRs: England and Wales, 1940–85

Age group	Year									
	1940	1945	1950	1955	1960	1965	1970	1975	1980	1985
15–19	15	17	22	24	34	45	49	37	31	30
20–24	91	103	126	137	166	180	156	115	114	95
25–29	108	118	136	142	172	181	155	123	136	128
30–34	75	94	89	84	101	103	80	59	71	76
35–39	43	58	48	44	46	48	35	20	23	24
40–44	15	19	14	12	14	13	9	5	4	5
45–49	1	1	1	1	1	1	1	0	0	0
TFR	1.74	2.05	2.18	2.22	2.67	2.85	2.42	1.80	1.88	1.78

be determined by a combination of age, period and cohort influences.

Now, one can sum the columns of Table 5.1 to calculate the TFR for each period. Clearly, it is also possible to sum the ASFRs for a cohort in the same way as is done to calculate a TFR. This measure is the 'Cohort Fertility Rate' (CFR). To take the 1920–4 birth cohort as an example, we have, from Table 5.1 a CFR of:

$$\frac{15 + 103 + 136 + 84 + 46 + 13 + 1}{1,000} \times 5$$

$$= 1.99.$$

(This calculation actually assumes that the 1940 rates were experienced throughout 1940–4, a problem that is discussed below on page 55.)

The CFR is often called the 'Completed Family Size', but this is somewhat misleading as it has very little to do with the family. It can be interpreted as the average number of children women in the particular birth cohort will have borne by age 50. Care in interpretation is, however, necessary. Consider the women born in 1915–19. They will be 50–54 in 1970. If a census was taken in 1970 and women were asked how many births they had had, then it would be possible to calculate the average number of children born per woman aged 50–54. This is not, however, precisely the same as the Cohort Fertility Rate, partly because only those women who have survived to 50–54 can answer, whereas the CFR includes the fertility of women who die before 50. Migration can also have an impact since those alive in England and Wales in 1970 aged 50–54 will include some immigrants, and will exclude those born in 1915–19 who emigrated. Indeed, migration is often a serious problem in cohort analysis, and can produce otherwise impossible effects such as a cohort increasing in size over time.

Table 5.2 Cohort Fertility Rates: England and Wales, 1920–44 birth cohorts

Birth cohort	CFR
1920–4	1.99
1925–9	2.22
1930–4	2.37
1935–9	2.38
1940–4	2.28

Cohort Fertility Rates are generally less variable than TFRs as can be seen from a comparison of the TFRs in Table 5.1 and the CFRs in Table 5.2. This is because TFRs are affected by the tendency of couples to advance or postpone their births, whereas the CFRs are not. If couples have their children earlier (i.e. the mean age of childbearing falls), the period rate will rise, while if they have them later, it will fall. The cohort rate will not change. This raises one of the big problems of fertility analysis: how can demographers, particularly those trying to explain fertility or carry out population forecasts, tell whether a change in period fertility is simply due to a timing change — couples advancing or postponing births — or whether it is a 'real' change in fertility levels, that is, couples having smaller or bigger families? Put another way, if the TFR changes in a particular year, how can one tell whether the CFRs of the cohorts who are bearing children in that year also change? The simple answer is that one cannot tell until the relevant cohorts have completed childbearing.

A timing change is also known as a 'tempo' change. An extreme example is Japan in 1966. It was considered that a girl born then, the 'Year of the White Horse', would grow up ill-tempered and no one would want to marry her. The TFR for 1966 fell to 1.6, compared with 2.2 in 1965 and 2.1 in 1967 (Frejka 1973: 11). Another example, also in 1966, comes from Romania where the sudden introduction of a more restrictive abortion law produced a big jump in the birth rate, which quickly fell back again as methods of contraception were adopted. In Britain the 1946–7 post-war 'baby-boom', when births postponed during the war arrived, is yet another example.

Clearly, these sort of tempo effects have a dramatic effect on period fertility rates, but probably have comparatively little effect on cohort rates. Influences on fertility which do affect the cohort rates are called 'quantum effects'. These will, though, inevitably also affect period rates since one can consider period rates to be the cross-sectional consequences of the performances of cohorts (Ryder 1980: 16). To put this another way, the difficulty when trying to explain fertility levels and trends using period rates is just that changes in cohort tempo — the rate of family building — appear as changes in period quantum (TFR).

A large part of the difficulty is that we shall not know the CFRs of current cohorts until some time in the future, perhaps thirty years for the youngest ones. This 'censoring' is one of the features of cohort data which makes their analysis statistically complex. Often it is necessary to resort to life-table techniques, which are introduced in the more familiar context of mortality analysis, in the next chapter.

The manipulation and presentation of cohort data

It is possible to manipulate and present cohort data in various ways. First, one can adjust the usual period table so that the cohorts appear as rows. Then Table 5.1 become Table 5.3. Note that the labelling on this table implies an assumption that, for example, the 1940 ASFR actually applies to the whole of the five years from 1940 to 1944. This highlights a particular problem which often arises when trying to carry out cohort analysis. If one is using data classified only by age and not date of birth, then it is impossible to translate precisely from ages to year of birth. For example, if a woman has a birth at some unknown date during 1980 and states she was 20 years old, then she may have been born at any time during the two years between 1 January 1959 and 31 December 1960. Similar problems arise in the opposite direction if period analysis is attempted with data including year of birth but not age. Comparable difficulties occur when considering marriage cohorts if only one of year or duration of marriage is available. Only if the precise date of birth or marriage is available can exact translation between cohort and period be carried out.

Comparison of cohort family building can be made slightly easier by cumulating the figures given in Table 5.3 over age, as has been done in Table 5.4, though this does not, of course, solve the difficulties mentioned in the previous paragraph.

These figures are obtained from Table 5.3 by expressing the ASFRs as per woman, multiplying by 5 and cumulating across the rows. The cumulated fertility to age 50 is the Cohort Fertility Rate.

Table 5.3 ASFRs by birth cohort: England and Wales, 1920–69

Year of birth	15–19	20–24	25–29	Age group 30–34	35–39	40–44	45–49	CFR
1920–4	15	103	136	84	46	13	1	1.99
1925–9	17	126	142	101	48	9	0	2.22
1930–4	22	137	172	103	35	5	0	2.37
1935–9	24	166	181	80	20	4	0	2.38
1940–4	34	180	155	59	23	5	0	2.28
1945–9	45	156	123	71	24			
1950–4	49	115	136	76				
1955–9	37	114	128					
1960–4	31	95						
1965–9	30							

Table 5.4 Cumulated fertility by birth cohort: England and Wales, 1920–69

Year of birth	Exact age						
	20	25	30	35	40	45	50
1920–4	0.075	0.590	1.270	1.690	1.920	1.985	1.988
1925–9	0.085	0.715	1.425	1.930	2.170	2.215	2.217
1930–4	0.110	0.795	1.655	2.170	2.345	2.370	2.372
1935–9	0.120	0.950	1.855	2.255	2.355	2.375	2.377
1940–4	0.170	1.070	1.845	2.140	2.255	2.278	2.280
1945–9	0.225	1.005	1.620	1.975	2.095		
1950–4	0.245	0.820	1.500	1.880			
1955–9	0.185	0.755	1.395				
1960–4	0.155	0.630					
1965–9	0.150						

Marriage cohorts

One problem of trying to analyse or explain fertility using birth cohort data is that the members of any particular birth cohort will marry at different ages, some early, some late, so their fertility behaviour is likely to be different. One way of controlling for this diversity is to use marriage cohorts — women marrying in the same year — instead of birth cohorts, irrespective of their age. Their rate of family building and overall family size is likely to be less variable than that of birth cohorts.

The measure used to look at the fertility of marriage cohorts is a 'Marriage-Duration-Specific Fertility Rate', defined as:

$$MDSFR = \frac{\text{Births in year } x \text{ to women who married in year } y}{\text{Total women who married in year } y}.$$

Such rates can be calculated for each year and some Australian ones are tabulated in Table 5.5.

Comparing Table 5.5. with Table 5.4, down the side there is date of marriage rather than date of birth, and along the top marriage duration rather than age. Age does not appear in the table at all.

There are several problems associated with marriage-duration fertility rates. First, there are difficulties in dealing with divorces and remarriages. It is usual to avoid them simply by considering only unbroken first marriages, though this is not a very satisfactory solution, especially in places where divorce and remarriage is common. Second, within a single marriage cohort fertility is likely to vary substantially by age at marriage. Those marrying young will tend to have higher fertility than those marrying late. Because of this MDSFRs are often split into five-year age-at-marriage bands. Third, it is clear that most of the births

Table 5.5 Cumulated fertility by marriage cohort: Australia, 1911–65

Year of marriage	Duration of marriage (years)						
	1	2	5	10	15	20	25
1911–15	0.506	0.751	1.523	2.390	2.839	3.029	3.078
1921–5	0.440	0.700	1.399	2.057	2.337	2.456	2.492
1931–5	0.393	0.651	1.267	1.852	2.174	2.302	2.336
1941–5	0.261	0.524	1.175	1.849	2.151	2.267	
1951–5	0.333	0.646	1.478	2.301			
1961–5	0.382	0.684					

which occur in the first year or two after marriage are first births, while at longer durations they will be predominantly high-order births. Thus one could additionally disaggregate the data by birth order to produce rates which are parity as well as age and marriage-duration specific, though the amount of data required for such disaggregation is immense and the tables produced are voluminous.

Synthetic cohorts

In Chapter 3 the Total Fertility Rate was interpreted as the number of children a woman would have if she survived to age 50 and experienced, over her reproductive years, exactly the given ASFRs. But no real group of women every actually experience any particular set of period ASFRs. The imaginary, hypothetical group who are supposed to do so are called a 'synthetic cohort'.

The only difference, then, between a TFR and a CFR is that the former describes the imaginary experience of a synthetic cohort, while the latter is based on the actual experience of a real cohort. Synthetic cohorts are very widely used in demographic analysis. For example, with a conventional life table (see Ch. 6) one is considering a synthetic cohort of 1,000, or however many, births who experience the age-specific death rates for the year on which the life table is based. As Notestein puts it, measures which use the concept of a synthetic cohort:

summarize a single year's experience for the population of all ages as if it were the experience of a single class (cohort) that has passed through all ages. They are hypothetical values like the readings on a car's speedometer. The latter does not tell you how far you have come during the last hour, or how far you will go in the next hour. It gives you the highly hypothetical information that if you had travelled during the past hour at precisely the rate you are travelling now you would have by the end of an hour, travelled the indicated distance.

(Notestein, quoted by Frejka 1973: 30)

Synthetic cohorts create confusion between period and cohort modes of analysis. To avoid this simply remember that there are three different types of cohort commonly used in formal demography: birth, marriage and synthetic.

Parity Progression Ratios

So far nearly all the fertility measures discussed use vital statistics data. Little attention has been paid to census or survey-derived data, though one, the Child/Woman Ratio, was described in Chapter 4 (see p. 36). That ratio did not require any specific fertility question to be asked since it uses only the age and sex structure. If, however, there are questions on fertility, then they normally ask about the number of children born alive, children still living and children who have died. From these questions tables can be produced showing the average number of children ever borne broken down by age of mother. The average number of children ever borne to women aged 45–49 will be very similar to the Cohort Fertility Rate, as mentioned above. The difference is that the former does not include births to emigrants or to those members of the cohort who did not survive to the census or survey.

Data on children ever borne can be tabulated either by birth cohort, or by marriage cohort, and from such tables Parity Progression Ratios (PPRs) can be calculated. A PPR is simply the probability of having another child given that one has already had a certain number. For example, if a woman has already had three births it is the probability of her having a fourth. The way they are calculated is shown, for birth cohort-based data, in Table 5.6, though the principle is exactly the same for marriage cohorts.

The reason why older women are chosen here is that their PPRs will be close to their final PPRs, whereas if younger women are considered the calculated PPRs will not reflect their final fertility and thus will be too small. The calculations involved are straightforward. One first tabulates the women by parity, as

Table 5.6 Parity Progression Ratios, 1910–14 birth cohort: Thailand, 1960 census

Children ever borne	Women 45–49	Women 45–49 with at least CEB	PPR	
0	14 352	454 364	0.968	a_0
1	26 548	440 012	0.940	a_1
2	29 268	413 464	0.929	a_2
3	33 271	384 196	0.913	a_3
4	39 448	350 925	0.888	a_4
5	44 928	311 477	0.856	a_5
6	48 252	266 549	0.819	a_6
7	49 401	218 297	0.774	a_7
8	46 789	168 896	0.723	a_8
9	41 112	122 107	0.663	a_9
10+	80 995	80 995		

in the first column of Table 5.6. These figures are then cumulated from the bottom to give the number of women with at least n children ever borne. Lastly, one divides adjacent figures to give the probabilities. For example, $a_0 = 440012/454364 = 0.968$.

Note that a_0 is just the proportion of women in the cohort who become mothers. Also, it can be shown that the Cohort Fertility Rate can be expressed as an arithmetic series of products of PPRs. That is:

$$CFR = a_0 + a_0a_1 + a_0a_1a_2 + a_0a_1a_2a_3 + \ldots$$

In highly developed societies, where two-child families are the norm, the a_2 PPR — the proportion of couples who go on to have a third child having already had two — is of critical importance in determining fertility levels.

Birth intervals

Parity Progression Ratios measure only the extent to which women are having first, second and higher-order births, not their timing. Yet, as has already been pointed out, the timing of births has an extremely important influence on period fertility rates. If women start having their first births earlier, or if the interval between successive births becomes shorter, then period fertility will rise, even if the Cohort Fertility Rate remains unchanged. Similarly, if the start of childbearing is delayed, or if the intervals lengthen, then period fertility will drop while the cohort quantum stays the same. Clearly, therefore, the analysis of birth intervals is of considerable importance in understanding fertility trends.

A birth interval is defined as the time between successive live births and is usually measured in months. Stillbirths and abortions are not counted. A birth interval is not the same as an inter-pregnancy interval, which is the period from the end of one pregnancy to the start of the next, and which is used mainly for measuring the length of exposure to the risk of conception, for use in studies of such matters as contraceptive effectiveness.

The first birth interval is the time between the first and second live birth, *not* the interval from marriage to first birth. Each interval begins with a period of post-partum amenorrhoea prior to the return of menstruation after confinement. This lasts at least 1.5 months and can be extended greatly by prolonged lactation. This may then be followed by a period of contraception, and then by a period of 'waiting' between stopping contraception and conception. Finally, there is the pregnancy, normally lasting nine months. Intervals can, however, be rather more complicated than this due to abortions and stillbirths. The minimum possible length of an interval is thus ten months, allowing for prematurity, but they are normally substantially longer and can be ten or twenty years. For a more detailed discussion, see Bongaarts and Potter (1983).

The data required for birth interval analysis are usually collected in a census or survey in the form of a 'birth history' or, if all pregnancies rather than just live births are asked about, a 'maternity history'. The simplest way to analyse birth interval data is just to calculate mean lengths, though because of the skewed distribution of interval lengths, caused by a small number of very long intervals, the median is a better measure in most circumstances. Analysis is, however, greatly complicated by the problem of censoring, mentioned earlier (see p. 54). Many women will not have completed their childbearing at the time of data collection. They will therefore have a final 'open' interval which is censored by the survey or census. Moreover, the intervals which are censored in this way will tend to be longer ones on average. Thus mean birth intervals computed for groups of women who have not completed childbearing will tend to be underestimates of the ultimate mean intervals. In order to avoid this bias when comparing different age groups it is necessary either to exclude the more recent experience of the older age group, or to estimate in some way the future experience of the younger group.

Other complications which often arise in birth interval analysis relate to the fact that stillbirths, abortions and infant deaths both affect, and are affected by, the length of the interval. These, the problems of censoring and selectivity mentioned above, and the difficulty of obtaining complete and accurate birth history data, even in developed countries, make the analysis of birth intervals one of the more difficult and statistically complex areas of formal demography (Page and Lesthaeghe 1980).

Exercises

1. This exercise is adapted from the problems given in Pressat (1974: 180–3). Table 5E.1 shows Parity Progression Ratios for birth cohorts of white, native-born US women, derived from the 1960 census. Complete this table using the information in Table 5E.2 by calculating the PPRs for the cohorts born in 1901–5 and 1906–10. Consider the patterns described in the completed table.

More detailed study has made it possible to predict the PPRs for the 1931–5 birth cohort, shown in Table 5E.3. Compare these figures with those for 1871–5 and 1896–1900 by graphical means. Why might the patterns you observe be occurring?

2. The PPRs shown in Table 5E.4 were calculated from data collected in a British survey conducted in 1967–8 (Langford 1976). They refer to women who married in 1941–50 and are disaggregated by their husbands' occupational status. Estimate the mean family size achieved by the non-manual group of women.

The data in Table 5E.5, from the same source, refer to women married in 1951–60. Calculate PPRs for these two groups of women. Compare the results with the figures in the earlier table. What differentials and trends in cohort fertility are apparent? In what ways are they limited or misleading?

Table 5E.1 Parity Progression Ratios, United States, 1960 census

Birth cohort	Parity Progression Ratio						
	0–1	1–2	2–3	3–4	4–5	5–6	6–7
1871–5	830	802	790	770	760	780	755
1876–80	826	795	758	748	735	760	740
1881–5	817	782	731	726	715	745	725
1886–90	805	768	717	706	695	735	705
1891–5	792	756	696	686	680	710	695
1896–1900	772	753	666	664	670	690	680
1901–5							
1906–10							

Table 5E.2 Live births by birth order per 1,000 women, United States, 1901–10

Birth cohort	Birth order								
	1	2	3	4	5	6	7	8+	All
1901–05	764	557	352	224	144	96	63	115	2315
1906–10	773	561	335	200	122	78	50	89	2208

Table 5E.3 PPR: Parity Progression Ratio: United States, 1931–5 cohort

Birth cohort	Parity Progression Ratio						
	0–1	1–2	2–3	3–4	4–5	5–6	6–7
1931–5	900	900	750	600	500	550	640

Table 5E.4 PPRs: women marrying in 1941–50 in England and Wales, by husband's occupational status

	a_0	a_1	a_2	a_3	a_{4+}
Non-manual	0.887	0.735	0.405	0.424	0.357
Manual	0.916	0.888	0.560	0.558	0.632

Table 5E.5 Children ever borne, 1951–60, in England and Wales, by husband's occupational status

Children ever borne	Number of women	
	Non-manual	Manual
0	25	40
1	38	66
2	93	137
3	62	73
4	10	40
5+	10	24

6 Mortality and life tables

Perhaps because death is a precise, easily definable event which occurs just once to each individual, the techniques for analysing mortality have a longer history and are more developed than those for analysing fertility. More likely reasons, though, are the actuarial demands of insurance companies during the eighteenth and nineteenth centuries. It was only in the early part of the twentieth century that fertility began to be studied to any great extent, but the history of mortality analysis goes back as far as the work of Graunt in the late seventeenth century, and even to Roman times.

This chapter is primarily concerned with the basic measures used in mortality analysis. It includes a discussion of the various simple mortality rates and a description of the technique of standardisation whose usefulness extends far beyond mortality analysis. But the main purpose of this chapter is to introduce the concepts, notation, calculation and application of life tables. First the procedure for calculating a life table from raw data is outlined, and then the various life-table columns are explained — how they are defined, calculated and interpreted. Good introductions to mortality analysis are given by Barclay (1958, Chs 4 and 5) and by Shryock and Siegel (1976, Chs 14 and 15).

Basic mortality measures

A more detailed discussion of these, including prevalence and incidence rates can be found in most introductory epidemiology texts.

The Crude Death Rate

The Crude Death Rate (CDR) is simply the deaths in a year divided by the total population at mid-year and multiplied by 1,000. That is:

$$CDR = \frac{\text{Deaths in year}}{\text{Population at mid-year}} \times 1,000.$$

It is, of course, possible to use periods shorter or longer than a year, but then the calculation becomes more complex, involving estimation of years of exposure to the risk of dying.

Although it is easily computed and understood, it is generally a poor measure of mortality as it does not take age structure into account. In many developing countries it is lower than in highly developed countries just because the former have a much younger age structure. For example, in England and Wales in 1983 the CDR was 11.7, while in Mexico, where mortality is higher, it was just 7.1. The CDR also covers all ages, yet a crucial aspect of mortality is the way it varies by age.

One important use of the CDR is to calculate the Crude Rate of Natural Increase — the difference between the CBR and the CDR — a measure of the current rate of population growth if net migration is not substantial.

The Infant Mortality Rate

This is usually defined as:

$$IMR = \frac{\text{Deaths under age 1 in year}}{\text{Live births in year}} \times 1,000.$$

Calculated in this way the IMR is not a proper rate but a ratio, as the denominator is not the population at risk of the events in the numerator: some of the deaths under 1 may be of births which occurred during the previous year, while some of the births which occurred during the year may die in the next year, before their first birthday. Shryock and Siegel (1976: 235) call this the 'conventional' IMR to distinguish it from other measures which more precisely relate the births and deaths. If date of birth is asked on death registration forms rather than just age, then the year of birth of those dying is available, so a 'true' IMR — the probability of dying during the first year of life — can be calculated. The extent to which the 'conventional' IMR approximates the 'true' IMR will depend principally on the magnitude of short-term fluctuations in the number of births over time, but usually they are very similar. In highly developed countries IMRs normally range from about 7 up to about 15, while in the poorest countries they vary between perhaps 50 and 200 per 1,000 or even higher. For example, in Sweden there were, in 1985, 98,463 births and 666 infant deaths. The IMR was thus 6.8. According to UN estimates for the early 1980s in developing countries there are, each year, about 104,000,000 births and 9,500,000 infant deaths. The IMR is thus about 91.

Neonatal Mortality Rates

Deaths occurring during the first year of life tend to be concentrated in the first week or month. Also, during these early weeks the causes of infant deaths tend to be different from those which occur later. Because of this the IMR is often broken down into three parts: the Early, Late, and Post-Neonatal Mortality Rates:

$$\text{Early Neonatal MR} = \frac{\text{Deaths under 1 week}}{\text{Live births}} \times 1,000$$

$$\text{Late Neonatal MR} = \frac{\text{Deaths 1–4 weeks}}{\text{Live births}} \times 1,000$$

$$\text{Post-Neonatal MR} = \frac{\text{Deaths 4–52 weeks}}{\text{Live births}} \times 1,000$$

The Late Foetal Death Rate

Popularly, and in many parts of the world, this is called the 'Stillbirth Rate'. It is defined as:

$$\text{Late Foetal Death Rate} = \frac{\text{Late foetal deaths}}{\text{Late foetal deaths} + \text{Live births}} \times 1,000$$

There are, however, problems with the identification of a late foetal death or stillbirth, a problem compounded by the fact that different countries also often use slightly different definitions. According to the World Health Organisation, a late foetal death occurs after the twenty-eighth week of gestation. Early foetal deaths (popularly known as 'miscarriages') are defined to occur before the twentieth week of gestation, and 'intermediate' foetal deaths between the twentieth and twenty-eighth week. Such boundaries are both arbitrary and, in practice, very difficult to determine precisely. Another difficulty is in demarcating the difference between a foetal death and a live birth which dies very soon after birth.

The Perinatal Mortality Rate

This widely used rate avoids the problems of defining a live birth and puts together late foetal and early neonatal deaths because they are thought to be determined by similar causes. It is defined as:

$$\text{Perinatal MR} = \frac{\text{Stillbirths} + \text{Deaths under 1 week}}{\text{Still} + \text{Live births}} \times 1,000.$$

Specific Death Rates

Crude rates are so called because they include all persons of all ages and groups in their denominator. Specific rates relate to a particular group, usually defined at least by age and sex. They may cover all causes of death, or just one. While they can be very precise, allowing very detailed analyses to be done, they are also very difficult to compare, simply because they are not single-figure indices. Comparing two columns of Age-Specific Death Rates can become very complex. It is this problem that can often be overcome by standardisation.

Standardisation

A detailed introduction to standardisation is available in many statistics texts so only a brief discussion will be given here. (See, for example, Armitage 1971: 384–91.) It is a general statistical technique and is used in many areas other than mortality analysis.

The aim of standardisation is to allow more precise comparison of two or more 'crude' rates by eliminating the effect of, say, the differences in age structure between two or more populations. Usually rates are age-standardised, but many other attributes can also be used.

There are two kinds of standardisation, known as 'direct' and 'indirect', though the reasons for using these names are not obvious. Direct standardisation involves taking a standard population and applying to it the specific rates for the populations being compared. This produces a number of expected events which can be compared with the actual number observed in the *standard* population and the ratio Exp./Obs. gives, directly, the standardised rate. The ratio of two such standardised rates is a very useful measure. It is known by various names, most commonly the 'Comparative Mortality Ratio' (CMR). Thus:

$$\text{Direct standardised rate} = \frac{\text{Expected from index rates}}{\text{Observed in standard population}}$$

With indirect standardisation, on the other hand, one takes a set of standard rates and applies these to the populations being compared to produce a number of expected events. The ratio Obs./Exp. then gives, not a standardised rate, but a 'Standardised Mortality Ratio' (SMR). Thus:

$$\text{SMR} = \frac{\text{Observed in index population}}{\text{Expected from standard rates}}$$

Then, to calculate the indirectly standardised rates for the index populations being compared one simply multiplies the crude rate in the *standard* population by the SMRs. Thus whereas in direct standardisation the standardised rates are found immediately (i.e. 'directly') before the CMR is calculated, in indirect standardisation they are only computed after the SMR has been found (i.e. 'indirectly').

The main advantage of indirect over direct standardisation is that it is not necessary to know the specific rates in the populations being compared. In general, the two methods of standardisation will give similar results as long as the standard chosen is not very strange. The World Health Organisation produce standard Standards. Note also that if the specific rates being compared vary systematically by age or whatever, then this is important and it should not be hidden by standardising and reporting only the single standardised rate. Instead, comparisons should be made within each age group.

Standardisation has been met earlier in this book, most obviously in Coale's Indices, which is just indirect standardisation, where the standard is the Hutterite ASFRs. But the TFR is also a standardised rate, as can be seen from Table 6.1, where the Bangladesh ASFRs from Table 4.2 (see p. 40) are directly standardised on a population with one woman in each age group. Remember that each woman will experience the ASFRs for five years.

Table 6.1 The TFR as a standardised rate: Bangladesh, 1974

Age group	ASFRs	Standard population	Expected births
15–19	0.2004	1	1.0020
20–24	0.3373	1	1.6865
25–29	0.3109	1	1.5545
30–34	0.2615	1	1.3075
35–39	0.1970	1	0.9850
40–44	0.0954	1	0.4770
45–49	0.0135	1	0.0675
			= 7.0800
			= TFR

Constructing a life table

A life table is simply an elegant and convenient way of analysing Age-Specific Death Rates (ASDRs), though the technique is now used in many other areas, where it is often called 'survival analysis'. It comprises a set of columns, most of which can be calculated from any of the others. The only raw data involved are the ASDRs.

When constructing a life table, the column calculated first is q_x. It gives the probability of dying between exact ages x and $x+1$. That is:

$$q_x = \frac{\text{Deaths during year of persons aged } x \text{ at start of year}}{\text{Population aged } x \text{ at start of year}}$$

Note that the denominator is the number alive at the *beginning* of the year. Thus assume 1,000 persons are born at exactly the same moment. Then there may be, say, 950 left alive at exact age 30. If ten die before they reach 31, then:

$$q_{30} = \frac{10}{950} = 0.010.$$

Now q_xs cannot generally be calculated directly because population estimates normally relate to the middle rather than the start of the year. Instead, they have to be estimated from simple ASDRs. If ASDRs are called M_x, as is conventional, then:

$$ASDR = M_x = \frac{\text{Deaths during year of persons aged } x}{\text{Population aged } x \text{ at mid-year}}.$$

The difference between M_x and q_x is simply that with the former the denominator is the population at the middle of the year while with the latter it is the beginning of the year. M_x and q_x will thus generally be very similar to each other with q_x slightly smaller than M_x in growing populations, larger in declining ones. So, to construct the life table we have to adjust the M_xs slightly to produce the q_xs. To explain how this is done it is necessary to introduce some notation:

Let D_x be the number of deaths in the year of persons aged x.
Let N_x be the population age x at the start of the year.
Let P_x be the population aged x at mid-year.

Then:

$$q_x = \frac{D_x}{N_x}$$

and

$$M_x = \frac{D_x}{P_x}.$$

Now, N_x is just P_x plus those dying between the start and the middle of the year. For most ages this will be close to $0.5D_x$ since deaths occur roughly evenly throughout the year.

Thus:

$$N_x = P_x + 0.5D_x.$$

Putting D_x over both sides we get:

$$\frac{D_x}{N_x} = \frac{D_x}{P_x + 0.5D_x}$$

$$\Rightarrow q_x = \frac{D_x}{P_x + 0.5D_x}.$$

Dividing top and bottom by P_x gives:

$$q_x = \frac{D_x/P_x}{P_x/P_x + 0.5(D_x/P_x)}$$

$$= \frac{M_x}{1 + 0.5M_x}.$$

However, if the ASDRs (M_xs) are expressed per 1,000 population rather than per 1, then the equation becomes:

$$q_x = \frac{M_x}{1,000 + 0.5M_x}.$$

Thus it is possible to estimate q_xs from M_xs using this formula. However, it is only an approximation and its accuracy depends on the extent to which reality differs from the assumption that those who die in the year live, on average, half of a year during that year. This will be fairly accurate for all ages except the very young and, to a lesser extent, the very old. The young will, on average, live less than half a year because their deaths will tend to be concentrated in the early part of the year. This fraction of a year lived is usually denoted by a_x.

It is therefore possible to generalise the equation to:

$$q_x = \frac{M_x}{1 + (1 - a_x) \cdot M_x}.$$

The values that $a_0, a_1 \ldots$ take vary from country to country and according to the level of mortality. For developing countries, where mortality is high, values of 0.3 for a_0, 0.4 for a_1 and 0.5 for all the others are normally used. Where mortality is low, 0.1 is a better figure for a_0. In general the values chosen are not critical, except for a_0. Moreover, there is another way to estimate q_0 without using the formula above, for it is just the Infant Mortality Rate i.e. it is possible to use:

$$q_0 = \frac{D_0}{\text{Births in year}}.$$

As an example, Table 6.2 shows the top and bottom parts of a life table for California, 1970.

Table 6.2 Life table for California, 1970

Age interval x to $x+1$	Mid-year population P_x	Deaths in year D_x	Age-specific Death Rate M_x	Fraction of last year lived a_x	Probability of dying q_x
0–1	340 483	6 234	0.018309	0.09	0.018009
1–2	326 154	368	0.001128	0.43	0.001127
2–3	313 699	269	0.000858	0.45	0.000858
3–4	323 441	237	0.000733	0.47	0.000733
4–5	338 904	175	0.000516	0.49	0.000516
5–6	362 161	179	0.000494	0.50	0.000494
6–7	379 642	171	0.000450	0.50	0.000450
.	.	.	.	.	.
.	.	.	.	.	.
.	.	.	.	.	.
83–4	34 439	3 753	0.108975	0.50	0.103344
84–5	31 009	3 669	0.118320	0.50	0.111711
85+	142 691	22 483	0.157564	—	1.000000

Source: Chiang (no date: 76–8)

Thus, for example:

$$q_3 = \frac{0.000733}{1 + (1 - 0.47)0.000733}$$

$$= 0.000733.$$

There are several points worth noting in this example. First, M_x and q_x are generally very close to each other, especially in populations with low mortality such as California. However, M_x is always slightly larger in growing populations. Second, the a_xs used here were calculated from Californian registration data and are specific to California, 1970. They are not generally applicable. Third, the last, open-ended age group, here 85+ has to be treated differently. Because all those alive at the start of the interval will die before its end, simply because it has no end, the last probability, q_{x+}, will always be 1.00. Fourth, although the general formula has been used here for q_0 the 'conventional' IMR (see p. 64) could have been used as an estimate of the true probability. Finally, the life table is extremely unusual in that it is for both sexes combined. Almost always the sexes are treated separately because their mortality is different.

There are other methods of adjusting M_xs to estimate q_xs. One is the Reed–Merrell method (though this was designed specifically for US data in the 1930s and incorporates adjustments for underreporting at young ages), and another is Greville's (Shryock and Siegel 1976: 254). Computer programs which calculate life tables such as that by Keyfitz and Flieger (1971) use iterative methods to find the closest fit between the M_x and q_x which avoid the need to make assumptions about a_xs. However, the general view is that these alternative methods are not significantly better or easier to use than the method described above. Deficiencies in the raw data are almost certainly a far more important source of error.

Abridged Life Tables

The Californian life table (see Table 6.2) is an example of a 'complete' life table because single-year age groups are used throughout. Often, though, it is preferable to construct 'abridged' life tables where most of the age groups are five years. This might be because the data being used are not sufficiently reliable for a complete life table, or because a more concise picture of mortality is preferred. In fact, in demography abridged life tables are far more common than complete ones.

Usually abridged life tables begin with age groups 0 to 1 and 1 to 5, then five-year groups until the last, open-ended interval. The way they are constructed is very similar to that for complete life tables, but instead of calculating q_x one calculates $_nq_x$, where n is the length of the interval, not its start. This notation is, to say the least, a little confusing but is used universally. $_5q_{20}$, for example, refers to the interval 20 to 25 *not* 5 to 20. The equation used is:

$$_nq_x = \frac{n \cdot {_nM_x}}{1 + n(1 - {_na_x}) \cdot {_nM_x}}.$$

It should be noted that normally, as is done here, $_na_x$ is taken to be the proportion of the interval lived by those who die, but sometimes it is defined as the average number of years lived by those who die. Thus for normal five-year intervals $_na_x$ may be 0.5 or 2.5. If the latter convention is used, then the denominator of the formula above changes slightly.

Fortunately, choosing the correct value of a_x to use in this equation is not critical, except at young ages. The convention is to assume a_0 is 0.1 in low-mortality countries and 0.3 in high-mortality countries, while 0.4 is used for all $_4a_1$s. (Chiang does, however give figures for a large number of countries, and, as stated earlier, computer programs can avoid entirely any need to make assumptions about a_x.)

Normally, much more important sources of error are age misstatement, the underreporting of young children and the omission of deaths. Even in highly developed countries age misstatement by the elderly is a problem.

Having covered how to calculate $_nq_x$ from raw data, it is now possible to describe the calculation, interpretation and uses of the other columns of a life table. So far in this chapter a real population and real deaths have been used to construct what is a mathematical model called the life table. It is now that mathematical model which is of interest. It should always be remembered that, even though it is based on real data, within the life table itself one is always dealing with an imaginary population, having imaginary births and deaths.

Life-table functions

Table 6.3 shows the abridged life table for females in England and Wales in 1985. Each column has been calculated from the first $_n q_x$ column, which itself was calculated using ASDRs ($_n M_x$s). Apart from a few assumptions, no other data are used.

Table 6.3 Abridged life table: England and Wales, females, 1985

x	n	$_n q_x$	$_n p_x$	l_x	$_n d_x$	$_n L_x$	T_x	e_x
0	1	0.008252	0.991748	100 000	825	99 258	7 756 261	77.563
1	4	0.001630	0.998370	99 175	162	396 311	7 657 003	77.207
5	5	0.000905	0.999095	99 013	89	494 842	7 260 692	73.331
10	5	0.000935	0.999065	98 924	93	494 388	6 765 850	68.394
15	5	0.001409	0.998591	98 831	139	493 808	6 271 462	63.456
20	5	0.001534	0.998466	98 692	152	493 080	5 777 654	58.542
25	5	0.001818	0.998182	98 540	179	492 253	5 284 574	53.629
30	5	0.002826	0.997174	98 361	278	491 110	4 792 321	48.722
35	5	0.004410	0.995590	98 083	432	489 335	4 301 211	43.853
40	5	0.007199	0.992801	97 651	693	486 523	3 811 876	39.036
45	5	0.012348	0.987652	96 958	1 197	481 798	3 325 353	34.297
50	5	0.020831	0.979169	95 761	2 005	473 793	2 843 555	29.694
55	5	0.035455	0.964545	93 756	3 324	460 470	2 369 762	25.276
60	5	0.058507	0.941493	90 432	5 291	438 933	1 909 292	21.113
65	5	0.087310	0.912690	85 141	7 434	407 120	1 470 359	17.270
70	5	0.139189	0.860811	77 707	10 816	361 495	1 063 239	13.683
75	5	0.220993	0.779007	66 891	14 782	297 500	701 744	10.492
80	5	0.352367	0.647633	52 109	18 362	214 640	404 244	7.758
85+		1.000000	0.000000	33 747	33 747	189 604	189 604	5.618

The following paragraphs describe how each column was calculated, and how it is interpreted and used.

$_n q_x$

This is the probability of dying between exact ages x and $x + n$. As stated earlier (see p. 64), $_1 q_0$ is the 'true' Infant Mortality Rate (IMR) and the IMR, as conventionally calculated, is a very good estimate of this. Recall also that the figure for the last, open-ended age group q_x will always be 1.0 as everyone alive at the start of the interval dies during it.

One minor detail worth noting here is that occasionally $_n q_0$ is written as $q(n)$

or $Q(n)$, particularly when using Brass-type indirect techniques, or on computers, which cannot easily cope with subscripts. Very confusingly, the n often then becomes an x.

$_nP_x$

This is the probability of surviving between exact ages x and $x + n$. It is just the complement of $_nq_x$. Thus:

$$_nP_x = 1 - {}_nq_x \quad \text{or} \quad _nP_x + {}_nq_x = 1.$$

Often $_nP_x$, like $_nq_x$, is expressed per 1,000 or 10,000 population in order to avoid lots of zeros.

l_x

This is the number of persons alive at exact age x. It is different from the functions discussed so far in that it refers to an exact age, rather than to an age interval. l_0 is an arbitrary number called the _radix_. Usually it will be a round number such as 1 or 1,000 or 100,000. l_x is thus the number remaining alive at age x out of the original l_0.

To calculate l_x, first choose a suitable radix, then work down the table using the formula:

$$l_x = l_{x-n} \cdot {}_nP_{x-n}.$$

In words, the number of persons surviving to age x is just the number surviving to age $x - n$ multiplied by the probability of surviving from age $x - n$ to age x. For example, using the figures from Table 6.3:

$$l_{20} = l_{15} \cdot {}_5P_{15}$$

$$= 98,831 \times 0.998591$$

$$= 98,692.$$

It is important to understand that this number bears no relationship to the actual number of 20-year-old females in England and Wales in 1985. It is the number of females, out of the original 100,000 imaginary births, who would survive to their twentieth birthday *if* they were to experience exactly the mortality rates prevailing in England and Wales in 1985. It thus only has meaning when related to the radix.

Note that by rearranging the formula above one can obtain:

$$_{n}p_{x} = \frac{l_{x+n}}{l_{x}}.$$

In words, the probability of surviving from age x to age $x + n$ is just the number of persons alive at age $x + n$ divided by the number alive at age x.

$$_{n}d_{x}$$

This is the number of persons dying between exact ages x and $x + n$. It is just the difference between two l_{x}s. Algebraically:

$$_{n}d_{x} = l_{x} - l_{x+n}.$$

Thus, from Table 6.3:

$$_{5}d_{10} = l_{10} - l_{15}$$

$$= 98{,}924 - 98{,}831$$

$$= 93.$$

Note that for the last, open-ended age group the number of persons dying is the same as the number alive at its start. That is:

$$d_{x+} = l_{x}. \quad = l_{o} = radix$$

But $_{n}d_{x}$ can also be calculated using:

$$_{n}d_{x} = l_{x} \cdot {_{n}q_{x}}.$$

In words, the number of persons dying during the interval is equal to the number alive at its start multiplied by the probability of dying during the interval. For example:

$$_{5}d_{10} = l_{10} \cdot {_{5}q_{10}}$$

$$= 98{,}924 \times 0.000935$$

$$= 93 \text{ as before.}$$

This is defined as the average proportion of the time lived in the interval x to $x + n$ by those who die during that interval. It is not calculated from other life-table columns but is either calculated from raw data, or, more frequently, assumed. For most age groups a value of 0.5 is adequate, but for the very young it is necessary to use other values. As stated above (see p. 69), it is common to use $a_0 = 0.3$ and $_4a_1 = 0.4$, though in low-mortality countries $a_0 = 0.1$ is better. The measure is used both in the estimation of life tables from raw data, and in the calculation of the next function, $_nL_x$.

This is the number of persons-years lived between exact ages x and $x + n$. Each person surviving through the interval contributes n person-years, while those who die during the interval will contribute only $n \cdot _na_x$ years. The calculation of $_nL_x$ thus involves an assumption about $_na_x$. The formula is:

$$_nL_x = n(l_{x+n} + _na_x \cdot _nd_x).$$

Now if $_na_x$ is assumed to to be 0.5, then the formula becomes:

$$_nL_x = n(l_{x+n} + 0.5_nd_x)$$

which, since $l_{x+n} = l_x - _nd_x$

$$= n(l_x - _nd_x + 0.5_nd_x)$$

$$= n(l_x - 0.5_nd_x)$$

$$= n(l_x - 0.5(l_x - l_{x+n}))$$

$$= n(0.5l_x + 0.5l_{x+n})$$

$$= \frac{n(l_x + l_{x+n})}{2}$$

and this is a much easier formula to use when calculating $_nL_x$ than the one above. In words, one simply takes the average of two l_xs and multiplies by n. Of course, this is not valid for L_0 or $_4L_1$ as $_na_x$ is not 0.5 at these ages.

Thus for England and Wales females, 1985:

$$_5L_5 = \frac{5(l_5 + l_{10})}{2}$$

$$= 5 \times \frac{99{,}013 + 98{,}924}{2}$$

$$= 494{,}842$$

and, assuming $a_0 = 0.1$, we have:

$$L_0 = l_1 + 0.1_1 d_0$$

$$\Rightarrow L_0 = 99{,}175 + 0.1 \times 825$$

$$\Rightarrow L_0 = 99{,}258.$$

There is a problem with the last, open-ended age group in that it is necessary to make an additional assumption about how many more years, on average, those alive at its start live for. There are several ways of doing this, and the method is not crucial because relatively few person-years are lived in the interval. Of course, if the old ages are of particular interest, then more care has to be taken. The usual method involves M_{x+}, the Age-Specific Death Rate in the open-ended interval. First, it is approximately true that:

$$_nM_x = \frac{_nd_x}{_nL_x}$$

In words, the ASDR is the number of life-table deaths divided by the number of person-years lived. Rearranging the equation gives:

$$_nL_x = \frac{_nd_x}{_nM_x}$$

so

$$L_{85+} = \frac{d_{85+}}{M_{85+}}$$

but $d_{85+} = l_{85}$ since everyone eventually dies so:

$$L_{85+} = \frac{l_{85}}{M_{85+}}.$$

Thus for England and Wales females, 1985, where $M_{85+} = 0.177987$:

$$L_{85+} = \frac{33{,}747}{0.177987}$$

$$= 189{,}604.$$

If M_{x+} is not available, then it is probably best to estimate L_{x+} using model life tables (see Chs 12 and 13), or a life table for a country with a similar level of mortality.

This is the total number of person-years lived after exact age x. It is thus simply the $_nL_x$ column cumulated from the bottom. That is:

$$T_x = T_{x+n} + {}_nL_x$$

Thus:

$$T_{85} = L_{85+}.$$

From Table 6.3:

$$T_{80} = T_{85} + {}_5L_{80}$$

$$= 189{,}604 + 214{,}640$$

$$= 404{,}244.$$

The main purpose of this function is in the calculation of the next — the expectation of life.

This is the expectation of life at age x, or the average number of years a person aged x has to live. Strictly, it should be written as $\mathring{e}_x$ since in actuarial science the circle is used to distinguish the conventional expectation of life from a different expectation in which deaths occurring during the year are excluded from the calculations. Since this latter statistic is not used at all in demography, the circle has become optional.

Since the total number of years left to be lived by l_x people is T_x, the expectation of life is just one divided by the other. Thus:

$$e_x = \frac{T_x}{l_x}.$$

Thus the expectation of life at birth is:

$$e_0 = \frac{T_0}{l_0}$$

So, for England and Wales, females, 1985:

$$e_0 = \frac{7,756,261}{100,000}$$

$$= 77.563 \text{ years.}$$

Finally, one function of the life table which has not been mentioned so far, but which is often useful, particularly in population projections, is the Survivorship Ratio. There are really two ratios, one between exact ages and one between intervals. The first, the probability of surviving between exact ages, is just the $_nP_x$ column described above, but it is the second, the survivorship between age groups, which is more commonly required. Unfortunately, the notation for this is not quite standardised, though normally S or P is used. Shryock and Siegel (1976: p. 262) use s. There are also notational problems about identifying the age groups involved since one needs at least three subscripts or superscripts.

The ratio is calculated simply as the ratio of any two $_nL_x$s. For example, the probability of surviving from the 5–9 age group into the 15–19 age group is

$$P = \frac{_5L_{15}}{_5L_5}$$

which, for England and Wales, females, 1985 is:

$$P = \frac{493,800}{494,842}$$

$$= 0.997910.$$

Interpretation of the life table

The way the life-table functions have been described so far has assumed that 1, 1,000, 100,000 or however many babies, are all born at one instant, and are then gradually killed off until eventually none are left. l_x is just the number of persons alive at exact age x, because everyone has their birthday simultaneously. $_nL_x$ is the number of person-years lived.

There is, however, an alternative interpretation which may be labelled as the 'dynamic', as opposed to the 'static' one outlined above. In this 'dynamic' interpretation, 1, 1,000 or 100,000 babies are assumed to be born at a constant rate during the year, and this carries on for many years, l_0 being born each year. With this interpretation the l_x and $_nL_x$ columns take on slightly different meanings. l_x becomes the number of persons having their birthday during the year, and $_nL_x$ is just the population aged between x and $x + n$. Now, the population described by the $_nL_x$ column is known as a 'Stationary' population. It has a constant age structure and a constant size with l_0 being born each year and exactly the same number dying. More details of the attributes of this important population are given in Chapter 11, which looks at 'model' age structures such as this more generally.

Exercises

1. Table 6E.1 is derived from OPCS (1984). The first two 'Population' columns give the 1982 estimated mid-year home population of England and Wales by age and sex. The two 'Deaths' columns give the deaths registered in 1982 by age and sex. Use these data to calculate the $_nq_x$ column of an abridged life table for females.

Table 6E.1 Population and deaths, by age: England and Wales, 1982

Age	Population Males	Females	Deaths Males	Females
0 –4	1 571 400	1 491 400	4 566	3 346
0	317 000	300 800	3 914	2 861
1	323 000	308 400	287	208
2	325 900	309 500	149	140
3	314 900	298 100	121	75
4	290 500	274 600	95	60
5 –9	1 557 600	1 473 800	391	253
10–14	1 947 500	1 847 000	546	353
15–19	2 121 200	1 014 500	1 669	588
20–24	1 942 800	1 893 200	1 668	672
25–29	1 708 200	1 683 800	1 409	702
30–34	1 764 700	1 749 100	1 735	1 079
35–39	1 734 500	1 709 800	2 246	1 576
40–44	1 417 200	1 396 800	3 280	2 132
45–49	1 368 500	1 351 900	5 647	3 639
50–54	1 381 000	1 398 300	10 497	6 351
55–59	1 382 000	1 445 500	18 820	10 854
60–64	1 277 400	1 429 100	27 701	16 897
65–69	1 088 600	1 323 100	39 171	24 598
70–74	900 100	1 233 300	51 908	37 623
75–79	578 400	972 500	52 096	49 866
80–84	274 500	620 300	37 844	54 879
85–89	97 200	297 900	19 875	44 632
90+	32 700	130 100	9 119	31 655
Total	24 145 400	25 461 400	290 166	291 695

2. The estimates in Table 6E.2 were derived from data collected in a survey carried out in Lagos in 1976. They show the proportion of women still breast-feeding at exact monthly intervals after the birth of their children.

Table 6E.2 Proportion of women still breast-feeding: Lagos, 1976

Month	Proportion
0	1.000
1	0.988
2	0.972
3	0.955
4	0.937
5	0.908
6	0.880
7	0.844
8	0.795
9	0.735
10	0.680
11	0.578
12	0.485
13	0.392
14	0.366
15	0.334
16	0.306
17	0.232
18	0.169
19	0.108
20	0.105
21	0.101
22	0.099
23	0.072
24	0.047

From the estimates calculate the following life-table indices:

(a) $_6d_{12}$

(b) p_{20}

(c) l_{12}

(d) $_3L_{20}$

(e) $_6q_6$

(f) How many of a group of 100 breast-feeding women who had a child between three and six months ago will still be breast-feeding in three months' time?

State any assumptions you have to make in these calculations.

Table 6E.3 Graunt's life table: Londoners 1662

Exact age	Survivors
0	100
6	64
16	40
26	25
36	16
46	10
56	6
66	3
76	1

3. The life table for Londoners shown in Table 6E.3 was constructed in 1662 by John Graunt.

Stating what assumptions you make, estimate:

(a) The probability that a baby will not survive to 26 years.
(b) The probability that a person aged 26 will survive to age 46.
(c) The average number of years that a baby is likely to survive under this mortality regime.
(d) How can you interpret the $_nL_x$ column of a life table?

7 Migration

This chapter is somewhat different from the others in that it aims to provide a general introduction to migration rather than considering only its formal aspects. It begins with a discussion of the importance of migration as a component of population change. Second, the terms commonly used in the study of migration are defined, particular attention being paid to the problem of defining a migrant. Then the various possible sources of migration statistics are considered, and finally there is a short discussion of the typical characteristics of migrants.

The importance of migration

The Basic Demographic Equation, discussed in Chapter 1, can be written as

$$P_{t+1} - P_t = \text{Births} - \text{Deaths} + \text{In} - \text{Out}$$

or, similarly, as

$$\text{Population change} = \text{Natural increase} + \text{Net migration}.$$

Thus population change in an area is determined partly by the level of natural increase, the difference between births and deaths, and partly by the level of net migration, the difference between the numbers moving in and moving out.

In some parts of the world natural increase is very much more important than net migration as a determinant of population change. This is particularly true of countries currently in the middle of their demographic transition where fertility is much higher than mortality. It tends also to be true when considering whole countries rather than parts of countries, simply because migration across international frontiers is generally much less than migration between areas within a country. It also tends to be the case when considering big countries rather than small countries.

In some parts of the world, on the other hand, net migration is more important than natural increase. This is generally true of developed countries, where both mortality and fertility are at very low levels, and of the smaller developing countries. But, importantly, as soon as one begins to look below the national level, at population change in provinces, districts, cities or whatever, migration is almost certain to assume great importance. Academic demographers rarely consider sub-national aggregates, but planners and administrators who use demographic data, particularly for population projections, are normally primarily interested in particular regions or urban areas. For them migration assumes great importance.

Basic measures and concepts

Migration is a huge subject. In fact, it is in many respects four different subjects based on two dichotomies. The first is between the developed and the developing world, and the second is between internal and international migration.

The reasons for distinguishing these are, first, that the sources of data are different (as will be shown below). Thus the measures and methods used to analyse them tend also to be different. Second, the four subjects must be considered separately because the causes of migration, and consequently the patterns produced, are frequently very different in each. For example, whereas migration is predominantly from rural areas to urban areas in developing countries, it is either urban to urban or urban to rural in developed countries.

Despite these differences, the terminology used in the study of migration is common to all. As with all technical subjects, certain words take on more precise, sometimes even quite different, meanings than in everyday English. Several will be discussed here.

Who is a migrant?

Defining precisely who is, and who is not, a migrant is extremely difficult. Is a student going to New York from India to study for a year a migrant, or is he just a visitor? Is a Turk going to work in a car factory in Munich for perhaps ten years, before returning to Turkey to set up a business, a migrant? Is someone who moves house, from one part of a city to another, a migrant or only a mover? The problem is essentially that being a migrant is not simply a matter of moving a certain distance for a certain length of time. It also involves an attitude of mind — the concept of intention. Thus a British executive going to work in Saudi Arabia for a couple of years thinks of himself as a visitor, not as a migrant, because he has no intention of staying there permanently. Contrast this with a family who travel from the UK to Australia, then three months later return because they didn't like it there. They intended to stay and so thought of themselves as migrants.

The fact that being a migrant involves future intentions about whether to stay, creates many problems for statistics gatherers. Among other things, it means that the event of migration is not clear-cut or precisely locatable in either time or space. To illustrate this, consider again the executive in Saudi Arabia. He may, having spent two years there, decide that he likes it, and stay. Does he then become a migrant, even though he has not moved anywhere, or was he a migrant two years before, when he first left his previous home? These and other problems mean that statistics-gathering organisations are inevitably forced to adopt somewhat arbitrary criteria for deciding who is a migrant and who is not. Different organisations often use very different criteria, depending on the way the data is collected and the purpose for which it is intended. For example, the definition used by the UK immigration authorities are quite different from those used in the census. Moreover, definitions used by the same organisation may vary over time. Some of the more commonly used ones are discussed below.

Emigrants and immigrants

To try to overcome some of the problems associated with determining who actually is a migrant, demographers have agreed on an arbitrary definition: 'An immigrant is a person who has resided abroad for a year or more and, on entering the country, has declared an intention to stay for a year or more'. There is a similar definition for emigrants. This definition is, however, used rather infrequently since migration data are rarely collected solely, or even primarily, for demographic purposes.

Inmigrants and outmigrants

A person moving from one part of a country to another part of the same country is said to be an 'outmigrant' from their origin and an 'inmigrant' to their destination. Thus the terms 'immigrant' and 'emigrant' refer to international moves while 'inmigrant' and 'outmigrant' refer to internal moves. But with internal migration there is also the problem of distance. Below a certain distance people are really only movers, not migrants. They will be moving for housing rather than job-related reasons. When gathering data on internal migration this problem is usually overcome in an arbitrary way by defining migrants as those who cross administrative boundaries. This is often very useful for those wanting to produce population projections for the administrative areas, and it enables area authorities, such as local government, to get some idea of population change in their area. Note, though, that this method of defining inmigrants and outmigrants means that some people who have only moved a very short distance, but who happen to cross a boundary, will be classed as migrants, while others who move long distances within an area will not. It also means that the numbers of migrants will depend not only on the level of mobility in the population but also on the number and size of areas being used.

Return migrants

If, having migrated from country A to country B, an individual then returns permanently to A, he is called a 'return migrant'. Note that he will be a return migrant from the national point of view wherever in country A he resettles — he does not have to have returned to his precise place of origin. Return migration is very common since wherever a flow of migrants develops it is inevitable that there will also develop a smaller counterflow of return migrants.

Lifetime migrants

Often in a census there is no direct question asked about migration, but sometimes it is possible to get some useful information about the level and pattern of migration using a question on birthplace. The place of birth is compared with the place of enumeration to produce a measure of 'lifetime migration'. Clearly it is a very crude measure, since neither the timing of any move nor the possibility of intermediate moves is considered. One individual might have moved soon after birth and then spent the last 50 years at the place of enumeration. Another might have returned to his birthplace shortly before the census, having spent most of his life elsewhere. A third might have led a near-nomadic life of frequent moves. None of the variety of these three individuals' experience can be captured by measurement of lifetime migration.

Gross and net migration

Gross migration is the sum of immigration and emigration, or, if one is consider-ing internal migration, the sum of inmigration and outmigration. Net migration is the difference between the two flows. Almost always the level of gross migra-tion is very much greater than the level of net migration (it can never be less) because of the tendency for counterstreams of returning migrants to develop. It is often easier to estimate net rather than gross migration, using perhaps the Basic Demographic Equation. Note that even if net migration is zero, gross migration may still be affecting substantially the structure and composition of a population.

The collection of migration data

The nature of migration within and across international boundaries means that no single source is adequate for measuring all types of migration stocks and flows. Registers, censuses, surveys and official administrative statistics can all be important sources of data on different aspects of migration. Each will be considered in turn.

Population registers

In some countries such as in Scandinavia, the Soviet bloc, and elsewhere, individuals have to register moves just as they register births, marriages and deaths. From such a register it is possible to obtain complete migration histories for individuals. This has the great advantage of being comprehensive, but it is extremely difficult to analyse such data successfully.

A population register is not maintained in the UK but the 'Central Register' of the National Health Service, located in Southport near Liverpool, has many of the characteristics of a general population register. One of its main purposes is to maintain General Practitioner patient lists, and, since a change of doctor nearly always implies a migration, this can be used to estimate internal migration flows. These are of very great importance for sub-national population estimates. It has been successfully used in Scotland for many years, but its use is more recent in England and Wales.

Censuses

These are very major sources of information on internal migration, less so for international migration. Because of its cross-sectional nature a census generally gives information on stocks of migrants only, not on flows.

At the simplest level one can obtain some estimates of migration without asking any specific questions. This can be done by comparing two censuses and using the Basic Demographic Equation. One takes the population aged, say, 15–19 at the first census. If the censuses are ten years apart these people will be aged 25–29 at the second census. The difference in size of these two figures, after subtracting the deaths that occurred during the inter-censal period, yields an estimate of net migration for that cohort. This method is, however, very unreliable even for entire populations, let alone subgroups, because it requires that each of the two censuses and the registration data are extremely accurate. Small errors in just one of these sets of data can easily produce large errors in the migration estimates. Nevertheless, it has been widely used in quite sophisticated ways. (For more details see Shryock and Siegel 1976: 357–62.)

Turning to census questions that are specifically designed to measure migration, the use of a birthplace question, which yields a measure of lifetime migration, has already been mentioned. This is generally not a very satisfactory measure, and its use is primarily confined to historical demography where early censuses containing a birthplace are an important source. The main problems are that people of different ages are exposed to the risk of moving for different lengths of time, that multiple moves are not recorded and that moves which occurred up to a lifetime ago are included with very recent moves.

Birthplace and related questions can also be used to look at stocks of immigrants, usually to try to obtain information on ethnic minorities, but there are many problems about this, both of a political and a practical nature. Such questions are often resented, and the extent to which birthplace reflects membership of an ethnic minority depends to a great extent on how long ago the immigration occurred. Many members of ethnic minorities in Britain were born in the UK so that birthplace is no longer a sensible indicator of ethnicity. In the opposite direction, a substantial number of white 'British' people now living in the UK were born in India before Independence in 1947. Using birthplace to indicate their ethnicity would classify them as Indian.

Specific migration questions, designed to obtain information on flows of migrants within a country, usually take one of two forms. Either they ask about one's previous address, together with duration of residence, or about one's address at a specific date in the past, usually one or five years ago. The former suffers from the disadvantage that some information on moves occurring many years ago is included. This is not normally of much interest. The latter is easier to analyse and questions of this form have been asked in UK censuses since 1961. In 1961 and 1971 addresses one and five years ago were asked for, but in 1966 and 1981 only the one-year question was included.

There are several difficulties with this form of migration question. First, some people simply cannot remember their address one or five years ago; second, some people move and then die before the census; third, some babies are born and then move between the reference date and the census — nobody under 5 can be a 'five-year migrant'. Fourth, multiple moves are not recorded.

Due to the extent of return migration the volume of migration measured using the five-year question is often only three or four times that measured using the one-year question, rather than five times as one might expect. It was partly this which led to the dropping of the five-year question from the 1981 UK census. Other factors were the expense and difficulty of coding, and the relative lack of interest in moves which, by the time the results were published, might have occurred up to eight or ten years ago.

Surveys

A census, or census-like survey, cannot gather information on emigration at all. Nor can it measure flows over time unless complex retrospective questions are asked. To do these things it is necessary to use surveys or official administrative statistics. In the UK there are two main sources — Home Office immigration statistics and the International Passenger Survey.

The Home Office and Department of Employment statistics on immigration are a by-product of the system of immigration controls, residence and work permits, and so on. These data are based on the legal definition of an immigrant, and include changes of status of individuals who have lived here for some time, such as a student who has been allowed to settle permanently. Such data are of rather limited use for demographic purposes.

The International Passenger Survey is a continuous sample survey of a small fraction of passengers entering or leaving the UK by the main sea and air ports. It began in 1964, primarily to measure tourism, but has become a useful source of migration statistics. Individuals are interviewed as they pass through customs and asked about such topics as their age, occupation, purpose of journey and intention to stay. It is generally regarded as producing rather unreliable data. This is because of large sampling errors and a low response rate. However, it is one of the few sources of information on emigrants (see OPCS 1975; Bulusu 1986).

The analysis of migration data

Given the variety of sources and types of data mentioned above, it is inevitable that the methods and measures used in migration analysis are not nearly as standardised or well developed as in other areas of formal demography.

However, the starting point for most analysis is a 'flow matrix' such as in Table 7.1. This gives the numbers of moves from each area to every other area. The marginals give the total numbers moving into and out of each area. Net migration can be calculated by subtracting gross flows. The leading diagonal sometimes is left empty, or it can be used to give the number of internal moves within each area. An additional column and row can be added giving moves from and to the rest of the world, thus 'closing' the matrix.

Table 7.1 Internal migration flow matrix: Scotland, 1971–2

Outmigrants from:	Inmigrants to:								
	H	NE	T	E	F/S	G	SW	B	Total
Highlands	—	. 1 603	760	1 523	283	2 360	166	77	6 772
North-East	1 547	—	1 496	1 828	298	1 334	107	106	6 716
Tayside	654	1 343	—	3 293	665	1 816	158	125	8 054
Edinburgh	1 498	1 596	3 344	—	1 927	5 413	607	1 110	15 495
Falkirk/Stirling	296	277	828	1 798	—	1 755	86	44	5 084
Glasgow	3 176	1 740	2 403	9 177	3 137	—	1 515	389	21 537
South-West	122	110	174	694	94	1 338	—	137	2 669
Borders	127	99	129	1 119	57	328	120	—	1 979
Total	7 420	6 768	9 134	19 432	6 461	14 344	2 759	1 988	68 306

Source: NHS Central Register

By using the figures in Table 7.1, together with some population estimates, it is straightforward to calculate various Gross and Net Migration Rates in the same way as birth and death rates. However, the problem is that these rates are strongly affected by the size of the area being considered. This is because the vast majority of moves in any population tend to be short distance, and often only moves which cross boundaries are recorded. Small areas will thus tend to have relatively high rates, as will areas whose boundaries are densely populated so that many moves cross them. Large, sparsely populated areas will, on the other hand, have relatively low rates. Migration rates are thus generally not comparable between areas, though the problems of comparison over time are less. For definitions of various rates see Kosinski (1975).

Note the similarity of opposing flows in Table 7.1. For example, the 1,603 moving from the Highlands to the North-East is almost balanced by the 1,547 moving in the opposite direction. This emphasises the extent to which, because of return migration, net migration flows are usually very small in relation to the overall level of gross migration. In this case gross migration is 3,150, but net migration is a mere 56.

The characteristics of migrants

Migrants tend to be a very select group in many ways, both when compared with the population at origin and with the population at destination. Only in the case of large-scale, forced moves — refugees — is this less true because then the whole population is involved. In the following discussion only voluntary migration is considered. Inevitably, the characteristics of migrants vary enormously throughout the world, so here only a few very broad generalisations can be made. For more details see, for example, White and Woods (1980) or Kosinski (1975).

First, not all ages tend to move equally. There is usually a big peak among young adults, and few people move after age 45, though there is a small peak at retirement in developed countries. Young children also move a lot as they are generally part of families headed by the mobile young adults. Older children move less as parents are perhaps less willing to disrupt their education.

Sometimes there is a substantial sex differential to migration, though often less than expected. Males tend to dominate labour migration flows to, for example, the Middle East from India, to South African mines from surrounding areas, or to manufacturing plants in Western Europe from the Mediterranean countries. In some cases, such as the Pakistani migration to the UK, the males move first and are later followed by the females.

The unmarried tend to move more than the married, as they are generally younger and have fewer roots. In many countries migration occurs at marriage, perhaps when the wife joins the husband's household, or as a new household is formed.

Migrants tend also to be generally fitter, more highly educated, richer and more ambitious than non-migrants, though some migration flows are dominated by the poorest sections of the community such as the landless and homeless.

8 Marriage and divorce

Marriage, separation, divorce, widowhood and remarriage, collectively called 'nuptiality' in demography, are not in themselves of particular interest to demographers. Rather, their importance arises partly from their relationship with the age at which sexual relations begin and end, and partly with the formation and dissolution of families and households. If the main focus of interest is really fertility patterns, then the interest in nuptiality will be mainly to do with when a woman first becomes exposed to the risk of childbearing, and thus with her age at first marriage. The extent of, and age at, separation is also important in some populations. Alternatively, if the interest is in the formation and break-up of families, a subject known as 'family demography', then separation, divorce, widowhood and remarriage are likely to be of at least equal interest as marriage, and male figures are as important as female ones. Family demography has attracted wide attention in developed countries in recent years because of the implications of, for example, changing patterns of divorce and widowhood for such things as housing demand, labour-force participation and the demands placed on social security systems.

Of course, there are also good reasons for studying nuptiality itself, especially since in many countries, both developed and developing, the patterns of marriage and divorce are changing, often quite rapidly, both as a consequence of, and themselves affecting, broader social changes.

Concepts and data sources

Whereas birth and death are clear-cut, biologically identifiable events, marriage is a much more complex culturally and socially defined event. In many places, including England and Wales, it is a well-defined, religious and/or legal ceremony. Consequently, it is possible to collect data on marriage using a system of registration, just like births and deaths. This does not work, however, in many parts of the world. In the Caribbean and parts of Latin America what are known as consensual, common law, or visiting unions are very common. These are more or less stable unions which are recognised by society, sometimes in much the same way as a marriage, but which involve no legal or religious ceremony. In parts of South and East Asia marriage is more of a process than a single event, involving several stages and ceremonies, sometimes spread out over a long period. In some highly developed, Western societies, particularly Sweden and Denmark, legal/religious marriages have somewhat fallen out of fashion. Perhaps one way of trying to overcome these definitional problems, though not necessarily a very good one, would be simply to ask people if they considered themselves to be married or not.

But, as well as obtaining information on marriage and divorce from registration (flow data), one can also collect data using censuses and surveys on the current marital status characteristics of the population (stock data). It is also possible to use censuses and surveys to retrospectively collect flow data by asking respondents to report their dates of marriage and divorce.

The United Nations, in their recommendations for the 1980 round of censuses, suggested that the minimum categories of marital status recorded should be:

1. Single (i.e. never married).
2. Married.
3. Widowed, not remarried.
4. Divorced, not remarried.
5. Remarried.

Note that those married more than once are distinguished from those married only once. It is important for demographers to be able to distinguish first marriages from remarriages, mainly because the impact of marriage on fertility is primarily determined by the age at first marriage. Some surveys and censuses also have additional categories for those who are separated but not divorced, and for those living together as married couples. What demographers frequently really want information on is not actually age at marriage but the age at which sexual relations begin, because that is when couples become 'exposed to the risk' of childbearing. In most societies marriage is a reasonable measure of this, but in some it is not — sexual relations may instead begin either some time before or some time after marriage.

Turning briefly to separation and divorce — the break-up of marriages — these concepts are even more culture-specific than marriage, making comparative studies virtually impossible. Even if reliable data can be collected, there are very great problems of interpretation. Partly this is because in many cultures there is a stigma associated with them so that some people will state that they are married or single when in fact they are separated or divorced. What demographers are interested in, essentially, is the break-up of sexual unions, yet often this is not a clear-cut event. Moreover, divorce is often a very poor indicator of this because legal obstacles to obtaining a divorce are often very great. For example, the law may require couples to have lived separately for several years before they can divorce. In England and Wales in 1970 some of the restrictions on divorce were relaxed, and there was suddenly a big jump in the number of divorces taking place. In general, therefore, it is wise to be very wary about data on marriage and divorce, particularly when it involves cross-cultural comparisons.

Having briefly covered the basic concepts of marriage and divorce, and the ways in which information on them can be gathered, it is now possible to look at the way they are measured.

The measurement of marriage and divorce

Just as it is possible to compute a Crude Birth Rate or a Crude Death rate for a population, so one can also calculate a Crude Marriage Rate as:

$$\text{Crude Marriage Rate} = \frac{\text{Marriages}}{\text{Population}} \times 1,000.$$

Conventionally, the numerator is the number of marriages occurring during a year, and the denominator is the population at mid-year, but longer or shorter time periods can be used. Note that the numerator is the number of marriages, not the number of persons getting married. The latter is used only rarely, in which case the rate is exactly twice as large. Like the Crude Birth Rate, the CMR is labelled 'crude' because its magnitude is determined not only by the amount of marriage occurring but also by the age structure of the population. It does, however, have the advantage of being a very simple measure to understand and very easy to calculate.

When dealing with more sophisticated rates than the CMR it becomes especially important to define exactly how the indices are calculated. This is partly because the names used are not standardised, but also because it is crucial to distinguish between rates for males and females. Although marriage (or divorce) happens simultaneously to two people, they are likely to be quite different in terms of characteristics such as their age and former marital status. General Marriage Rates, like General Fertility Rates, improve upon crude rates by eliminating from the denominator groups not at risk of marriage. Ideally, for females one wants to use only unmarried women over the legal minimum age of marriage. If this is, say, 15 then the GMR for females is:

$$\text{GMR (females)} = \frac{\text{Marriages}}{\text{Unmarried females aged } 15+} \times 1,000.$$

A similar rate can also be calculated for males, as with all the other indices defined here.

If information on the marital status of the population is unavailable, or unreliable, then an alternative, though inferior, specification of the GMR can be used. This is:

$$\text{GMR (females)} = \frac{\text{Marriages}}{\text{All females aged } 15+} \times 1,000.$$

A third alternative is to restrict coverage to only first marriages and calculate a general First Marriage Rate. This can be calculated as:

$$\text{GFMR (females)} = \frac{\text{Marriages to single females}}{\text{Single females aged } 15+} \times 1{,}000.$$

Note that it is impossible to produce a Crude First Marriage Rate because it is impossible to define a 'first marriage'. A marriage may be the first for both bride and groom, or for just one or for neither. In most developed countries a substantial and increasing proportion of marriages now involve remarriage of one or both partners.

One other measure which should be recalled here is Coale's Index of marriage, I_m — a fertility-weighted mean of the proportions of females aged 15–49 who are married. For details of this see Chapter 4 (pp. 47–8).

Because marriage is very highly age-specific, and demographers are particularly interested in age patterns of marriage, it is commonplace to produce Age-Specific Marriage Rates. These can in fact be calculated in two distinct ways, and it is important to distinguish between them because they lead to different ways of summarising marriage patterns. One method involves thinking of marriage as an event like fertility. Thus one can marry again, just like one can have another birth. The denominators of rates computed using this method include both the unmarried and the married. The other, more frequently used method involves treating marriage more like mortality, removing people from exposure to risk on marriage. This latter, conventional approach produces ASMRs with denominators which include only the unmarried. The conventional ASMR for females aged 20 is thus:

$$\text{ASMR (F, 20)} = \frac{\text{Marriages to females aged } 20}{\text{Unmarried females aged } 20} \times 1{,}000.$$

The analogy with mortality rates is not, however, perfect since it is possible to re-enter the unmarried state through divorce or widowhood, but it is impossible to rise from the dead! However, if attention is restricted to first marriages, then the analogy *is* perfect as it is impossible to return to the single (i.e. never married) state having left it. A typical Age-Specific First Marriage Rate is:

$$\text{ASFMR (F, 20)} = \frac{\text{Marriages to single females aged } 20}{\text{Single females aged } 20} \times 1{,}000.$$

Using these ASMRs graphs like that in Figure 8.1 can be drawn. Mathematical models describing such curves have also been developed and they are introduced in Chapter 14.

Just as it is possible to summarise Age-Specific Death Rates by constructing

A.S.F.M.R.

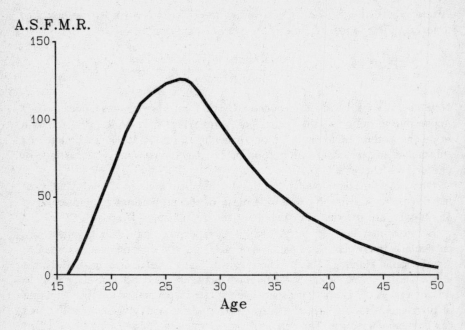

Age

Figure 8.1 Age-Specific First Marriage Rates, England and Wales, 1985

a life table, so it is possible to summarise Age-Specific First Marriage Rates by producing a life table for marriage — a 'Nuptiality table'. One begins calculating a probability of marrying during a year using Age-Specific First Marriage Rates, in the same way that a probability of dying, q_x, is derived from Age-Specific Death Rates.

Starting with, say, 1,000 female births, then after perhaps fifteen years there will still be 1,000 single because none marries before 15, or whatever the legal minimum age for marriage is. But by age 20 a few will have married, say 150, leaving 850 unmarried. This can be continued until eventually, say by age 50, almost all who will ever marry have done so. A small proportion, 5 per cent perhaps, will never marry.

There are two problems with this sort of table. First, it assumes no mortality among the original 1,000 births. Second, marriage, unlike death, is not necessarily a once-and-for-all event. Some who marry will later divorce, or become widowed, and thus become exposed to the risk of marrying again. The exclusion of mortality can be remedied in a straightforward way by including a death column in the table. For example, out of the original 1,000, perhaps fifty might die by age 15, leaving 950 unmarried survivors. Between ages 15 and 20 another twenty might die and 130 marry, and so on. A table which takes mortality into account in this way is called a 'net nuptiality table', as opposed to a 'gross nuptiality table' which leaves mortality out.

The problem of remarriage can be coped with using what are known as increment–decrement life tables, where an extra column is added giving those re-entering the state of being exposed to risk. This is, however, rarely done in studies of nuptiality, mainly because of lack of data and poor reporting of divorce, but also because, even if the data are perfect, the nuptiality table may nevertheless be very misleading simply because of its synthetic nature. To understand this, consider England and Wales. As stated earlier, divorces became much easier to obtain from 1971, so divorce rates rose suddenly, then fell back as the backlog of separations were formalised. Thus, if a nuptiality table was produced which was based on 1971 or 1972 data, it would not be at all representative of the past or likely future extent or pattern of divorce. Nuptiality tables, like life tables, are generally period rather than cohort measures. They use the concept of a synthetic cohort and reflect the current rates, not the rates experienced by any real cohort. Of course, it is theoretically possible to produce a cohort nuptiality table, just as it is possible to produce a cohort life table, but the data requirements for it are huge.

If, as mentioned above, marriage is thought of like fertility rather than mortality, then Age-Specific Marriage Rates can be calculated which include all women, both married and unmarried, in the denominators. A typical ASMR calculated in this unconventional way would be:

$$\text{ASMR (F, 20)} = \frac{\text{Marriages to females aged 20}}{\text{All females aged 20}} \times 1,000.$$

Such rates can be summed to form a Total Marriage Rate (TMR) in an analogous way to the Total Fertility Rate. The TMR can be interpreted as the average number of marriages a woman would have if subject to the age-specific rates that go to make it up. This is not a very useful measure at all, but a much more useful one can be obtained if the rates are restricted to first marriages. One can sum unconventional Age-Specific First Marriage Rates such as

$$\text{ASFMR (F, 20)} = \frac{\text{First marriages to females aged 20}}{\text{All females aged 20}} \times 1,000$$

= TFMR

to form a Total First Marriage Rate. This can be interpreted as the proportion of women who would eventually marry if the age-specific rates prevailed. However, as with all synthetic measures, this will only indicate the likely experience of true cohorts if age-specific first-marriage rates have been fairly constant for a long time. This is unlikely to be the case in many populations.

The mean age at marriage

If information on the number of marriages, broken down by age, are available, perhaps from a registration system, then it is straightforward to calculate a mean age of marriage. Because first, second and subsequent marriages occur at very different mean ages, it is sensible, if possible, to consider them separately. Similarly the sexes must be treated separately as in most societies males tend to marry later than females.

Table 8.1 Mean age at first marriage: England and Wales, males, 1985

Age last birthday	Mid-point of age (a)	Bachelors marrying (b)	(a) × (b)
16	16.5	255	4 207.5
17	17.5	871	15 242.5
18	18.5	3 267	60 439.5
19	19.5	7 288	142 116.0
20	20.5	13 783	282 551.5
21	21.5	21 422	460 573.0
22	22.5	26 468	595 530.0
23	23.5	28 997	681 429.5
24	24.5	27 758	680 071.0
25	25.5	24 378	621 639.0
26	26.5	20 320	538 480.0
27	27.5	16 561	455 427.5
28	28.5	12 769	363 916.5
29	29.5	9 854	290 693.0
30–34	32.5	24 580	798 850.0
35–39	37.5	8 517	319 387.5
40–44	42.5	2 873	122 102.5
45–49	47.5	1 388	65 930.0
50–54	52.5	784	41 160.0
55+	60.0*	1 163	69 780.0
		253 296	6 609 526.5

* Estimated

The method is simple. It is just the calculation of a weighted average of the ages, where the weights are the numbers marrying. This is done most easily using the statistical functions of a calculator, but is fully worked out in Table 8.1. One problem is that using five-year rather than single-year age groups will often give very imprecise results because the grouping is too coarse. Generally, it is better to use single-year age groups, up to at least age 25. Note that, because age 16 last birthday, for example, covers the whole year from exact age 16 to exact age 17, the average age of 16 year olds at the time of marriage is 16.5. With the last, open-ended age group, 55+, an estimate of the mid-point has to be made.

The calculations involve first multiplying the values (ages) by the weights (bachelors marrying), then summing the results, and finally dividing the total by the sum of the weights. Thus:

$$\text{Mean} = \frac{6,609,526.5}{253,296}$$

$$= 26.09 \text{ years.}$$

The Singulate Mean Age at Marriage

If no system of marriage registration exists, or if it is incomplete or very inaccurate, then it is impossible to calculate directly a mean age at marriage. Fortunately, though, there are methods for estimating the mean age at marriage indirectly using data derived from a census or survey. Of course, it is possible to ask a direct, retrospective question about age at marriage, but in most parts of the world there are likely to be many who simply do not know, or who, for other reasons, give wrong or no answers. The solution is to use data on current marital status.

Several indices have been developed, but the measure invented by Hajnal (1953), and known as the 'Singulate Mean Age at Marriage' (SMAM), is by far the most common and widely used. It was originally developed for a historical study of marriage patterns in Europe, and Hajnal discovered that, from probably the sixteenth century until the 1930s, Western and Southern Europe experienced a unique pattern of late marriage and high proportions never marrying (Hajnal 1965).

The SMAM is in many respects a similar measure to the Total Fertility Rate in that it is age-standardised and is a period measure, describing the behaviour of an hypothetical, synthetic cohort. The data used are the proportions single (*not* the proportions married) classified by age. The details are a little difficult to grasp at first, so two examples will be given. The best way to understand the calculations is to remember that the mean age at marriage is the same as the mean number of years spent single before marriage. The mean number of years single can be calculated by dividing the total number of years spent single by the number of people eventually marrying out of a group of, say, 100. This is best understood through the following example. Table 8.2 gives the data required for males in England and Wales in 1981.

The procedure is as follows. First, calculate the years of singleness lived by 100 persons up to age 15:

$$15 \times 100 = 1,500$$

Then calculate the years of singleness lived between exact ages 15 and 50:

Table 8.2 Percentage single: England and Wales, males, 1981 census

Age	% single
15–19	98.96
20–24	74.81
25–29	34.09
30–34	16.60
35–39	11.17
40–44	9.28
45–49	8.95
50–54	8.72

$$= (98.96 + 74.81 + 34.09 + 16.60 + 11.17 + 9.28 + 8.95) \times 5$$

$$= 1,269.30.$$

Note that the figure for 50–54 is *not* included. The sum is up to exact age 50 only. Thus the total years of singleness lived before age 50 is:

$$1,500 + 1,269.30 = 2,769.30.$$

Now, calculate the percentage still single at exact age 50. This is usually estimated by taking the average of the percentage single in the age groups 45–49 and 50–54:

$$(8.95 + 8.72)/2 = 8.835.$$

The total number of years of singleness lived before age 50, as calculated above, includes some that were experienced by those never marrying. These thus have to be calculated and subtracted from the total. The number of years of singleness lived by those not marrying by exact age 50 is:

$$8.835 \times 50 = 441.75.$$

Thus those who married experienced:

$$2,769.30 - 441.75 = 2,327.6$$

years of singleness.

Finally, the number who married by age 50 is:

$$100 - 8.835 = 91.165$$

Thus 91.165 men experienced 2,327.6 years of singleness before they married. The mean is thus:

$$\frac{2,327.6}{91.165} = 25.39 \text{ years} = \text{SMAM}$$

The calculation of the total years of singleness can perhaps be better understood from the graph in Figure 8.2. The total area under the curve is calculated by first adding that before age 15 and that between 15 and 50. From

% Single

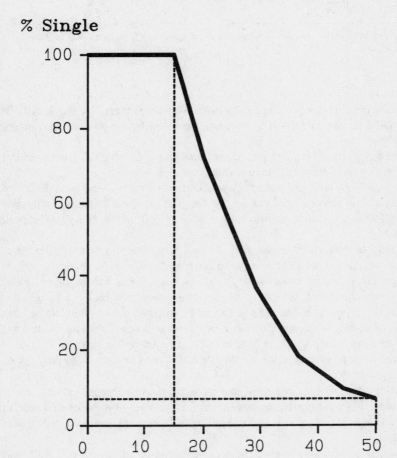

Figure 8.2 Calculation of the Singulate Mean Age at Marriage

Table 8.3 Proportions of females never married: Nigeria and Mali

Age group	% single	
	Mali	Nigeria
10–14	—	73.01
15–19	69.5	17.73
20–24	13.4	5.21
25–29	1.1	3.03
30–34	0.7	2.26
35–39	0.0	0.85
40–44	0.0	2.02
45–49	0.0	2.78

Note: The Mali figures relate to a sample of Delta Rimaibe, the Nigerian data to the Northern Region.

this is subtracted the area occupied by those who never marry by the age of 50. The SMAM is then calculated by dividing the result by the number who marry by age 50.

Table 8.3 shows two other sets of proportions single which illustrate several points over which particular care should be taken.

First, the Nigerian figures start at age 10 rather than 15. There is no difficulty with this if it is remembered that in the first step of the calculations only 100 $\times$ 10 = 1,000 years of singleness lived before age 10, rather than 1,500 should be used.

Second, the Nigerian figures show a frequently observed pattern of increasing proportions single at later ages. This may be due to a declining age at marriage during the previous twenty to thirty years, or it may be due to older persons reporting themselves as single when they are really widowed or divorced. In either case, the SMAM cannot be calculated using the data as it is. No real or synthetic cohort can show proportions single increasing with age. Either the proportions single at high ages must be altered to make them consistent with a cohort interpretation, or the SMAM should be calculated only up to, say, age 40 or 45.

Third, both sets of figures show that most marriages occur in just one or two age groups. It would clearly be better here to use a single-year breakdown, at least up to age 25. This is done for Mali in the following example, using data in Table 8.4.

The number of years of singleness experienced up to age 15 is 1,500, and that experienced between 15 and 40 is 406.6. Thus the total years of singleness is 1,906.6. Since all 100 in the hypothetical cohort marry by age 40, there is no need to subtract the experience of those not marrying. Thus the SMAM is:

Table 8.4 Percentage single: Delta Rimaibe females, Mali

Age	% never married
15	88.9
16	79.8
17	71.2
18	59.0
19	37.1
20	22.7
21	16.4
22	12.8
23	6.6
24	3.1
25–29	1.1
30–34	0.7
35–39	0.0

$$\frac{1,906.6}{100.0} = 19.1 \text{ years.}$$

In interpreting the SMAM it should be remembered, first, that again the measure is a synthetic one, using data derived from a cross-sectional census or survey. The proportions single at high ages are a result of marriages occurring over perhaps the last thirty years. The SMAM does not, therefore, measure current marriage patterns as the ordinary mean age at marriage in Table 8.1 does. The SMAM will only be identical to the ordinary mean if marriage patterns have remained constant for the previous twenty or thirty years. If the marriage age has been rising in the past, then the SMAM will be an underestimate of the current mean age. It will be a true estimate of the mean at some unknown time in the past.

Remarriage and divorce rates

If data on marriage is collected, as was recommended earlier, so that first marriages are distinguishable from subsequent ones, then it is possible to look at remarriage, using rates and means very similar to those discussed earlier. A Crude Remarriage Rate can be calculated for females as:

$$CRR = \frac{\text{Females remarrying}}{\text{Divorced and widowed females}} \times 1,000$$

The male CRR may well be very different from that of females, as in India, where remarriage of males is quite common, but for females it is very rare.

Age-specific remarriage rates can also be calculated as:

$$\text{ASRR (F, 30)} = \frac{\text{Females aged 30 remarrying}}{\text{Widowed and divorced females aged 30}} \times 1,000$$

Turning briefly to divorce rates, these can be computed in exactly the same way as marriage rates. However, male and female rates will always be exactly the same, unless the population is polygamous, since the same number of males and females must divorce, and the same numbers will be married at any given time.

It is very often the case that the focus of interest in analyses of divorce, widowhood and remarriage is not so much on the extent to which they are occurring, but on the proportions of men and women who experience these events during their lifetime. Such figures can be readily calculated, but of even greater interest is often the implications of current rates for the future. To do this one uses a life table technique. To look, for example, at what would happen to a cohort of marriages if they were to experience the divorce rates for a particular year one can calculate a gross divorce table. Mortality can also be taken into account by including widowhood rates.

Exercises

1. From the data given in Tables 8E.1 and 8E.2 calculate:

(a) The mean age at marriage of females marrying in England and Wales in 1981.
(b) The median age at marriage of females marrying in England and Wales in 1981.
(c) The Singulate Mean Age at Marriage for females from the 1981 census of England and Wales.

Why are the three measures different? Is the median a better measure than the mean in this case? Would the SMAM and the mean age at marriage be the same if the mean was calculated using only first marriages (i.e. excluding marriages of widows and divorcees)?

Table 8E.1 Females marrying in 1981, England and Wales

Age	Marriages
15	0
16	2 685
17	7 852
18	21 660
19	31 146
20	35 903
21	35 139
22	31 222
23	26 139
24	20 649
25	16 395
26	13 276
27	11 143
28	9 248
29	8 121
30–34	30 122
35–39	17 174
40–44	10 837
45–49	7 637
50–54	5 205
55+	10 420

Table 8E.2 Females by marital status and age, England and Wales, 1981

Age group	Single	Married	Widowed and divorced
15–19	1 877 926	87 767	495
20–24	945 341	781 760	32 420
25–29	312 682	1 220 771	93 643
30–34	157 891	1 531 978	131 671
35–39	92 276	1 318 860	126 890
40–44	74 654	1 186 132	126 292
45–49	76 095	1 129 956	132 019
50–54	90 421	1 145 657	78 320
55–59	104 554	1 123 748	245 741

2. Calculate a net nuptiality table using the data for males in England and Wales, in 1980 given in Table 8E.3. At age 16, 97.9 per cent had never married.

Table 8E.3 Probability of marrying and of dying: males, England and Wales, 1980

Age	Probability of marrying between ages x and $x+1$ g_x	Probability of dying between ages x and $x+1$ q_x
16	0.00059	0.00052
17	0.00360	0.00110
18	0.01644	0.00115
19	0.03457	0.00106
20	0.06073	0.00105
21	0.09078	0.00096
22	0.11081	0.00089
23	0.12716	0.00090
24	0.13191	0.00102
25	0.13395	0.00114
26	0.12396	0.00107
27	0.11914	0.00127
28	0.11964	0.00160
29	0.11414	0.00162

3. Table 8E.4 gives the proportion of Swedish women who were single in 1935, 1940 and 1945.

Table 8E.4 Proportion of Swedish women single, 1935, 1940 and 1945

Age group	1935	1940	1945
10–14	1 000	1 000	1 000
15–19	988	981	970
20–24	783	716	636
25–29	486	394	304
30–34	337	272	204
35–39	270	248	190
40–44	240	231	204
45–49	231	222	210
50–54	221	222	210

Source: Hajnal (1953)

(a) Describe the trend in nuptiality indicated by these data.
(b) Calculate the SMAM for each year. Will the crude average age at marriage in 1945 be higher or lower than the SMAM?
(c) How might one go about using these data to produce indices of nuptiality relating specifically to the periods 1935–40 and 1940–5?

9 Reproductivity

Reproductivity is the name given to that part of formal demography which considers the extent to which one generation is reproducing itself.

This chapter is essentially a continuation of Chapter 4 on period fertility. It introduces two new period measures of fertility levels — that is, the Gross and Net Reproduction Rates — and also two new period measures of fertility timing or location — that is, the mean of the age-specific fertility distribution and the mean age of childbearing.

The Gross Reproduction Rate

This measure is very similar to the Total Fertility Rate (TFR) except that it considers only female rather than all births. It is calculated in the same way as the TFR but uses female age-specific fertility rates. The female ASFRs are summed and — because each age group covers five years — multiplied by five. The figure of 3.4 for Bangladesh, given in Table 9.1 is towards the upper end of the range of values the Gross Reproduction Rate (GRR) can take. At the lower end, the figure for England and Wales, 1981 was 0.88.

Table 9.1 Gross Reproduction Rate: Bangladesh, 1974

Age group	Women	Total births	Female births	Female ASFR
10–14	4 533 000	9 066	4 410	0.001
15–19	3 777 000	747 846	363 738	0.096
20–24	3 101 000	1 045 037	508 286	0.164
25–29	2 636 000	819 796	398 733	0.151
30–34	2 161 000	566 182	275 380	0.127
35–39	1 793 000	353 221	171 800	0.096
40–44	1 484 000	140 980	68 570	0.046
45–49	1 222 000	17 108	8 321	0.007
		3 699 236	1 799 238	0.688
			× 5 =	3.440
			=	GRR

Source: ODM (1977)

There is another way of calculating the GRR which involves the Sex Ratio at Birth (see p. 27). One can estimate the GRR just by multiplying the TFR by the proportion of births that are female. Thus for Bangladesh, 1974, where the TFR was 7.08 and there were 1,799,238 female and 1,899,998 male births (ODM 1977: 76), the GRR was:

$$7.08 \times \frac{1,799,238}{3,699,236}$$

$$= 3.44.$$

If the true Sex Ratio at Birth is not known, 105 is usually quite acceptable as an estimate.

The GRR can be interpreted as the average number of daughters a women would have if she survived to at least age 50, and experienced the given female ASFRs. Remember the GRR, like the TFR, is a period rate and so says nothing about any real cohort. Instead, it considers an hypothetical, synthetic cohort.

A GRR of 1.0 suggests that the women are approximately replacing themselves, while a figure of 2.0 may be taken to imply that the population is doubling itself in a generation; that is, each woman is producing, on average, two daughters. However, it is important to be very careful in the interpretation of the GRR, not only because it is a period measure, but also because it assumes no mortality either before age 15 or between ages 15 and 50. Clearly, though, not all daughters will survive to replace their mothers, and not all mothers will survive to the end of the childbearing years, particularly in areas of high mortality. Thus a GRR greater than 1.0 is required to achieve replacement, perhaps 1.15 though the figure depends on the level of mortality. Incidentally, the same applies to the TFR. A figure of over 2.0 is required to ensure that in the long term the population maintains its size. It is this impact of mortality that is controlled for in the next measure to be considered, the Net Reproduction Rate.

The Net Reproduction Rate

Essentially, the Net Reproduction Rate (NRR), sometimes denoted by R_0, is a GRR adjusted for mortality. The adjustment is performed by multiplying each female ASFR by the probability of surviving from birth to that age, before summing and multiplying by five as usual. The NRR will thus always be slightly less than the GRR, the extent of the difference being dependent on the level of mortality.

The probability of surviving to age x is just l_x so to calculate the NRR requires both female ASFRs and a life table. Note that a precise life table for females for the year in question is not essential. Any reasonable estimate is adequate. The calculations for Bangladesh, 1974, are shown in Table 9.2.

Table 9.2 Net Reproduction Rate: Bangladesh, 1974

Age group	Female ASFRs	Exact age x	l_x	$_5L_x$	Female births to women in Stationary population (2) × (5)	Mid-point of age group	(2) × (7)	(6) × (7)
(1)	(2)	(3)	(4)	(5)	(6)	(7)	(8)	(9)
15–19	0.097	15	0.755	3.725	0.3613	17.5	1.698	6.323
20–24	0.164	20	0.735	3.610	0.5920	22.5	3.690	13.320
25–29	0.151	25	0.709	3.480	0.5255	27.5	4.153	14.451
30–34	0.127	30	0.683	3.350	0.4255	32.5	4.123	13.829
35–39	0.096	35	0.657	3.213	0.3084	37.5	3.600	11.565
40–44	0.046	40	0.628	3.060	0.1408	42.5	1.960	5.984
45–49	0.007	45	0.596	2.885	0.0202	47.5	0.333	0.960
		50	0.558					
	0.688				2.3737		19.557	66.432
× 5 =	3.440 = GRR >				= NRR			

Source: Derived from ODM (1977)

It should be noted that the female ASFRs are here expressed per one woman rather than per 1,000. Similarly, the radix of the life table is 1.0. This is recommended as it avoids problems of remembering to divide or multiply by 1,000 in various places. Note also that the only 'raw' data are in columns 1 to 4. All the other columns are derived from these.

The first step is to calculate the $_5L_x$s — the Stationary population associated with the life table. Recall that the notation $_5L_{15}$ refers to the age group 15–19, not 5–15. $_5L_{15}$ is just the average of adjacent l_xs, multiplied by 5 since five-year age groups are being used. For example:

$$_5L_{15} = \frac{(l_{15} + l_{20})}{2} \times 5$$

$$= \frac{(0.755 + 0.735)}{2} \times 5$$

$$= 3.725.$$

This procedure is repeated for each age interval and thus column 5 is calculated from column 4. Next, to calculate the NRR one asks 'What if this Stationary population were to experience the fertility rates of the actual population?' This can be answered simply by multiplying the female ASFRs by the $_5L_x$s. This gives column 6, the expected female births, sometimes known as the 'Net Maternity Distribution'. Adding these gives the NRR. There is no need

here to multiply by five as this was done when the $_5L_x$s were computed. The
NRR for Bangladesh, 1974, is thus about 2.4. Compare this with the figure of
3.4 for the GRR. The difference between the two is a measure of the impact of
mortality on reproductivity in Bangladesh. Contrast this with England and Wales
where in 1983 the GRR was 0.86 and the NRR only slightly less, at 0.84. The
difference is very much less because mortality in England and Wales is much
lighter than in Bangladesh.

The NRR can be interpreted as the average number of daughters a woman
would have during her reproductive years given the assumptions of:

1. Fertility at the given rates.
2. Mortality at the given rates.

Both the fertility and mortality rates used are based on events occurring
during a particular period, and in thinking of the NRR as a number of female
births per woman one is considering an imaginary, synthetic cohort, not any real
cohort. This has several implications. The most important is that an NRR of less
than 1.0 does not necessarily mean that the population is declining in absolute
numbers. It would normally take NRRs of less than 1.0 for a considerable
number of years before that happened. Nor does it mean that any real cohort
will have that number of daughters. Postponement or advancement of births may
be taking place, causing the fertility rates for the particular year on which the
NRR is based to be unusually high or low. Alternatively, cohort fertility may
be rising or falling so that the fertility rates of the 15–19 age group will not be
the same as those experienced by the 45–49 age group thirty years earlier when
they were 15–19.

The history of the NRR is interesting and helps to reinforce some of the points
made here. It was popularised by Kuczynski and others in the 1920s and 1930s
(see Shryock and Siegel 1976: 324–6). Since fertility had, by that time, been
falling continuously for a long period in most industrialised countries, the low
NRRs came to be interpreted, for some reason, as indicating the level to which
fertility would eventually fall. The relatively high Crude Birth Rates of the time
were explicable by reference to the favourable age structure. Some countries,
particularly France, become worried by this. Then, after the war, period fertility
rose rapidly and with it the NRRs and the measure was accused of being
misleading. In fact, it was only that the rate was being interpreted in a naïve
way. It was thought that it indicated the likely achievement of real cohorts,
whereas it is really only a synthetic, period measure, saying nothing about real
cohorts. The NRR has never really recovered its popularity, and this, together
with the comparatively large amount of data required for its calculation, has
meant that the Total Fertility Rate is a much more widely used measure.

The above method is the conventional way of calculating an NRR. However,
another method does exist which normally provides a very good approximation

to the true value. It is not now practically useful since calculators and computers mean that the computations involved in the conventional method are no longer daunting. It is, however, included here because it serves to introduce one or two extra measures, and because it may aid understanding of the NRR. It is a slight modification of the method described by Coale (1955).

The 'quick' method of calculating the NRR involves first computing $\overline{m}$ ('m bar') — the mean of the age-specific fertility distribution. This is simply a weighted average of the mid-points of the age groups, the weights being the ASFRs. (It is immaterial whether both sexes or just female ASFRs are used.) The mid-points are multiplied by the weights, summed and then divided by the sum of the weights. This is done for Bangladesh in Table 9.2. The mid-points are given in column 7. Note that they are 17.5, 22.5, . . . , and not 17, 22, . . ., because the groups cover exact ages 15–20, 20–25 . . . Thus:

$$\overline{m} = \frac{\text{Sum of column 8}}{\text{Sum of column 2}}$$

$$= \frac{19.557}{0.688}$$

$$= 28.4 \text{ years.}$$

Then the NRR can be calculated using the approximate relationship:

$$\text{NRR} = \text{GRR} \times l_{\overline{m}}$$

In words, the NRR is approximately equal to the GRR multiplied by the probability of surviving to the mean of the age-specific fertility distribution.

To calculate $l_{28.4}$ one simply interpolates linearly between l_{25} and l_{30}. This can be done graphically or algebraically. One graphical method involves drawing a line, scaling it with both x and l_x, then reading off the value of l_x against 28.4. In Figure 9.1 it is approximately 0.690, so:

$$\text{NRR} = 3.440 \times 0.690$$

$$= 2.4,$$

which is close to the precise value that was computed above.

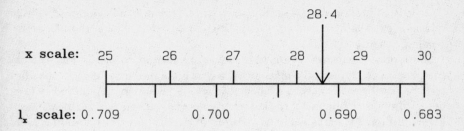

Figure 9.1 Calculating the Net Reproduction Rate

The timing of fertility

In some societies, particularly where fertility is low and contraception widespread, women tend to have their children at fairly young ages, while in other societies, particularly those with high, 'natural' fertility regimes, women have their children, on average, somewhat later. The measure defined above, $\overline{m}$, the mean of the age-specific fertility distribution, is but one of a whole series of measures of the timing or location of fertility. It is easy to get confused about these, partly because the names and algebraic symbols used are not entirely standardised, but especially because some are often used as approximations of others.

After $\overline{m}$, the most commonly used timing measure is the 'mean age of childbearing'. This can be thought of as the mean age of mothers at the birth of their children. The measure is labelled μ (mu) by Keyfitz (1968: 102), and $\overline{a}'$ ('a bar prime') by Barclay (1958: 220). Shryock and Siegel (1976: 320) do not give any name.

μ is, like $\overline{m}$, a weighted mean and is calculated in exactly the same way as $\overline{m}$ except that the weights this time are not the female ASFRs, but the births to the life table Stationary population, which, as was mentioned above, is also called the Net Maternity Distribution. Thus in Table 9.2 column 7 is multiplied by column 6 to give column 9. This is then summed and divided by the sum of the weights — the NRR — to give μ. That is:

$$\mu = \frac{\text{Sum of column 9}}{\text{Sum of column 6}}$$

$$= \frac{66.432}{2.3737}$$

$$= 28.0 \text{ years.}$$

This is a little less than $\bar{m}$, as it always will be because the two measures are related in exactly the same way as the GRR and the NRR. μ takes mortality into account, while $\bar{m}$ does not.

Two other measures of timing should be mentioned here, mainly for completeness and to avoid confusion. The first is the median of the age-specific fertility distribution, sometimes labelled $\tilde{m}$. It is sometimes preferable to $\bar{m}$ when the fertility distribution is very skewed. The second is the mean age of mothers giving birth and is perhaps the simplest of all the measures mentioned here. It is just the average of the ages of all the mothers giving birth during the year (or whatever period is being used). It is often labelled as M and is usually computed, again, as a weighted mean of the centres of the age groups, but now the weights are the actual numbers of births, rather than the ASFRs or the Net Maternity Distribution.

Finally, there are two or three points which need to be re-emphasised. Firstly, all the measures described here are period measures based on cross-sectional data, describing the experience of synthetic and not real cohorts. Secondly, it is possible and often useful to produce means separately for each birth order since, for example, first births occur, of course, at a much earlier age than subsequent births. Third, analogous measures for real cohorts can also be calculated, just as with period measures of fertility levels, though this is less commonly done. Last, if single-year figures are available and accurate, then using them will, of course, produce a more precise estimate than if five-year figures are used.

Chapter 11, which introduces Stable population models, is in many ways a continuation of this chapter. In it another measure of the timing of fertility, known as the 'Mean Length of Generation', will be described. It is different from all those described here.

Exercise

1. Calculate the Gross and Net Reproduction Rates for Hong Kong, 1973, from the data presented in Table 9E.1. Before calculating them, consider roughly what results you should obtain. What do the results tell you about fertility in Hong Kong?

Table 9E.1 Hong Kong data, 1973

Age group of women	Mid-year female population (000s)	Births in 1973*	Age x	l_x (Radix = 1)
15–19	234.0	3 986	15	0.97518
20–24	185.7	23 798	20	0.97258
25–29	112.5	27 433	25	0.96916
30–34	86.7	12 065	30	0.96524
35–39	107.0	7 642	35	0.96006
40–44	122.0	2 771	40	0.95209
45–49	112.6	354	45	0.94091
			50	0.92435

* Births of *both* sexes

Part II

Demographic models

10 Introduction to demographic models

It has been frequently observed that though we cannot hope to reach perfection in any thing, yet that it must be advantageous to us to place before our eyes the most perfect models.

(Malthus 1798, First Essay, Ch. 15: 174)

Like so many other words, the term 'model' is used in rather different senses in scientific and everyday usage. In ordinary English it can have several meanings such as in, 'She models the latest fashions', 'She is a model child' or 'He has a model aeroplane'. In scientific English, however, a model is different from all these. It is some sort of simplified representation of reality where some aspects of the truth are omitted or assumed to be unchanging so that other aspects can be observed more clearly. It is thus an idealisation, made necessary by the complexity of the real world. It is also frequently presented in a highly formalised way, often in algebraic notation.

It is convenient here to divide scientific models into two broad groups. First, there are 'normative' models which are concerned with describing what would occur under certain precisely specified, often wholly unrealistic conditions. Second, there are 'descriptive' models which try to reproduce reality as accurately as possible.

Normative models have been used in demography since long before Malthus wrote the above, but it is only in the last thirty or so years that the great power and usefulness of descriptive models has been realised. Today the development and testing of descriptive models of many kinds is one of the largest and most active areas of demography.

Normative models often exist both in a very simple form which deviates very much from reality, and also in more complex forms, where greater realism has been introduced by relaxing some of the simplifying assumptions. The oldest and most widely used normative models in demography are undoubtedly those based on the concept of the 'synthetic cohort', such as the Total Fertility Rate and the life table. In these models all except one of age structure, fertility, mortality, and migration, are fixed, often at zero, so that measures are obtained which are entirely determined by and accurately describe only one of these. Thus the TFR measures what fertility would be if mortality was zero and is unaffected by migration or age structure. Similarly, life table measures are independent of all except mortality. The Net Reproduction Rate and Stable Population models are similarly normative. The conditions, or assumptions, involved in these are more complex but just as closely specified. Most population projections are also normative models since they are based entirely on a fixed base population and a series of precisely stated assumptions.

These normative models so dominate formal demography that it is not often they are actually thought of as models; yet it should always be remembered that a move from ASFRs to a TFR, or from ASDRs to a life table, is a move from reality to a model. (normative)

There now exist a large number of descriptive models in demography. Those most widely used are concerned with the description of age structure itself, and with the age patterns of mortality, fertility and nuptiality. It is a characteristic of these phenomena that they are distributed by age in ways that are somewhat predictable. Mortality tends to be high in infancy, drops to low levels during childhood and early adulthood, then rises gradually to high levels in old age. Fertility rises rapidly to a peak somewhere in the twenties, then drops during the thirties reaching very low levels in the forties. Nuptiality follows very roughly the same pattern as fertility, though the peak may occur in the teens. It is this predictability within certain limits that makes demographic phenomena particularly suitable for descriptive modelling.

The uses of descriptive models

Descriptive models are used for several quite different purposes in demography. First, they can be used to smooth data. For example, a set of 'raw' ASDRs may be very irregular due perhaps to age-heaping, or because of small sample sizes. Smoothing by fitting models can produce better estimates.

Second, the fitting of models can be an extremely good way of assessing data quality. A set of data that cannot be fitted well should be treated with suspicion since, although a poor fit does not, of course, constitute absolute proof of the existence of errors or omissions, it does indicate that more careful investigation, or at the very least caution in analysis, is necessary.

Third, it is often the case that some data are missing, or simply not believable. Models can then be fitted to the partial data to complete them in a plausible way. For example, one may only have ASFRs in five-year age groups and want single-year figures. A model can be fitted to the five-year figures and then used to generate the single-year figures. Or, as another example, one may not trust reports of fertility given by, perhaps, very young or old women. A model can then be fitted to only those parts of the data that are trusted. Similarly, the data available may comprise only a few figures, perhaps a couple of child and two or three adult death rates. These can be used to fit a descriptive model and thereby to obtain estimates to replace the missing data. Historical demographers make extensive use of models in this way to build up plausible pictures of the past using scanty documentary or even archaeological evidence. It should be emphasised, though, that models used in this way are not magic. They cannot create data where none exist. They can merely provide estimates, or ranges of estimates and these have to be based on data which already exist. Otherwise one is merely guessing.

Fourth, models can be used in circumstances where data simply do not exist, either because they have not been collected, or because they relate to events occurring in the future. In population projections it is usually necessary to produce fertility, mortality and migration rates for dates in the future, and models are a convenient way of generating these. A closely related problem is the production of estimates for dates between censuses or surveys.

Fifth, models often provide a convenient way of describing some feature of a population in a very concise way. Overall mortality levels, for example, can be described using just an expectation of life at birth. Populations can then be compared using just that single 'parameter'.

Finally, models can be used for research into the effect of changes in the determinants of mortality, fertility, migration and so on. Given that it is extremely difficult and often unethical to carry out experiments in human populations, it is very useful to have some other way of assessing the likely impact of change. For example, it is possible to study the effect on fertility of rising ages at marriage or increasing contraceptive availability. Or one can assess the effect on mortality and age structure of the elimination of, say, cancer as a cause of death.

The growth in the availability, complexity and variety of demographic models has been one of the most important developments in demography in the last twenty years. In the following five chapters only the most important are mentioned. The emphasis is strongly on models which look at mortality and fertility by age, and which are useful for demographic estimation. For a somewhat wider discussion see Menken (1978), or the introduction in the United Nations' 'Manual X' (1983, Ch. 1).

11 Models of age structure

This chapter is essentially a continuation of Chapter 9 on reproductivity. It does not attempt to go into the field of Stable Population Theory to any great depth, but begins by describing the main features of Stable and Stationary populations, and goes on to show how to calculate, first the Intrinsic Rate of Natural Increase and, second, the Stable age distribution.

The concept of a 'Stable' population is generally regarded as having been invented by Alfred J. Lotka in 1907 and developed in a long series of papers published between then and 1925. However, work by Keyfitz has shown that Lotka's work was in fact pre-empted by Euler in the eighteenth century (1760). For details of this, and indeed many other important papers in mathematical demography, see Smith and Keyfitz (1977).

The extremely important discovery made by Euler and Lotka was that if, in any population, mortality and fertility remains constant for a long period, and if there is no migration, then eventually a fixed age structure will develop and, remarkably, that this 'Stable' age structure is completely independent of the initial age structure. To put this in another way, a set of age-specific mortality rates and a rate of growth together uniquely determine a certain Stable age distribution.

It is important at the outset to realise that the word 'Stable' describes the unchanging *shape* of an age distribution, not the total size of a population. A population which is Stable may, despite its name, actually be growing or declining in size very rapidly. The special case of a Stable population in which the growth rate is zero is known as a 'Stationary' population. One such has been met before in the $_nL_x$ column of the life table. In what follows the main characteristics of Stationary populations will be described first, and the discussion will then be generalised to all Stable populations.

The Stationary population

At the end of Chapter 6 on life table functions (see p. 79), it was pointed out that the $_nL_x$ column of a life table can be thought of as a Stationary population with a constant size, and a constant age structure. It is possible to say quite a lot about this population. First, its size is T_0. Secondly, there are l_0 babies being born each year, and, since the population size is unchanging, exactly the same number of persons are dying. From this it follows that the Crude Birth Rate in the Stationary population, known as the 'Intrinsic Birth Rate' (IBR), must be:

$$IBR = \frac{l_0}{T_0}$$

which must also be the <u>Intrinsic Death Rate</u>. Using again the data for England and Wales females, 1985 (see Table 6.3, p. 72), we have:

$$IBR = \frac{100,000}{7,756,261}$$

$$= 0.0129$$

$$= 13.0 \text{ per } 1,000.$$

Note that this figure bears no relation to the actual crude birth or death rates for England and Wales in 1985. It describes a hypothetical population derived solely from the mortality rates experienced by females of all ages in England and Wales during 1985.

One minor but interesting relationship which can be noted here is that since the expectation of life is calculated as:

$$e_x = \frac{T_x}{l_x}$$

(see p. 77) it must also be true that

$$IBR = IDR = \frac{1}{e_0} \quad = \frac{l_0}{T_0}$$

It is now possible to generalise the above from Stationary populations to cover Stable populations which are growing or declining in size.

The Stable population

In non-Stationary Stable populations the intrinsic birth and death rates will not be equal and so the difference between them, the <u>'Intrinsic Rate of Natural Increase'</u>, will not be zero. This measure is usually denoted by r and is sometimes called the <u>'True Rate of Natural Increase'</u>, or 'Lotka's r'.

Since the age composition of a Stable population is constant, and the growth rate is r per cent per year, then every age group must also be growing at the same rate of r per cent per year. Further, the numbers of births and deaths occurring each year must be growing at r per cent per year, and so must the number of deaths in each age group and births to mothers in each age group. But, while the absolute numbers continue to increase, all rates stay exactly the same so all mortality and fertility rates, crude, intrinsic and age-specific, and all life-table functions remain unchanging.

Having defined and described a Stable population, it is logical to turn now to the actual calculation of a Stable age structure from a set of mortality and fertility rates. The process involves first calculating the Stationary population and then adjusting it so that the rate of increase is r, rather than 0.0. The calculation of the Stationary population is straightforward since it is just the life table $_nL_x$ column, and the method is given in Chapter 6 (p. 75), but the calculation of r is more complex.

The Intrinsic Rate of Natural Increase

In Chapter 9 on reproductivity the Net Reproduction Rate was defined as the average number of daughters a woman would have if she was to experience the given mortality and fertility rates. It can thus be interpreted as a measure of the extent to which the population increases in a generation. For example, an NRR of 2.0 implies that each mother has, on average, two daughters and thus that a population doubles every generation.

Clearly, if the length of a generation was known as well as the NRR, then it would be possible to calculate the rate of population increase each year using a straightforward 'compound interest' formula. The mean length of a generation is an important measure. Here it will be denoted by T, because this is the symbol used by Shryock and Siegel (1976: 317), and by Coale (1955, 1957). It should be noted, however, that Barclay (1958: 220), uses $\bar{a}$ (a bar), while Keyfitz (1968: 102) uses A_r. Also, this T bears no relation to the life table function T.

The compound interest formula is:

$$NRR = e^{rT}$$

while can be rearranged as

$$Log_e\ NRR = rT$$

or

$$r = \frac{Log_e NRR}{T}$$

It turns out, though, that there is no simple way of calculating precisely the mean length of a generation. Instead, an approximation has to be used. In fact T can be closely approximated by μ (mu), the mean age of childbearing, which was described in Chapter 9 (see p. 111). The exact relationship between the two measures is that T relates to the Stable population, while μ describes the associated Stationary population.

On page 111 μ was calculated for Bangladesh, 1974, as being 28.0 years and the NRR was 2.3737, so:

$$r = \frac{\text{Log}_e 2.3737}{28.0}$$

$$= \frac{0.8644}{28.0}$$

$$= 0.0309$$

$$= 3.1 \text{ per cent per annum.}$$

This is in fact a quick way of calculating r, introduced by Coale (1955), which is only an approximation. The conventional method involves a huge equation. (For details, see Shryock and Siegel 1976: 316–17, or the excellent discussion in Glass 1940: 407.) That method produces a figure of 0.0306 for r, so the approximation above is, in this case, very close indeed. Coale (1957) gives another, somewhat more complex method which he considers gives an even better approximation than that above.

Again it is important to emphasise that the Intrinsic Rate of Natural Increase, r, bears no relationship to the Crude Rate of Natural Increase — the difference between the Crude Birth and Death Rates. They describe different populations which have the same age-specific fertility and mortality, but differing age structures. The CRNI relates to the real population, whereas r relates to the imaginary Stable population that would develop if the fertility and mortality rates on which the calculations are based were to remain constant indefinitely and there was no migration. Only if the real population was actually Stable would the crude and intrinsic rates be the same.

Calculation of the Stable age distribution

Having obtained the Intrinsic Rate of Natural Increase from the Bangladesh mortality and fertility rates, that rate of increase can now be applied to the Stationary population calculated from the 1974 Bangladesh female mortality rates in order to produce a Stable population with a growth rate of $r = 0.0309$.

The easiest way to explain and understand the procedure is to first assume that the population is growing, so that r is positive. Now, if there were, say, 1,000 $= l_0$ births during 1974, then there would clearly have been fewer than 1,000 births in earlier years. So, for example, those people aged 5 in 1974 would be the survivors of the births of 1969, of which there would have been fewer than

1,000. Successive age groups in the Stable population will thus comprise the survivors of progressively smaller and smaller birth cohorts. Of course, if r is negative, then the cohorts will be progressively larger.

In order to calculate the Stable population it is therefore necessary to find, for each age group, a factor by which the Stationary population must be adjusted in order to take account of the fact that they are not all the survivors of exactly 1,000 births, but of varying numbers of births. The factor will be a little less than 1.0 for young age groups, but closer to 0.0 for older age groups (again assuming that r is positive). Further, the factor will decrease exponentially since the number of births is, by definition, increasing by a factor of $1 + r$ per year ($100 + r$ if r is expressed as a percentage rather than a proportion.) This is therefore just another 'compound interest' problem. The factor will be e^{-ry} where y is the average age of the age group. This average age is normally assumed to be the midpoint of the age group, but for early years it will be less. For example, for the $0-1$s it might be 0.1 or 0.3, while for those aged between 1 and 5 it may be 2.6 rather than 3.0. generally, $y = x + {}_na_x$ (for a discussion of ${}_na_x$ see pp. 69 and 74).

Thus, to summarise, the main steps in producing a Stable population are:

1. Calculate the Stationary population, the ${}_nL_x$ column of the life table, in the normal way (see p. 75).
2. Calculate the Intrinsic Rate of Natural Increase, r.
3. Write down a column of y's, the average age of each age group, using appropriate assumptions.
4. Compute a column of factors e^{-ry}.
5. Multiply the Stationary population by the factors.

One problem, however, is that so far only females have been considered. To include males it is necessary to repeat the calculations separately for males using a male life table. One small complication is that the radix in this life table should not be the usual 10,000 or whatever, but instead should be increased to perhaps 10,500 so that the ratio of the radices of the male and female life tables is equal to the Sex Ratio at Birth. The calculations are shown in Table 11.1. The calculation will be done on the assumption that the rate of increase, r, is the same for males as for females. While this will normally be roughly the case, the extent of the difference will depend on the Sex Ratio at Birth and differential mortality. It is, of course, theoretically possible to calculate and use an r for males from a 'male' NRR and a 'male' Mean Length of Generation.

First, the Stationary population in columns 5 and 6 is computed from the l_xs in columns 2 and 3 using assumptions that $a_0 = 0.3$ and ${}_4a_1 = 1.6$. The

Table 11.1 Calculation of Stable age distribution: Bangladesh, 1974

Exact age x (1)	Female l_x (2)	Male l_x (3)	n (4)	Stationary population Female $_nL_x$ (5)	Male $_nL_x$ (6)	Average age y (7)	Factor (r=0.0309) e^{-ry} (8)	Female (9)	Stable population (Tot. = 10,000) Male (10)	Female (11)	Male (12)
0	1000	1056	1	899	938	0.3	0.9908	891	929	213	223
1	855	877	4	3 250	3 366	2.6	0.9228	2 999	3 106	718	744
5	784	811	5	3 880	4 010	7.5	0.7931	3 077	3 180	737	762
10	768	793	5	3 810	3 933	12.5	0.6796	2 589	2 673	620	640
15	756	780	5	3 730	3 848	17.5	0.5823	2 171	2 241	520	537
20	736	759	5	3 613	3 727	22.5	0.4989	1 803	1 859	432	445
25	709	732	5	3 480	3 590	27.5	0.4275	1 488	1 535	356	368
30	683	704	5	3 350	3 455	32.5	0.3663	1 227	1 266	294	303
35	657	678	5	3 213	3 315	37.5	0.3139	1 009	1 041	242	249
40	628	648	5	3 060	3 160	42.5	0.2689	823	850	197	204
45	596	616	5	2 885	2 982	47.5	0.2304	665	687	159	165
50	558	577	5	2 673	2 765	52.5	0.1975	528	546	126	131
55	511	529	5	2 410	2 498	57.5	0.1692	408	423	98	101
60	453	470	5	2 088	2 178	62.5	0.1450	303	316	73	76
65	382	399	5	1 595	1 778	67.5	0.1242	198	221	47	53
70	296	312	5	1 248	1 325	72.5	0.1064	133	141	32	34
75	203	218	5	790	860	77.5	0.0912	72	78	17	19
80	113	126	5	398	448	82.5	0.0781	31	35	7	8
85	46	53	5	1 586	1 804	90.0	0.0620	98	112	23	27
								20 513	21 239	4 911	5 089

Source: Derived from ODM (1977)

last, open-ended age groups were calculated using the relationship

$$L_{85+} = \frac{l_{85}}{M_{85+}}.$$

From the raw data M_{85+} = 0.029 for females and 0.028 for males. Note that the radix of the male life table is 1,056 as the Sex Ratio at Birth in Bangladesh is 105.6. The average ages, (y's) in column 7 use the same assumption as above at young ages. The figure of 90.0 for the 85+ age group is chosen arbitrarily. The factors in column 8 are calculated straightforwardly and the Stationary population in column 5 and 6 are multiplied by the factors to produce the Stable populations in columns 9 and 10.

However, the total size of this Stable population is not a round number such as 1,000 or 10,000. Normally, therefore, the entire Stable population is multiplied by a constant fraction to produce a rounded total. The total size of the population in columns 9 and 10 is 20,513 + 21,239 = 41,752. This is turned into a population with a total of 10,000 simply by multiplying each number in columns 9 and 10 by 10,000/41,752 = 0.2395. The result is shown in the last two columns of the table.

Stable population models such as this are very widely used in mathematical demography, in demographic estimation, in population projections and elsewhere, even though few real populations now have a Stable age structure, because of declines in mortality and, more recently, fertility. A population which was once approximately Stable, but which has subsequently experienced steady mortality decline, is said to be 'Quasi-Stable'. There exists a substantial literature on such models and they were once extensively used for demographic estimation. However, since in most real populations fertility has also fallen, producing rapid deviations from stability, there are few remaining populations which can even approximate quasi-stability.

Doubling time

One question often asked when considering rates of increase, either crude or intrinsic, is how long it would take for the population to double in size if the current rates were to continue. This can be answered using the now familiar compound interest equation. The calculation will here be done using intrinsic rather than crude rates.

If D is the doubling time, and P is the population, then the population will increase exponentially to $2P$ according to the formula:

$$2P = P \cdot e^{rD}$$

$$\Rightarrow D = \frac{\text{Log}_e 2.0}{r}.$$

For Bangladesh $r = 0.0309$ so:

$$D = \frac{0.693}{0.0309} = 22.4 \text{ years.}$$

Thus the population of Bangladesh would double in about twenty-two years *if* fertility and mortality levels were to continue indefinitely and *if* the population was already approximately Stable.

There is a quick way of doing this calculation. Since the value of $Log_e 2.0$ is roughly 0.7, then if r is expressed as a percentage, simply dividing 70 by r gives a close approximation to the doubling time. Here r is 3.09 per cent so the approximation is $70/3.09 = 22.7$ years, very close to the 22.4 years calculated above.

Exercises

1. The Crude Rate of Natural Increase among white females in the United States in 1920 was 1.01 per cent. Use the data in Table 11E.1 to calculate their Net Reproduction Rate, Mean Length of Generation and Intrinsic Rate of Natural Increase.

Table 11E.1 White female fertility and mortality, United States, 1920

Age group	Daughters per annum per 100,000	Probability of surviving to ages 12.5, 17.5 etc.
10–14	9	0.88567
15–19	2 202	0.87438
20–24	7 310	0.85509
25–29	7 481	0.82960
30–34	5 780	0.80181
35–39	3 898	0.77417
40–44	1 552	0.74664
44–49	172	0.71610
50–54	5	0.62937

Source: Dublin and Lotka (1936, Table 37: 245). Data are based on twenty-seven states.

On the basis of these results Dublin and Lotka commented, 'The natural rate of increase of a population, if measured directly by the excess of the birthrate over the deathrate, gives a misleading impression of its reproductive vitality'. Calculate the doubling time for this population, using both the Crude and Intrinsic Rates of increase.

Do you agree with Dublin and Lotka? Do the intrinsic measures of increase and doubling time give a better impression of the future growth of the white female population of the United States than the crude measures?

2. The Intrinsic Rate of Natural Increase in England and Wales in 1981 was approximately -0.57 per cent per annum. Assuming that fertility and mortality were to remain the same, how many years would it be before the population would have declined to 25 million (some 50 per cent of the current total), regarded by some as the optimum population. What other assumptions must you make to carry out this calculation?

3. Define precisely the Intrinsic Rate of Natural Increase and the Mean Length of Generation. Calculate these two measures for Norwegian females, 1984 using the data presented in Table 11E.2.

Table 11E.2 Female fertility and mortality, Norway 1984

Age group	Age-specific fertility (per 1,000)	Exact age x	l_x ($l_0 = 1,000$)
15–19	19.2	15	9 887
20–24	93.9	20	9 884
25–29	123.7	25	9 881
30–34	68.3	30	9 878
35–39	22.2	35	9 873
40–44	4.1	40	9 867
45–39	0.2	45	9 855
		50	9 834

Source: Norges Offisielle Statistikk (1985)

4. In 1972–3 the Net Reproduction Rate of England and Wales was 1.0. From the data in Table 11E.3, first calculate the female Stable age distribution. Second, compare it with the observed female age structure. Comment on and give possible reasons for the difference.

Table 11E.3 Female mortality and age distribution, England and Wales, 1972–3

Survivors to age x		Observed age distribution	
Exact age	l_x	Age group	%
0	1 000	0–4	7.61
5	982	5–9	7.93
10	981	10–14	7.12
15	980	15–19	6.54
20	978	20–24	7.39
25	976	25–29	6.44
30	973	30–34	5.63
35	970	35–39	5.50
40	964	40–44	5.84
45	955	45–49	6.25
50	938	50–54	5.92
55	914	55–59	6.11
60	878	60–64	5.97
65	826	65–69	5.31
70	747	70–74	4.32
75	629	75–79	2.97
80	459	80+	3.15
85	273		
90	81		

12 Empirical model life tables

It is important at the outset to realise that model life tables are identical to ordinary, real life tables in every way, except that they relate to no particular place or time.

The need for model life tables that could be used in the ways suggested in Chapter 10 became apparent in the 1950s. Since then at least eight different sets of models have been published. In this chapter only three will be discussed. They are the 1955 United Nations set (United Nations 1955, 1956), the Princeton Regional Model Life Tables, often known after their authors as the 'Coale–Demeny Set', (Coale and Demeny 1966, 1983), and the 'New' United Nations set for developing countries (United Nations 1982). They are all based on a distillation of the patterns of mortality found in collections of real life tables and are thus here described as 'empirical'. In the next chapter several other fundamentally different model life tables are described. They are generally known as 'relational' models for reasons that will become clear.

The determinants of mortality patterns

Any graph of age-specific death rates, such as that in Figure 12.1, will tend to show a roughly similar pattern. The graph starts at a high level in infancy, drops to low levels during childhood and early adulthood, then rises gradually into old age. The precise shape of the graph varies from country to country, over time and between sexes, but the general pattern will remain the same. It is this feature of mortality, the fact that it changes with age in regular, predictable ways, within certain limits, that makes it possible to produce good models of it.

In fact, Ledermann and Breas (1959) looked in detail at the way mortality patterns differ from each other and they found that most of the variation can be explained by just five factors. These are:

1. The overall level of mortality.
2. The ratio of child to adult mortality.
3. Old age mortality.
4. Infant Mortality.
5. Sex differences in mortality.

The various sets of model life tables differ greatly in the extent to which they take into account these different factors, or allow the user to choose them.

Mortality

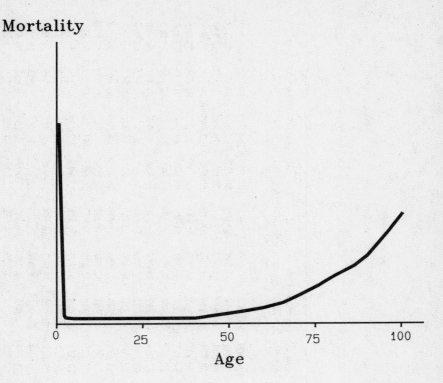

Figure 12.1 The typical age-pattern of mortality

However, it is the first, the overall level of mortality, that is by far the most important, and consequently it is the one that all sets are built around.

The 1955 United Nations set

These life tables are used only very rarely now, but are of interest because their simplicity makes them useful as an introduction to other model life-table sets. Also, they were the first to be published, initially in 1955, then in a revised form in 1956 (United Nations 1955, 1956).

The authors collected together 158 empirical life tables for each sex which they used as basic data. These were put into a complex regression analysis in order to distil out the basic pattern. The result was a set of twenty-four model life tables for each sex. The male ones are shown in Table 12.1. They run from level 0, corresponding to an expectation of life of just 20 years, up to level 115 which has an e_0 of 73.9.

These tables can be used in several ways. For example, if one has perhaps

Table 12.1 The 1955 United Nations model life tables, males

Sex and age (x) in years	Level 0 ($e_0=20$)	Level 5 ($e_0=22.5$)	Level 10 ($e_0=25$)	Level 15 ($e_0=27.5$)	Level 20 ($e_0=30$)	Level 25 ($e_0=32.5$)	Level 30 ($e_0=35$)	Level 35 ($e_0=37.5$)	Level 40 ($e_0=40$)	Level 45 ($e_0=42.5$)	Level 50 ($e_0=45$)	Level 55 ($e_0=47.5$)
MALES												
0	100 000	100 000	100 000	100 000	100 000	100 000	100 000	100 000	100 000	100 000	100 000	100 000
1	66 769	68 545	70 951	72 807	74 441	75 962	77 535	79 075	80 427	81 761	83 091	84 347
5	48 876	52 418	56 217	59 395	62 201	64 819	67 389	69 878	72 050	74 198	76 272	78 230
10	44 523	48 335	52 372	55 812	58 871	61 745	64 558	67 288	69 672	72 040	74 316	76 466
15	42 044	45 956	50 088	53 648	56 831	59 835	62 778	65 641	68 147	70 641	73 036	75 301
20	39 182	43 088	47 230	50 857	54 123	57 231	60 301	63 304	65 943	68 583	71 117	73 518
25	35 820	39 643	43 726	47 368	50 664	53 834	57 024	60 154	62 941	65 740	68 441	71 013
30	32 226	35 980	40 021	43 697	47 064	50 337	53 666	56 939	59 888	62 860	65 744	68 496
35	28 373	32 075	36 090	39 823	43 282	46 682	50 168	53 602	56 727	59 885	62 965	65 910
40	24 198	27 850	31 843	35 644	39 207	42 750	46 404	50 009	53 321	56 676	59 963	63 112
45	19 733	23 284	27 207	31 040	34 681	38 348	42 154	45 918	49 425	52 989	56 482	59 834
50	15 307	18 634	22 367	26 122	29 761	33 482	37 368	41 230	44 894	48 634	52 300	55 828
55	11 332	14 272	17 648	21 156	24 629	28 248	32 085	35 933	36 649	43 456	47 233	50 877
60	7 900	10 306	13 155	16 228	19 353	22 688	26 299	29 978	33 603	37 359	41 120	44 781
65	5 132	6 925	9 125	11 596	14 188	17 031	20 199	23 497	26 824	30 325	33 873	37 364
70	2 975	4 152	5 654	7 417	9 329	11 495	14 002	16 684	19 466	22 456	25 533	28 654
75	1 399	2 031	2 876	3 921	5 109	6 511	8 201	10 076	12 102	14 341	16 733	19 185
80	483	738	1 099	1 574	2 143	2 855	3 757	4 805	5 993	7 354	8 867	10 470
85	90	150	245	382	558	798	1 125	1 532	2 023	2 616	3 310	4 080

Sex and age (x) in years	Level 60 (e_0=50)	Level 65 (e_0=52.5)	Level 70 (e_0=55)	Level 75 (e_0=57.6)	Level 80 (e_0=60.4)	Level 85 (e_0=63.2)	Level 90 (e_0=65.8)	Level 95 (e_0=68.2)	Level 100 (e_0=70.2)	Level 105 (e_0=71.7)	Level 110 (e_0=73.0)	Level 115 (e_0=73.9)
MALES												
0	100 000	100 000	100 000	100 000	100 000	100 000	100 000	100 000	100 000	100 000	100 000	100 000
1	85 622	86 918	88 189	89 766	91 553	93 340	94 948	96 199	97 033	97 589	97 959	98 206
5	80 180	82 139	84 025	86 186	88 513	90 840	92 996	94 799	96 087	96 950	97 526	97 911
10	78 599	80 740	82 792	85 110	87 579	90 045	92 326	94 256	95 697	96 679	97 335	97 774
15	77 546	79 799	81 949	84 360	86 913	89 462	91 824	93 838	95 380	96 451	97 167	97 646
20	75 900	78 304	80 598	83 146	85 831	88 510	90 999	93 142	94 842	96 064	96 882	97 430
25	73 575	76 188	78 672	81 409	84 291	87 173	89 860	92 204	94 136	95 548	96 495	97 131
30	71 240	74 055	76 741	79 679	82 744	85 814	88 704	91 251	93 399	94 984	95 050	96 767
35	68 846	71 866	74 756	77 888	81 142	84 399	87 475	90 212	92 554	94 306	95 487	96 282
40	66 247	69 474	72 567	75 894	79 336	82 777	86 038	88 963	91 490	93 413	94 712	95 587
45	63 172	66 614	69 913	73 438	77 073	80 704	84 143	87 258	89 970	92 077	93 528	94 507
50	59 345	62 979	66 511	70 180	73 990	77 799	81 408	84 714	87 610	89 932	91 596	92 748
55	54 521	58 301	61 989	65 811	69 757	73 703	77 454	80 930	84 008	86 548	88 468	89 872
60	48 466	52 315	56 084	59 985	64 008	68 039	71 880	75 462	78 710	81 475	83 639	85 330
65	40 908	44 659	48 373	52 218	56 180	60 158	63 986	67 606	70 965	73 930	76 351	78 320
70	31 847	35 282	38 772	42 291	46 000	49 739	53 384	56 893	60 227	63 290	65 875	68 070
75	21 751	24 567	27 449	30 466	33 638	36 875	40 080	43 227	46 284	49 192	51 732	53 953
80	12 198	14 149	16 183	18 339	20 646	23 036	25 456	27 882	30 322	32 734	34 971	36 999
85	4 943	5 957	7 057	8 255	9 569	10 966	12 415	13 914	15 458	17 015	18 581	20 119

Source: United Nations (1956)

just one $_nq_x$ value for an area and no other information, but wants to estimate the entire life table, then it is possible to select the particular model life table that has a value of $_nq_x$ closest to the observed one. More realistically, if mortality rates up to, say, age 50 are known, and estimates for higher ages are required, then it might be appropriate to select the model life table which minimises the differences between the observed values and the model ones. For projections, one can use the tables by framing mortality assumptions in the form of a move from one model level to another model by a certain date.

This set of model life tables has been criticised quite severely since it was published, and is primarily of historical interest now. The main criticisms are as follows.

First, some of the 158 empirical life tables on which the models are based were not very accurate, particularly at young and old ages. Second, some of the life tables used had already been smoothed, adjusted or calculated using some sort of interpolation or other model themselves and so were not 'real'. Third, at a technical level, the regression methods used to derive the models were statistically biased. Fourth, the low levels, which have high mortality, are based on a particularly small number of life tables, which are also, inevitably, the least reliable. The models at these levels are thus themselves not very good.

Finally, and most importantly, the models are inflexible and rigid. Once a mortality level is chosen, then the entire model life table is selected. Yet, as Ledermann and Breas showed, two populations with identical mortality levels may well have very different age patterns of mortality. Perhaps in one adult mortality is high relative to childhood mortality, while in the other it is relatively low. On some occasions this rigidity is not a problem, such as when one has, say, an estimate of the overall level of mortality, but does not know anything about the age pattern. In such circumstances there is no way of choosing between models with different age patterns of mortality and so the lack of choice is unimportant. But such circumstances are very rare nowadays. Almost always some information about the pattern is available and the rigidity of these models then becomes a serious drawback. One has to turn instead to one of the other sets available.

The Princeton Regional Model Life Tables

These are still the most widely used model life tables, despite having been published as long ago as 1966 (Coale and Demeny 1966). A new, revised edition was published in 1983.

They are similar to the United Nations set in that they comprise twenty-five Levels for each sex (twenty-four in the 1966 edition), though these are called Levels 1 to 25 rather than 0, 5, 10, . . . 115. They correspond to e_0s for females ranging from 20.0 to 80.0. Their greater flexibility compared with the UN set comes from there being a set of models for each of four 'families' of 'regions' called 'North', 'South', 'East' and 'West'. The age patterns of mortality in each of the regions differ, each having relatively high or low infant, childhood, adult or old age mortality. Before describing their characteristics in more detail, it is useful to consider briefly how they were constructed.

The raw data used by Coale and Demeny were a collection of 326 male and 326 female real life tables. They had excluded any that were thought to be inaccurate, affected by war or epidemics, or which had been adjusted in some way and were thus not based solely on raw data. This meant that the vast majority of the 326 tables came from Europe and other developed countries.

The 326 tables were then divided into nine groups on the basis of the patterns of mortality they showed. Five of these groups were then rejected either because they comprised life tables that were clearly inaccurate (mainly those from Africa and Latin America), because they were affected very strongly by tuberculosis mortality, because they were pre-1870 or because they were very small. This left four groups on which the four families of model life tables are based.

The model life tables were then generated using regression procedures. The precise details are given in Coale and Demeny (1966: 20–3), but, roughly, a simple regression of the form

$$_nq_x = a + be_{10}$$

was calculated for each age, for each sex and region separately, and the coefficients then used to compute the model $_nq_x$s. The expectation of life at age 10, e_{10} was chosen as the independent variable because it was considered to be a good indicator of the overall level of mortality, and relatively unaffected by the mortality rates for any one age group. The final result was that a set of twenty-four models were produced for each region for each sex, making 192 in all.

For the 1983 revisions the upper limit of the age range was raised from 80 to 100 years. This was achieved using a Gompertz formula (Coale and Demeny 1983: 20). It did, however, necessitate a very slight revision to the figures below age 80 so the 1966 and 1983 models are not absolutely identical below age 80, though the differences are extremely small. The other extension was that the mortality range was extended up to a female expectation of life at birth of 80 years. Previously, the maximum had been 77.5 years. This was done by adding a new 25th Level.

The characteristic features of the four regions are as follows:

1. *North:* This region is based on nine life tables from Norway, Sweden and Iceland. It is characterised by relatively low infant and old age mortality, but high adult mortality caused by an unusually high incidence of tuberculosis.
2. *South:* This is derived from twenty-three Mediterranean life tables from Portugal, Spain, Sicily and southern Italy. It has high mortality under age 5, particularly among infants, low adult mortality and high mortality over age 65.

Table 12.2 Princeton regional model life table, West, level 12

LEVEL 12

FEMALES

Age (x)	1000 q(x)	d(x)	1000 m(x)	l(x)	L(x)	P(x)	T(x)	e(x)	Age (x)
0	132.25	13 225	144.69	100 000	91 404.	0.83896*	4 750 000.	47.500	0
1	83.06	7 208	21.97	86 775	328 078.	0.93573†	4 658 596.	53.686	1
5	24.28	1 932	4.92	79 567	392 523.	0.97994	4 330 518.	54.426	5
10	18.94	1 470	3.82	77 635	384 647.	0.97794	3 937 995.	50.724	10
15	25.51	1 943	5.16	76 165	376 162.	0.97122	3 553 347.	46.653	15
20	32.41	2 406	6.58	74 222	365 337.	0.96561	3 177 186.	42.806	20
25	36.61	2 629	7.45	71 816	352 772.	0.96110	2 811 848.	39.153	25
30	41.48	2 870	8.46	69 187	339 050.	0.95627	2 459 076.	35.542	30
35	46.27	3 068	9.46	66 318	324 225.	0.95136	2 120 026.	31.968	35
40	51.34	3 247	10.53	63 249	308 453.	0.94523	1 795 802.	28.392	40
45	58.67	3 520	12.07	60 002	291 560.	0.93247	1 487 349.	24.788	45
50	77.72	4 390	16.15	56 481	271 871.	0.91091	1 195 788.	21.171	50
55	102.44	5 336	21.55	52 091	247 651.	0.87608	923 917.	17.736	55
60	149.84	7 006	32.29	46 755	216 963.	0.82407	676 266.	14.464	60
65	209.17	8 314	46.50	39 749	178 793.	0.75034	459 304.	11.555	65
70	305.14	9 592	71.50	31 435	134 155.	0.63884	280 511.	8.923	70
75	430.57	9 405	109.74	21 843	85 703.	0.49964	146 356.	6.700	75
80	583.37	7 256	169.45	12 438	42 821.	0.34468	60 653.	4.876	80
85	749.66	3 885	263.21	5 182	14 760.	0.19250	17 832.	3.441	85
90	888.16	1 152	405.52	1 297	2 841.	0.07981	3 073.	2.369	90
95	968.73	141	619.78	145	227.	0.02072‡	232.	1.596	95
100	1 000.00	5	945.62	5	5.	0.0	5.	1.058	100

Age (x)	1000 q(x)	d(x)	1000 m(x)	l(x)	L(x)	P(x)	T(x)	e(x)	Age (x)
MALES									
0	155.99	15 599	174.20	100 000	89 549.	0.81679*	4 450 415.	44.504	0
1	83.94	7 085	22.22	84 401	318 844.	0.93430†	4 360 866.	51.668	1
5	23.61	1 825	4.78	77 316	381 563.	0.98108	4 042 022.	52.279	5
10	17.18	1 297	3.46	75 491	374 345.	0.97938	3 660 459.	48.488	10
15	24.42	1 812	4.94	74 195	366 625.	0.97076	3 286 114.	44.290	15
20	34.59	2 503	7.03	72 383	355 906.	0.96379	2 919 489.	40.334	20
25	38.04	2 658	7.75	69 879	343 018.	0.95932	2 563 583.	36.686	25
30	43.65	2 934	8.92	67 221	329 064.	0.95258	2 220 565.	33.034	30
35	51.68	3 322	10.60	64 287	313 461.	0.94269	1 891 501.	29.423	35
40	63.74	3 886	13.15	60 965	295 496.	0.92966	1 578 040.	25.885	40
45	77.98	4 451	16.20	57 079	274 710.	0.91070	1 282 544.	22.470	45
50	102.60	5 400	21.58	52 627	250 178.	0.88344	1 007 834.	19.150	50
55	133.42	6 301	28.51	47 228	221 017.	0.84357	757 656.	16.043	55
60	185.20	7 580	40.65	40 927	186 443.	0.78593	536 640.	13.112	60
65	252.46	8 419	57.45	33 347	146 531.	0.70832	350 197.	10.502	65
70	348.51	8 688	83.70	24 928	103 791.	0.59517	203 666.	8.170	70
75	478.53	7 772	125.81	16 241	61 774.	0.45230	99 875.	6.150	75
80	625.08	5 294	189.47	8 469	27 940.	0.30818	38 101.	4.499	80
85	780.85	2 479	287.93	3 175	8 611.	0.16827	10 161.	3.200	85
90	904.51	629	434.39	696	1 449.	0.06858	1 550.	2.228	90
95	973.60	65	651.01	66	99.	0.01779‡	101.	1.523	95
100	1 000.00	2	974.73	2	2.	0.0	2.	1.026	100

* P(birth)
† P(0–4)
‡ T(100)/T(95)

Source: Coale and Demeny (1983)

3. *East:* This set of models was generated from thirty-one primarily Central European life tables from Austria, Germany, Bavaria, Prussia, north Italy, Poland and Czechoslovakia. It has high infant and high old-age mortality, relative to childhood and adult rates.

4. *West:* This region may be regarded as describing some kind of 'average' mortality pattern, and is consequently by far the most frequently used. Coale and Demeny recommend its use when no reliable information on the age pattern of mortality is available. The models are based on a large 'rag-bag' of 130 life tables which were considered to be accurate but which did not fit into any of the other three groups. It includes life tables from, among others, the Netherlands, Finland, France, England and Wales, Japan, Ireland, Israel, Australia, Canada and South Africa.

Table 12.2 illustrates the way the models are presented. It shows West region, Level 12. The top panel gives the females, with an expectation of life at birth of 47.5, while the bottom panel gives the males, with an e_0 of 44.5. The only slightly unusual column is that labelled $P(x)$ which is just the survivorship rates, the ratios between adjacent $_nL_x$s as described in Chapter 6 (see p. 75).

It is important to realise that, although there are separate life tables for males and females at each Level, there is no reason why one should not use any life table, however labelled, to describe any mortality pattern, whether male, female or both sexes combined. There is no peculiar characteristic of the life tables for one sex that makes them appropriate for modelling the mortality of the other sex, or both sexes combined. If a 'female' model life table happens to fit a set of male data better than any 'male' model does, then it should be used.

Even more importantly, there is no strong connection between the life tables for males and females for a particular region and Level. If, say, West, Level 1, males fits some observed male data best, then West, Level 1, females will not necessarily fit the observed female data at all well. For example, it was stated in Chapter 3 (see p. 30) that in India and some other parts of South Asia female mortality is heavier than male mortality; yet in the Coale–Demeny models female mortality is lighter than male at every Level.

Computer programs exist which make the using of these models relatively easy. Fitting a model to some observed data for smoothing, or to produce a complete life table from partial data, can be carried out using standard curve-fitting procedures.

The survivorship column, $P(x)$ is particularly useful for population projections. Note that the first two values in this column are rather strange. The first, in the $P(0)$ position, gives the probability of five years of births surviving to become the 0 to 4 age group (i.e. up to exact age 5). In life-table notation it is:

$$\frac{_5L_0}{5(l_0)}$$

The second, in the $P(1)$ position, gives the probability of surviving from the 0–4 age group into the 5–9 age group. In other words, it is just the ratio:

$$\frac{{}_5L_5}{{}_5L_0}.$$

The main criticism that has been made of these tables is that, because they are based almost exclusively on European mortality patterns, they may not be appropriate for studying mortality patterns in developing countries and elsewhere, where causes of death and disease patterns are probably substantially different. Additionally, it seems that the availability of just four different sets of models provides insufficient flexibility to cope with the variety of patterns observed in the real world. Often, none of the four regions fits an observed pattern satisfactorily. For example, it is thought that in parts of West Africa childhood mortality is higher relative to infant mortality than in any of the Coale–Demeny regions.

The 1982 United Nations Set

The United Nations (1982) have attempted to overcome some of the limitations of the Princeton models mentioned above by producing a new set of model life tables which are very similar in form to the Coale–Demeny set but are based entirely upon empirical life tables from developing countries. Like Coale and Demeny, the authors collected together as many accurate life tables from developing countries as they could find. A total of seventy-two tables (thirty-six male and thirty-six female) were found from India, Iran, Kuwait, Israel, Tunisia and countries in Central and Latin America and South-East Asia. There was none from sub-Saharan Africa.

These life tables were then divided into several groups using a battery of sophisticated statistical techniques. Four major patterns emerged. These were labelled the 'Latin American', 'Chilean', 'South Asian' and 'Far Eastern' patterns. A fifth 'General' pattern was also produced which is an average of all the original empirical life tables. A comparison of these patterns with the Coale–Demeny West region models indicates that the different patterns have roughly the following characteristics:

1. *Latin American:* These have relatively high infant and child mortality due mainly to excess diarrhoeal and parasitic diseases. Adult mortality is high due to accidents. Old-age mortality is relatively low due to low mortality from cardiovascular disease.
2. *Chilean*: This family has extremely high infant mortality, due mainly to

deaths from respiratory disease and possibly early weaning.

3. *South Asian*: This has high mortality under 15 and over 55, but relatively low mortality at adult ages.

4. *Far Eastern*: The old ages in this family show very high mortality, particularly among males. This is perhaps ascribable to a past history of tuberculosis. Some Caribbean as well as Asian populations appear to exhibit this pattern.

5. *General*: This is very similar to the Coale–Demeny West region.

The models are published for each of the five patterns, for each sex, and are given for expectations of life at birth from 35 to 75 years in single-year intervals in a form very similar to the Coale–Demeny Levels (see Table 12.2).

The following chapter describes two much more flexible systems of 'relational' model life tables, derived in a very different way from those described above and capable of generating a much wider variety of mortality patterns.

Exercises

1. As part of the investigations carried out jointly by the British Medical Research Council and the government of Gambia, since the 1950s births and deaths occurring in the Gambian village of Keneba have been accurately recorded. From these data the death probabilities shown in Table 12E.1 have been calculated. The total number of children observed was 865.

Table 12E.1 Death probabilities, Keneba, Gambia

Age x	% surviving to x
1 week	94.1
1 month	90.8
1 year	76.1
2 years	64.3
3 years	56.5
4 years	52.3
5 years	50.1

Use Tables 12E.2 and 12E.3 to fit an appropriate Coale–Demeny model life table and thus estimate the expectation of life at birth and at age 5 in Keneba. What factors may cause your figure for e_0 and e_5 to be poor estimates of the true values? What is the probability that a Keneban child, currently aged 0–4 will survive to 5–9?

2. In Table 12E.4 each of the four Princeton regional model life-table families have been fitted to the Icelandic life table for males, 1856–65. What is a model

life table and why is it useful? Which of the four families of models fits the data for Iceland best? In the light of these fits, comment on the age-pattern of mortality in childhood in Iceland during the nineteenth century.

Table 12E.2 Values of l_x by single years of age from 1 to 5 for regional model life tables ($l_0 = 100,000$) at mortality Levels 1-25

MODEL
WEST

LEVEL	Females					Males				
	l_1	l_2	l_3	l_4	l_5	l_1	l_2	l_3	l_4	l_5
1	63 445	54 958	51 154	48 696	46 836	58 050	50 262	46 851	44 617	42 957
2	66 601	58 514	54 891	52 549	50 776	61 614	54 105	50 817	48 663	47 062
3	69 444	61 785	58 353	56 135	54 456	64 826	57 643	54 497	52 437	50 906
4	72 027	64 811	61 578	59 488	57 907	67 743	60 918	57 929	55 972	54 517
5	74 389	67 625	64 593	62 634	61 152	70 411	63 965	61 142	59 293	57 919
6	76 562	70 251	67 423	65 596	64 213	72 865	66 812	64 160	62 424	61 133
7	78 571	72 713	70 088	68 391	67 107	75 135	69 481	67 004	65 382	64 177
8	80 438	75 028	72 604	71 037	69 852	77 243	71 992	69 691	68 185	67 066
9	82 178	77 211	74 986	73 547	72 459	79 209	74 360	72 237	70 846	69 813
10	83 807	79 276	77 246	75 933	74 940	81 049	76 601	74 654	73 378	72 430
11	85 336	81 233	79 394	78 206	77 307	82 775	78 726	76 953	75 791	74 928
12	86 775	83 092	81 441	80 374	79 567	84 401	80 745	79 144	78 096	77 316
13	88 121	84 865	83 405	82 462	81 749	85 983	82 816	81 428	80 520	79 844
14	89 396	86 646	85 413	84 616	84 013	87 487	84 756	83 560	82 777	82 194
15	90 606	88 290	87 242	86 559	86 037	88 804	86 446	85 414	84 738	84 235
16	91 769	89 864	88 987	88 407	87 954	90 084	88 086	87 208	86 632	86 203
17	92 884	91 352	90 635	90 153	89 772	91 322	89 716	88 976	88 477	88 098
18	93 949	92 759	92 192	91 806	91 496	92 517	91 266	90 662	90 244	89 921
19	94 965	94 089	93 664	93 372	93 134	93 666	92 736	92 266	91 933	91 672
20	95 931	95 347	95 059	94 859	94 693	94 767	94 129	93 791	93 547	93 353
21	96 884	96 531	96 355	96 231	96 127	95 866	95 460	95 236	95 070	94 937
22	97 718	97 507	97 400	97 324	97 260	96 901	96 648	96 501	96 391	96 302
23	98 470	98 361	98 305	98 264	98 230	97 838	97 699	97 616	97 552	97 499
24	99 095	99 048	99 024	99 007	98 992	98 652	98 588	98 548	98 517	98 492
25	99 555	99 540	99 533	99 527	99 522	99 289	99 266	99 252	99 240	99 231

MODEL NORTH

	Females					Males				
LEVEL	l_1	l_2	l_3	l_4	l_5	l_1	l_2	l_3	l_4	l_5
1	68 005	59 681	54 557	50 689	47 753	62 858	54 755	49 828	46 166	43 381
2	70 766	62 905	58 061	54 403	51 626	66 052	58 313	53 606	50 109	47 449
3	73 263	65 852	61 290	57 847	55 232	68 919	61 570	57 101	53 780	51 254
4	75 516	68 564	64 285	61 055	58 602	71 515	64 572	60 350	57 212	54 826
5	77 570	71 074	67 074	64 055	61 763	73 883	67 354	63 382	60 432	58 187
6	79 456	73 407	69 683	66 871	64 737	76 057	69 943	66 224	63 461	61 359
7	81 196	75 585	72 130	69 523	67 543	78 062	72 362	68 895	66 319	64 360
8	82 808	77 625	74 434	72 025	70 197	79 920	74 631	71 413	69 023	67 205
9	84 308	79 542	76 608	74 394	72 712	81 650	76 764	73 793	71 586	69 906
10	85 709	81 349	78 665	76 639	75 101	83 264	78 777	76 048	74 019	72 477
11	87 022	83 056	80 615	78 772	77 373	84 777	80 679	78 187	76 335	74 927
12	88 253	84 670	82 464	80 799	79 535	86 196	82 479	80 218	78 538	77 261
13	89 398	86 244	84 302	82 837	81 724	87 529	84 247	82 250	80 767	79 638
14	90 441	87 729	86 046	84 770	83 796	88 709	85 835	84 087	82 789	81 801
15	91 453	89 164	87 717	86 609	85 751	89 858	87 367	85 852	84 726	83 870
16	92 431	90 521	89 291	88 340	87 595	90 975	88 909	87 598	86 608	85 846
17	93 372	91 802	90 773	89 971	89 335	92 054	90 376	89 258	88 399	87 730
18	94 274	93 012	92 170	91 508	90 978	93 094	91 759	90 827	90 099	89 526
19	95 136	94 153	93 487	92 959	92 531	94 091	93 061	92 309	91 712	91 237
20	95 956	95 230	94 729	94 330	94 003	95 043	94 286	93 706	93 240	92 866
21	96 736	96 246	95 904	95 628	95 401	95 950	95 437	95 026	94 691	94 420
22	97 487	97 221	97 032	96 879	96 753	96 826	96 534	96 290	96 089	95 925
23	98 122	97 974	97 867	97 780	97 708	97 580	97 408	97 258	97 134	97 032
24	98 723	98 648	98 593	98 548	98 510	98 321	98 230	98 148	98 079	98 022
25	99 219	99 187	99 163	99 144	99 127	98 944	98 904	98 866	98 834	98 807

Table 12E.2 Contd.

					MODEL EAST					
	Females						Males			
LEVEL	l_1	l_2	l_3	l_4	l_5	l_1	l_2	l_3	l_4	l_5
1	57 180	49 795	46 656	44 596	43 167	49 453	42 922	40 206	38 482	37 222
2	60 636	53 494	50 458	48 466	47 084	53 511	47 063	44 382	42 680	41 436
3	63 788	56 935	54 022	52 111	50 784	57 211	50 920	48 305	46 644	45 431
4	66 680	60 150	57 375	55 554	54 290	60 606	54 530	52 003	50 399	49 227
5	69 350	63 168	60 540	58 815	57 619	63 741	57 920	55 500	53 963	52 840
6	71 827	66 009	63 536	61 913	60 786	66 649	61 115	58 814	57 353	56 286
7	74 135	68 692	66 378	64 860	63 806	69 358	64 135	61 963	60 584	59 577
8	76 292	71 232	69 081	67 670	66 690	71 891	66 997	64 962	63 670	62 725
9	78 317	73 643	71 657	70 353	69 448	74 268	69 715	67 822	66 620	65 742
10	80 221	75 936	74 115	72 920	72 090	76 504	72 302	70 555	69 445	68 635
11	82 003	78 166	76 535	75 464	74 722	78 599	74 819	73 247	72 249	71 520
12	83 663	80 270	78 828	77 881	77 225	80 519	77 144	75 741	74 850	74 199
13	85 260	82 285	81 020	80 191	79 615	82 373	79 387	78 145	77 357	76 781
14	86 794	84 213	83 117	82 397	81 897	84 161	81 547	80 461	79 770	79 266
15	88 267	86 059	85 120	84 504	84 077	85 882	83 626	82 688	82 092	81 657
16	89 677	87 823	87 035	86 518	86 159	87 536	85 624	84 829	84 324	83 956
17	91 028	89 531	88 885	88 455	88 151	89 123	87 544	86 887	86 470	86 166
18	92 318	91 160	90 650	90 305	90 055	90 643	89 406	88 879	88 539	88 288
19	93 548	92 706	92 328	92 069	91 877	92 095	91 200	90 797	90 529	90 325
20	94 721	94 176	93 927	93 753	93 622	93 480	92 897	92 620	92 429	92 282
21	95 904	95 546	95 380	95 262	95 171	94 852	94 462	94 266	94 127	94 018
22	96 939	96 718	96 614	96 539	96 481	96 111	95 868	95 741	95 648	95 574
23	97 861	97 739	97 681	97 638	97 605	97 245	97 110	97 035	96 980	96 935
24	98 640	98 583	98 555	98 535	98 518	98 219	98 154	98 116	98 088	98 065
25	99 245	99 223	99 212	99 204	99 198	98 989	98 963	98 948	98 936	98 926

MODEL SOUTH

LEVEL	Females					Males				
	l_1	l_2	l_3	l_4	l_5	l_1	l_2	l_3	l_4	l_5
1	69 279	55 503	49 161	45 812	43 909	66 423	53 927	48 164	45 074	43 368
2	71 532	58 606	52 655	49 512	47 727	68 857	57 056	51 612	48 964	47 083
3	73 567	61 479	55 913	52 974	51 304	71 056	59 951	54 829	52 083	50 567
4	75 420	64 152	58 964	56 225	54 668	73 058	62 645	57 842	55 267	53 846
5	77 119	66 651	61 832	59 287	57 842	74 894	65 163	60 675	58 269	56 941
6	78 685	68 997	64 537	62 181	60 843	76 586	67 526	63 347	61 107	59 870
7	80 136	71 206	67 094	64 923	63 689	78 154	69 750	65 874	63 796	62 649
8	81 487	73 291	69 518	67 525	66 394	79 613	71 850	68 270	66 351	65 291
9	82 748	75 265	71 820	70 001	68 968	80 975	73 838	70 546	68 781	67 807
10	83 916	77 145	74 028	72 382	71 447	82 229	75 650	72 616	70 990	70 092
11	84 937	78 890	76 106	74 636	73 801	83 337	77 434	74 711	73 252	72 446
12	85 933	80 569	78 099	76 795	76 054	84 419	79 153	76 724	75 422	74 702
13	86 903	82 184	80 011	78 863	78 211	85 474	80 809	78 657	77 504	76 867
14	87 848	83 738	81 845	80 846	80 278	86 501	82 405	80 515	79 502	78 943
15	88 764	85 232	83 606	82 748	82 260	87 498	83 941	82 300	81 420	80 935
16	89 651	86 670	85 297	84 573	84 161	88 463	85 419	84 015	83 262	82 846
17	90 509	88 068	86 936	86 334	85 986	89 397	86 841	85 663	85 031	84 682
18	91 342	89 424	88 523	88 038	87 751	90 303	88 235	87 270	86 749	86 457
19	92 266	90 774	90 064	89 676	89 440	91 361	89 859	89 132	88 727	88 493
20	93 180	92 044	91 496	91 193	91 004	92 369	91 237	90 668	90 344	90 150
21	94 089	93 256	92 849	92 620	92 475	93 372	92 551	92 123	91 872	91 718
22	94 988	94 405	94 116	93 952	93 846	94 367	93 799	93 491	93 306	93 190
23	95 868	95 484	95 292	95 181	95 180	95 343	94 973	94 765	94 637	94 555
24	96 716	96 483	96 365	96 296	96 249	96 287	96 064	95 934	95 853	95 799
25	97 514	97 386	97 321	97 282	97 255	97 178	97 057	96 984	96 937	96 906

Table 12E.3 Regional model life tables: South, Levels 3 and 4

Level 3

Age (x)	1,000 q(x)	d(x)	1,000 m(x)	l(x)	L(x)	P(x)	T(x)	e(x)	Age (x)
FEMALES									
0	264.33	26 433	319.16	100 000	82 819.	0.63124*	2 500 000.	25.000	0
1	302.62	22 263	95.63	73 567	232 801.	0.77965†	2 417 181.	32.857	1
5	74.06	3 799	15.44	51 304	246 073.	0.94681	2 184 380.	42.577	5
10	39.83	1 892	8.12	47 505	232 984.	0.95324	1 938 307.	40.802	10
15	54.59	2 490	11.21	45 613	222 089.	0.93918	1 705 323.	37.387	15
20	67.97	2 931	14.05	43 123	208 581.	0.92969	1 483 234.	34.395	20
25	73.03	2 935	15.14	40 192	193 915.	0.92555	1 274 653.	31.174	25
30	76.11	2 836	15.80	37 257	179 478.	0.92202	1 080 738.	29.008	30
35	80.17	2 759	16.67	34 421	165 482.	0.91911	901 260.	26.183	35
40	81.74	2 588	17.02	31 662	152 097.	0.91602	735 778.	23.239	40
45	86.63	2 519	18.08	29 074	139 323.	0.90166	583 681.	20.076	45
50	112.22	2 980	23.72	26 555	125 623.	0.87008	444 358.	16.733	50
55	151.51	3 572	32.68	23 575	109 302.	0.80943	318 735.	13.520	55
60	240.45	4 810	54.37	20 003	88 472.	0.71393	209 433.	10.470	60
65	351.14	5 335	84.46	15 193	63 163.	0.58930	120 961.	7.961	65
70	510.14	5 029	135.11	9 858	37 222.	0.42580	57 798.	5.863	70
75	687.24	3 319	209.40	4 829	15 849.	0.25331	20 576.	4.261	75
80	790.00	1 193	297.11	1 510	4 015.	0.16506	4 727.	3.130	80
85	900.88	286	431.19	317	663.	0.07373	713.	2.247	85
90	967.39	30	622.46	31	49.	0.02282‡	50.	1.590	90
95	1 000.00	1	898.27	1	1.	0.0	1.	1.113	95

Age (x)	1,000 q(x)	d(x)	1,000 m(x)	l(x)	L(x)	P(x)	T(x)	e(x)	Age (x)
MALES									
0	289.44	28 944	359.07	100 000	80 608.	0.61656*	2 466 119.	24.661	0
1	288.36	20 489	89.99	71 056	227 674.	0.79021†	2 385 511.	33.572	1
5	66.34	3 355	13.77	50 567	243 609.	0.95413	2 157 837.	42.673	5
10	32.01	1 511	6.50	47 212	232 434.	0.96044	1 914 229.	40.545	10
15	48.01	2 194	9.83	45 701	223 238.	0.94071	1 681 795.	36.800	15
20	72.13	3 138	14.94	43 507	210 001.	0.92785	1 458 557.	33.525	20
25	72.18	2 914	14.95	40 368	194 849.	0.92803	1 248 556.	30.929	25
30	71.73	2 686	14.86	37 455	180 826.	0.92508	1 053 707.	28.133	30
35	78.64	2 734	16.34	34 768	167 279.	0.91481	872 882.	25.106	35
40	92.90	2 976	19.45	32 034	153 028.	0.90008	705 603.	22.027	40
45	108.31	3 147	22.85	29 058	137 737.	0.87913	552 575.	19.016	45
50	136.14	3 527	29.13	25 911	121 088.	0.84554	414 838.	16.010	50
55	177.44	3 972	38.79	22 383	102 384.	0.78978	293 750.	13.124	55
60	253.39	4 665	57.69	18 412	80 861.	0.70584	191 366.	10.394	60
65	353.32	4 857	85.10	13 746	57 075.	0.59209	110 505.	8.039	65
70	499.35	4 439	131.36	8 889	33 794.	0.43871	53 430.	6.010	70
75	667.51	2 971	200.38	4 450	14 826.	0.27182	19 636.	4.412	75
80	774.70	1 146	284.46	1 480	4 030.	0.17851	4 811.	3.251	80
85	889.51	297	412.23	333	719.	0.08283	781.	2.342	85
90	961.45	35	594.36	37	60.	0.02706‡	61.	1.663	90
95	1 000.00	1	856.77	1	2.	0.0	2.	1.167	95

Table 12E.3 Contd.

Level 4

Age (x)	1,000 q(x)	d(x)	1,000 m(x)	l(x)	L(x)	P(x)	T(x)	e(x)	Age (x)
FEMALES									
0	245.80	24 580	292.53	100 000	84 023.	0.65682*	2 750 000.	27.500	0
1	275.15	20 752	84.92	75 420	244 385.	0.80162†	2 665 977.	35.348	1
5	67.07	3 667	13.93	54 668	263 258.	0.95183	2 421 592.	44.296	5
10	36.20	1 846	7.37	51 002	250 577.	0.95743	2 158 334.	42.319	10
15	49.73	2 444	10.19	49 155	239 910.	0.94455	1 907 757.	38.811	15
20	61.98	2 895	12.78	46 711	226 607.	0.93583	1 667 847.	35.706	20
25	66.69	2 922	13.78	43 816	212 066.	0.93199	1 441 240.	32.893	25
30	69.53	2 843	14.39	40 894	197 644.	0.92869	1 229 174.	30.058	30
35	73.38	2 792	15.21	38 050	183 551.	0.92580	1 031 529.	27.110	35
40	75.16	2 650	15.59	35 258	169 932.	0.92260	847 978.	24.050	40
45	80.03	2 610	16.64	32 608	156 779.	0.90898	678 047.	20.794	45
50	103.97	3 119	21.89	29 999	142 509.	0.87942	521 268.	17.376	50
55	140.66	3 781	30.17	26 880	125 325.	0.82276	378 759.	14.091	55
60	223.37	5 160	50.04	23 099	103 112.	0.73304	253 434.	10.972	60
65	327.77	5 880	77.79	17 939	75 585.	0.61400	150 322.	8.379	65
70	479.84	5 787	124.68	12 059	46 409.	0.45515	74 737.	6.197	70
75	653.05	4 097	193.94	6 273	21 123.	0.28421	28 327.	4.516	75
80	767.10	1 669	278.09	2 176	6 003.	0.18402	7 204.	3.310	80
85	866.41	449	406.69	507	1 105.	0.08468	1 201.	2.369	85
90	961.11	55	591.50	58	94.	0.02708‡	96.	1.670	90
95	1 000.00	2	859.90	2	3.	0.0	3.	1.163	95

Age (x)	1,000 q(x)	d(x)	1,000 m(x)	l(x)	L(x)	P(x)	T(x)	e(x)	Age (x)
MALES									
0	269.42	26 942	328.76	100 000	81 949.	0.64231*	2 700 735.	27.007	0
1	262.98	19 213	80.32	73 058	239 206.	0.81047†	2 618 786.	35.845	1
5	60.38	3 251	12.49	53 846	260 288.	0.95822	2 379 580.	44.193	5
10	29.32	1 483	5.95	50 595	249 413.	0.96376	2 119 292.	41.888	10
15	43.98	2 160	8.98	49 111	240 374.	0.94564	1 869 879.	38.074	15
20	66.12	3 105	13.66	46 952	227 307.	0.93387	1 629 505.	34.706	20
25	66.13	2 900	13.66	43 847	212 276.	0.93390	1 402 198.	31.979	25
30	66.07	2 705	13.65	40 947	198 244.	0.93094	1 189 922.	29.060	30
35	72.54	2 774	15.03	38 242	184 552.	0.92124	991 678.	25.932	35
40	86.03	3 051	17.95	35 468	170 017.	0.90722	807 127.	22.757	40
45	100.79	3 267	21.18	32 417	154 242.	0.88714	637 110.	19.654	45
50	127.40	3 714	27.14	29 149	136 834.	0.85502	482 868.	16.565	50
55	166.81	4 243	36.27	25 436	116 996.	0.80192	346 034.	13.604	55
60	238.73	5 059	53.93	21 193	93 821.	0.72190	229 039.	10.807	60
65	334.12	5 390	79.59	16 133	67 730.	0.61219	135 217.	8.381	65
70	475.16	5 105	123.11	10 743	41 464.	0.46194	67 488.	6.282	70
75	641.17	3 615	188.74	5 638	19 154.	0.29591	26 024.	4.616	75
80	756.44	1 530	270.03	2 023	5 668.	0.19380	6 870.	3.396	80
85	877.55	432	393.69	493	1 098.	0.09199	1 203.	2.441	85
90	955.95	58	570.89	60	101.	0.03080‡	104.	1.728	90
95	1 000.00	3	827.66	3	3.	0.0	3.	1.208	95

* P(birth)
† P(0–4)
‡ T(95)/T(90)

Table 12E.4 Actual and fitted survival probabilities, Iceland males 1856–65

Exact age x	Observed	Probability of survival (l_x) West	North	East	South
1	0.832	0.845	0.868	0.829	0.856
5	0.776	0.775	0.783	0.774	0.771
10	0.761	0.756	0.751	0.759	0.756
15	0.745	0.743	0.734	0.751	0.745

13 Relational model life tables

This chapter is very much a continuation of the previous one, but the model life-table systems described here are based on an entirely different, 'relational' principle. The most important, the 'Brass two-parameter logit system' is described first, and is followed by a brief discussion of two systems which extend this to four parameters.

The Brass relational two-parameter logit system

The relational system of model life tables is unlike the United Nations' or Coale–Demeny sets in that it is derived from a mathematical relationship rather than from empirical life tables. As a preliminary to explaining the system, it is necessary to understand what a 'parameter' is, and what a 'logit transformation' is.

Parameters

Buying a shirt or a pair of shoes involves specifying just one measurement: the collar or shoe size. But to buy a pair of trousers you need two measurements: waist and leg length. The shirt and shoes can thus be described as one-parameter garments, while trousers are two-parameter garments. The 1955 United Nations model life-table system is thus a one-parameter system. Specifying just one figure, whether it be e_0, l_{25} or whatever, determines entirely the model life table to be selected. The Coale–Demeny set can be thought of as a two-parameter system because picking a model involves choosing both a Region, and a Level. However, since there are only four Regions it is not considered to be truly a two-parameter system.

The Logit transformation

Any series of numbers can be turned into another series of numbers using a mathematical rule or 'transformation'. If the rule is 'square it', then the series 1, 2, 3, 4, . . . becomes 1, 4, 9, 16 . . . Some other examples are:

Reciprocal:

$$1, 2, 3, 4 \ldots \text{becomes } 1, 1/2, 1/3, 1/4 \ldots$$

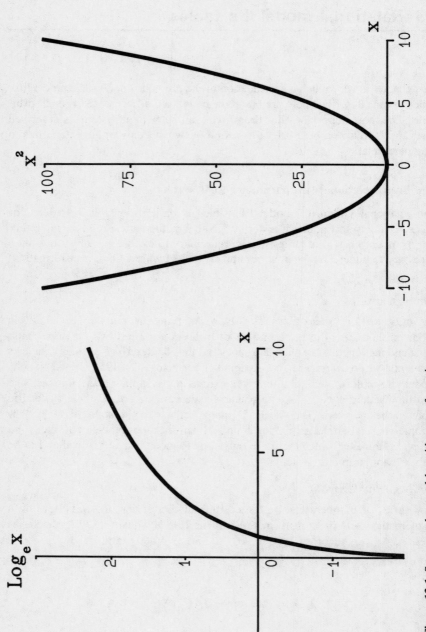

Figure 13.1 Square and natural logarithm transformations

Common Logarithm — Log_{10}

    1, 2, 3, 4 . . . becomes 0.0, 0.3010, 0.4771, 0.6021 . . .

Natural Logarithm — Log_e or Ln:

    1, 2, 3, 4 . . . becomes 0.0, 0.6931, 1.0986, 1.3863 . . .

Transformations can be graphed as in Figure 13.1.

The logit transformation, which is of interest here, is slightly more complicated than those above. The formula is:

$$\text{Logit}(p) = 0.5 \, Log_e \left(\frac{1-p}{p} \right)$$

It is also different from those mentioned above in that it can be used only for transforming proportions. Hence the use of p rather than x in the equation.

The transformation has some interesting properties:

When $p = 0$ then $\text{logit}(p) = 0.5 Log_e(1/0) = +$infinity.
When $p = 1$ then $\text{logit}(p) = 0.5 Log_e(0/1) = -$infinity.
When $p = 0.5$ then $\text{logit}(p) = 0.5 Log_e(0.5/0.5) = 0.0$.

The graph of the logit transformation is given in Figure 13.2. It can be seen that the possible range of the transformed values is from minus infinity to plus infinity, whereas, of course, the range of the original proportions is from 0.0 to 1.0.

Occasionally, the transformation is expressed as

$$\text{Logit}(p) = 0.5 Log_e \left(\frac{p}{1-p} \right)$$

rather than as above and this changes the sign of all the values. Also, the 0.5 in the transformation is omitted in most statistics books. These differences have no fundamental effect, but, of course, it is essential to be consistent, and it is best to follow demographic convention and use the first form given above.

To return to model life tables, a set of l_x values are just proportions if the radix is 1.0. l_{10}, for example, is just the proportion surviving to age 10. Thus it is possible to take logits of l_xs. This is very useful because it has been found by Brass (1971) that if one takes two life tables, and takes logits of their l_xs, then the relationship between the two sets of logits is remarkably linear, that is drawing a graph of one against the other, as in Figure 13.3, produces a straight line. This important discovery is essentially an empirical rather than a

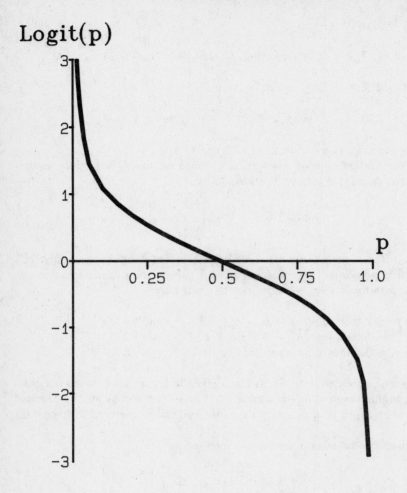

Figure 13.2 The logit transformation

theoretical finding though Brass (1975: 91–6) gives some justification. Sometimes it does not give exactly a straight line, especially at the extremes of the age range.

The equation of a straight line can be written as:

$$y = a + bx$$

so it is possible to describe one set of logit(l_xs) by using another set of logit(l_x)s and the appropriate values of a and b. Thus with one set of l_xs and an a and a b it is possible to produce another set of l_xs. Alternatively, from any one

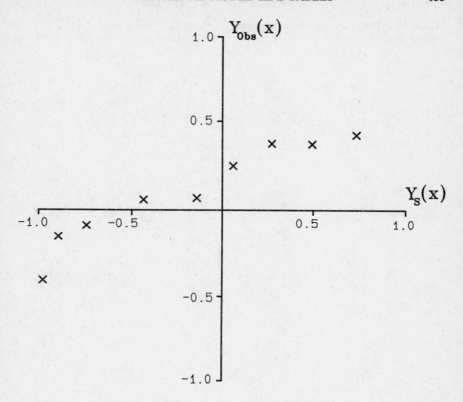

Figure 13.3 A typical relationship between two sets of logit(l_xs)

'standard' life table it is possible to generate a whole series of other related life tables just by varying a and b. It is this aspect of the models that makes the system 'relational'.

The two 'parameters', a and b, are in fact known by the Greek letters α (alpha) and β (beta).

If logit(l_x) is denoted by $Y(x)$ and the logits of the standard as $Y_s(x)$, as has become conventional in the literature, then the equation of the straight line can be rewritten as:

$$Y(x) = \alpha + \beta \, Y_s(x).$$

Before looking at α and β consider the standard. Any standard can be chosen, but it is sensible to choose one that shows some sort of average pattern of mortality. In fact, two standards are in common use. They are known as the General and African Standards, and are shown in Table 13.1.

Note that the two standards are identical after age 10, but in the African Standard childhood mortality is higher, relative to infant mortality, than in the

Table 13.1 General and African Standard life table l_xs and logits

x	General Standard l_x	$Y_s(x)$	x	African Standard l_x	$Y_s(x)$
0	1.0000		0	1.0000	
1	0.8499	−0.8670	1	0.8802	−0.9972
2	0.8070	−0.7153	2	0.8335	−0.8053
3	0.7876	−0.6553	3	0.8101	−0.7253
4	0.7762	−0.6218	4	0.7964	−0.6820
5	0.7691	−0.6016	5	0.7863	−0.6514
10	0.7502	−0.5498	10	0.7502	−0.5498
15	0.7362	−0.5131	15	0.7362	−0.5131
20	0.7130	−0.4551	20	0.7130	−0.4551
25	0.6826	−0.3829	25	0.6826	−0.3829
30	0.6525	−0.3150	30	0.6525	−0.3150
35	0.6223	−0.2496	35	0.6223	−0.2496
40	0.5898	−0.1817	40	0.5898	−0.1817
45	0.5535	−0.1073	45	0.5535	−0.1073
50	0.5106	−0.0212	50	0.5106	−0.0212
55	0.4585	0.0832	55	0.4585	0.0832
60	0.3965	0.2100	60	0.3965	0.2100
65	0.3210	0.3746	65	0.3210	0.3746
70	0.2380	0.5818	70	0.2380	0.5818
75	0.1516	0.8611	75	0.1516	0.8611
80	0.0768	1.2433	80	0.0768	1.2433
85	0.0276	1.7810	85	0.0276	1.7810
90	0.0059	2.5634	90	0.0059	2.5634
95	0.0006	3.7090	95	0.0006	3.7090
100	0.0000		100	0.0000	

Source: Carrier and Hobcraft (1973). (These are the smoothed and extended versions of the original standards.)

General Standard. There is nothing special about these standards. They are just ordinary life tables, and it is quite possible to use other life tables as the standard, though this seems to be rarely done.

Now, consider α and β. Recall that in the simple equation of a straight line a is the intercept — the point at which the line crosses the y-axis, and b is the slope or gradient of the line. Varying a will raise or lower the line, as in Figure 13.4a, while varying b makes the line more or less steep as in Figure 13.4b.

Thus in the equation

$$Y(x) = \alpha + \beta \cdot Y_s(x)$$

altering α will affect the level of mortality, while altering β will affect the relationship between childhood and adult mortality.

As for the values α and β can take, clearly, if $\alpha = 0.0$ and $\beta = 1.0$ then $Y(x)$ will equal $Y_s(x)$. Thus the derived life table will be identical to the standard, so these are the neutral values. If either the General or African Standard

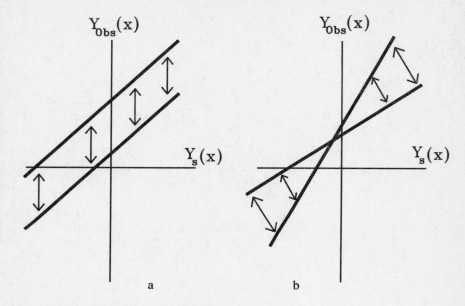

Figure 13.4 The effects of varying α and β

is used, this gives an expectation of life at birth in the middle forties. Putting α at about $+0.8$ gives an e_0 around 18 years, while setting it at -1.5 gives an e_0 about 79 years. Thus the range of reasonable values for α is about $+0.8$ to -1.5. A high (i.e. positive) value indicates high mortality relative to the standard, while a low (i.e. negative) value indicates low mortality relative to the standard.

For β, a reasonable range of values is roughly from 0.6 to 1.4, though it depends to some extent on which standard is being used. A low value gives a line with a gentle gradient and thus indicates high infant and child mortality and low adult mortality relative to the standard. A high value, on the other hand, gives a steep slope, implying low infant and child mortality and high adult mortality relative to the standard. In fact, altering β pivots the life table round age 51, where the standard $l_{51} = 0.5$ so $Y_s(51) = 0.0$. If one chooses to leave β at 1.0, then one is effectively using just a one-parameter system, the parameter being α.

Table 13.2 shows nine logit model life tables for selected values of α and β based on the African Standard. Comparing the e_0s for models with the same values of β shows the effect of varying α, while comparing the models with the same values of α shows the effect of varying β.

Table 13.2 Selected logit model life tables

Age x	α = +0.8			α = 0.0			α = −0.8		
	β = 0.7	β = 1.0	β = 1.4	β = 0.7	β = 1.0	β = 1.4	β = 0.7	β = 1.0	β = 1.4
0	10 000	10 000	10 000	10 000	10 000	10 000	10 000	10 000	10 000
1	4 492	5 973	7 671	8 016	8 802	9 423	9 524	9 733	9 878
2	3 840	5 026	6 581	7 554	8 335	9 051	9 386	9 612	9 793
3	3 579	4 627	6 061	7 341	8 101	8 840	9 318	9 548	9 742
4	3 441	4 413	5 768	7 221	7 964	8 710	9 279	9 509	9 710
5	3 345	4 262	5 557	7 134	7 863	8 610	9 250	9 480	9 684
10	3 036	3 774	4 849	6 835	7 502	8 234	9 145	9 370	9 585
15	2 929	3 604	4 593	6 723	7 362	8 080	9 104	9 325	9 542
20	2 763	3 340	4 192	6 541	7 130	7 814	9 035	9 248	9 465
25	2 566	3 028	3 710	6 309	6 826	7 450	8 944	9 142	9 354
30	2 338	2 749	3 278	6 085	6 525	7 072	8 850	9 029	9 229
35	2 226	2 496	2 889	5 865	6 223	6 680	8 754	8 908	9 088
40	2 066	2 250	2 513	5 632	5 898	6 245	8 646	8 769	8 917
45	1 901	2 002	2 143	5 375	5 535	5 746	8 520	8 599	8 700
50	1 722	1 740	1 764	5 074	5 106	5 148	8 361	8 379	8 402
55	1 523	1 460	1 379	4 709	4 585	4 420	8 151	8 075	7 969
60	1 303	1 171	1 008	4 270	3 965	3 571	7 868	7 649	7 334
65	1 067	871	661	3 718	3 210	2 594	7 457	7 007	6 344
70	821	593	381	3 069	2 380	1 640	6 869	6 074	4 927
75	570	348	178	2 305	1 516	823	5 974	4 695	3 077
80	342	165	62	1 492	768	299	4 649	2 918	1 322
85	164	57	14	763	276	68	2 904	1 233	327
90	55	12	2	269	59	8	1 204	286	38
95	11	1	0	55	6	0	268	30	2
e_0	16.66	18.53	21.54	43.16	43.59	44.62	69.37	66.55	64.13
e_{50}	19.52	15.95	12.94	22.85	18.92	15.54	29.62	25.16	21.15

Note: This table uses the African Standard.
Source: Carrier and Hobcraft 1973: 44

For example, in the first panel, where $\alpha = +0.8$, compare the values of l_1 and of l_{50}. It can also be seen from the e_0s in this panel that α and β do not alter level and 'tilt' entirely independently. Changing the value of β does have some small effect on the overall level of mortality.

Fitting a logit model life table

The aim is to discover which one of the infinite family of life tables that can be generated by varying α and β, the raw data are most like. The raw data may be a complete life table, or they may be just a handful of values.

Very briefly, the logits of the observed l_xs are first plotted on a graph against the logits of the standard life table. Then a straight line is fitted to the points in some way, and α and β, the intercept and slope of the line, are calculated. The fitted logits are then computed by putting α, β and the standard logits into the straight-line equation. Lastly, anti-logits are taken to produce a set of fitted l_xs — the model life table. The following example should make this clearer.

The 1976 Swaziland census asked questions on how many children female respondents had ever borne, and how many were dead. Analysis of the responses produced the following female childhood mortality estimates:

$$l_2 \quad 0.8102$$
$$l_3 \quad 0.8060$$
$$l_5 \quad 0.7885$$

A question on maternal orphanhood 'Is your mother alive?' yielded the following adult female mortality estimates:

$$l_{45} \quad 0.6843$$
$$l_{50} \quad 0.6484$$
$$l_{55} \quad 0.5952$$
$$l_{60} \quad 0.5363$$
$$l_{65} \quad 0.4773$$

The problem is to find the model life table that best fits these eight points. The procedure is to first plot the logits of the standard values against the logits of the observed values. Here the African Standard is used. The numbers are given in Table 13.3 and are plotted in Figure 13.5.

Conventionally, the standard values are plotted on the X-axis, the observed values on the Y-axis. The straight line can be fitted in a number of ways, normally by eye or by regression. The conventional method when using this specific kind of data which fall into two clearly-defined groups is called the 'Group Average Method'. This simply involves taking the average of the

Table 13.3 Fitting logit model life table, Swaziland females, 1976

x	Obs. l_x	Logit (Obs. l_x) $Y_{Obs}(x)$	African Standard l_x	Logit (Standard l_x) $Y_s(x)$
2	0.8102	−0.7257	0.8335	−0.8052
3	0.8060	−0.7121	0.8101	−0.7252
5	0.7885	−0.6580	0.7863	−0.6515
45	0.6843	−0.3868	0.5534	−0.1073
50	0.6484	−0.3060	0.5106	−0.0212
55	0.5952	−0.1928	0.4590	0.0832
60	0.5363	−0.0727	0.3965	0.2100
65	0.4773	0.0454	0.3221	0.3746

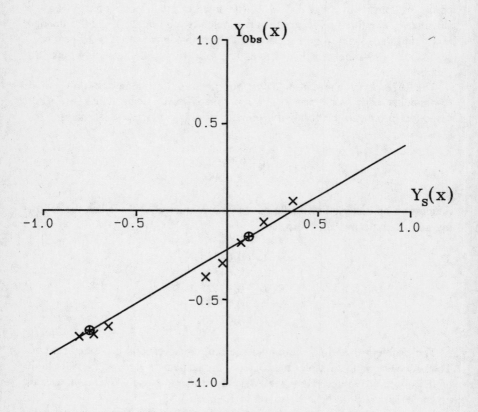

Figure 13.5 Fitting logit model life table: Swaziland females, 1976

childhood mortality points and the average of the adult mortality points and drawing a line between the two. The childhood point, (x_c, y_c), is calculated as

$$y_c = \frac{(-0.7257) + (-0.7121) + (-0.6580)}{3}$$

$$= -0.6986$$

and

$$x_c = \frac{(-0.8052) + (-0.7252) + (-0.6515)}{3}$$

$$= -0.7273.$$

Similarly, for the adult group the average point is:

$$(x_a, y_a) = (0.1079, -0.1826).$$

It should be re-emphasised that the use of the Group Average Method for fitting the line is not in any way an inherent part of the technique. It is simply a general procedure for fitting straight lines to points which happens to be particularly appropriate here because it is a very robust method.

Having fitted the line, the values of α and β can be calculated. For β, the slope, it is convenient, but not essential, to use the group average points. That is:

$$\beta = \frac{y_a - y_c}{x_a - x_c}$$

$$= \frac{(-0.1826) - (-0.6986)}{(0.1079) - (-0.7273)}$$

$$= 0.6178.$$

This value suggests that in Swaziland the relationship between child and adult mortality is very different from that described by the standard. The slope is substantially less than 1.0 so infant and child mortality is much higher relative to adult mortality than it is in the standard.

Then, for α we can also conveniently use the group average points:

$$\alpha = y_c - \beta \cdot x_c$$

$$= -0.2493.$$

This value, being less than 0.0 indicates that the overall level of mortality in Swaziland is somewhat lower than in the standard.

Having now calculated α and β, it is possible to calculate the logits of the fitted model using the equation

$$Y_{\text{Fit}}(x) = \alpha + \beta \cdot Y_s(x)$$

Then the fitted l_xs are computed by taking the anti-logits of $Y_{\text{Fit}}(x)$ using the equation

$$\text{Fitted } l_x = \frac{1}{1 + e^{2Y_{\text{Fit}}(x)}}$$

Table 13.4 Finding fitted logit model life table: Swaziland, females, 1976

x	$Y_s(x)$	$Y_{\text{Fit}}(x)$	Fitted l_x	Observed l_x
0			1.0000	1.0000
1	−0.9972	−0.8654	0.8495	
2	−0.8053	−0.7468	0.8166	0.8102
3	−0.7253	−0.6974	0.8014	0.8060
4	−0.6820	−0.6706	0.7927	
5	−0.6514	−0.6517	0.7864	0.7885
10	−0.5498	−0.5890	0.7646	
15	−0.5131	−0.5663	0.7563	
20	−0.4551	−0.5305	0.7429	
25	−0.3829	−0.4859	0.7255	
30	−0.3150	−0.4439	0.7084	
35	−0.2496	−0.4035	0.6915	
40	−0.1817	−0.3616	0.6733	
45	−0.1073	−0.3156	0.6528	0.6843
50	−0.0212	−0.2624	0.6283	0.6484
55	0.0832	−0.2426	0.6190	0.5952
60	0.2100	−0.1196	0.5595	0.5363
65	0.3746	−0.0194	0.5097	0.4773
70	0.5818	0.1101	0.4452	
75	0.8611	0.2815	0.3629	
80	1.2433	0.5154	0.2629	
85	1.7810	0.8453	0.1557	
90	2.5634	1.3306	0.0653	
95	3.7090	2.0628	0.0159	

This is done in Table 13.4, where the observed l_xs have been included for comparison.

Thus, having started out with three child and five adult mortality estimates, we have now estimated a complete life table for Swaziland females, 1976. It should, however always be remembered that, despite the sophistication of the estimation technique, this is nevertheless very much an estimate, based on a rather small amount of data. The true life table may actually be substantially different.

To conclude this discussion of the Brass two-parameter logit model life table system let us briefly compare it with the Coale–Demeny and old United Nations sets. First, it is apparent that the logit system is based not upon empirical, observed life tables but upon a mathematical formula which relates one life table with another. Second, it is more flexible than the others since it has two true parameters, allowing a great many patterns of mortality to be modelled. If, however, information on the pattern of mortality is unavailable, or very unreliable, then it can be used as a more rigid one-parameter system simply by setting β to 1.0. Third, the system has the advantage that it does not require large books of tables or complex computer programs for it to be used easily.

Four-parameter life table systems

Just as the Coale–Demeny and United Nations models were found to be insufficiently flexible to model well some observed mortality patterns, so was the two-parameter logit system. In particular, it could not produce models which fitted closely those mortality patterns which had unusually high or low infant or old-age mortality relative to childhood and early adult mortality, but which were nevertheless thought to be real. Consequently, the two-parameter system has been extended to a four-parameter system.

In fact, two four-parameter systems have been developed, both of which are essentially extensions of the two-parameter logit system. In both systems α and β are retained while the two extra parameters affect mainly the extremes of the age range.

The first is by Zaba (1979). In addition to α and β, there are two parameters which Zaba named ψ (psi) and χ (chi). The former has the effect of curving the mortality pattern of the standard in the same direction at old and young ages, while the latter tends to twist the pattern of mortality in opposite directions at each end of the age range. Unfortunately, because of this, the two parameters interact and therefore do not have separate interpretations in the way that α and β have. This is a major disadvantage of this system. Another problem is that the parameters do actually have some significant effect in the middle of the age range as well as at the extremes.

These two problems are to a great extent overcome in the other four-parameter system developed by Ewbank, Gomez de Leon and Stoto (1983). They call their two extra parameters $\varkappa$ (kappa) and λ (lambda) and say that these names were chosen because 'k' stood for 'kids' and 'l' for 'later'. Rather than using the logit transformation, they use:

$$\frac{\left(\dfrac{p}{1-p}\right)^{x} - 1}{2x} \quad \text{when } p \geqslant 0.5$$

and

$$\frac{1 - \left(\dfrac{1-p}{p}\right)^{\lambda}}{2\lambda} \quad \text{when } p < 0.5$$

This in fact simplifies to become the logit transformation when x and λ are both 0.0 (not 1.0) though this is not immediately obvious.

In the General and African Standards l_x reaches a value of 0.5 at about age 51 years. Since x is only used in the transformation for values greater than or equal to 0.5, it must only affect mortality at ages under 51. Similarly, λ only affects mortality at ages above 51 years. Increasing x increases childhood and early adult mortality relative to the standard, while increasing λ increases mortality at the oldest ages.

Ewbank, Gomez de leon and Stoto (1983: 112) also found that they could improve their model using a 'New' standard life table which is identical to the General and African Standards above age 15, but below age 15 the values lie largely between the two standards.

Discussion

At the start of the previous chapter it was stated that Ledermann and Breas (1959) had shown how variation in mortality patterns can be explained to a very great extent by just five factors. These were the overall level of mortality, the ratio of child to adult mortality, old age mortality, infant mortality. and sex differentials. The old 1955 UN set only allowed the user to choose the first of these. The Coale–Demeny and new 1982 UN sets are somewhat more flexible in that the different regions or families allow some choice of pattern. But the two-parameter logit system takes this a stage further by permitting much greater flexibility over the choice of pattern. The four-parameter systems outlined above allow even greater flexibility since they take account of the third and fourth of the factors.

Given all these different sets of model life tables, it is often difficult to choose which to use. The choice is not helped by the fact that no strict rules can be given: it is not possible to say, for example, that one should always use the system which produces the model with the closest fit. The one that fits best must always be the most flexible, namely one of the four-parameter systems, since they can certainly do no worse than two-parameter systems. Yet flexibility is not always what is wanted.

The general, but not always helpful, rule is to use a system which is flexible enough to let real features and irregularities through, but which is sufficiently robust to be unaffected by errors in the data. Thus, if one has bad data and so do not know the pattern of, say, infant or old-age mortality, then use a fairly rigid system, but if one has what are thought to be fairly good data, then use a more flexible one. Practical considerations such as the availability of computer programs and the desire to facilitate comparison with other work are also important.

Exercises

1. A prospective dual record demographic survey called the 'Population Change Survey' was carried out in Malawi during 1970–2. The life table was calculated directly from the data obtained by the survey.

Table 13E.1 Observed life table: Malawi, 1970–2

Age	l_x
0	1 000
1	858
5	653
10	603
15	592
20	559
25	548
30	528
35	511
40	492
45	460
50	435
55	404
60	381

First, find the parameters, α and β, of a two-parameter relational model life table, using the General Standard life table as the standard. Compare the fitted l_xs with the observed ones. What are the main differences? Discuss the accuracy of, and possible causes of errors in, the observed figures.

What do the data suggest about the age pattern of mortality in Malawi? Would a one-parameter model produce an adequate fit? Would a model which uses the African rather than General Standard improve the fit?

2. Estimate the values of α and β you would use to fit a two-parameter logit life table to the data in Table 13E.2.

Table 13E.2 Farr's 1841 English life table No. 1 for females

x	l_x
0	100 000
5	75 557
10	71 928
20	67 181
30	61 279
40	54 755
50	47 705
60	39 379
70	26 080

Comment on the fit you get. What is the fitted value for l_{15}? What considerations should be taken into account when deciding whether to use a one-, two- or four-parameter model?

3. What is the Infant Mortality Rate implied by the life table shown in Table 13E.3. Fit a logit relational model to these data and from it produce a new estimate of infant mortality. Is this new estimate more accurate than the observed figure? Give reasons for your answer. If you think that it is more accurate, what are the implications for the remainder of the life table?

Table 13E.3 Life table for Breslau, 1687–91

Age x	l_x
0	1 000
1	855
5	710
10	653
20	592
30	523
40	436
50	335
60	232
70	131
80	34

Source: Halley, 1693.

14 Models of nuptiality and fertility

Compared with the models of mortality described in the two previous chapters, models of marriage and fertility are generally more complex, less numerous and less widely used. The complexity is largely a reflection of the nature of marriage, divorce and fertility since they are influenced, to a greater extent than mortality, by the exercise of free will and because, unlike death, marriages and births can occur more than once to each individual. This, plus the fact that fertility and nuptiality are inherently more variable than mortality, means that fertility and nuptiality models will, on average, fit the data less closely than mortality models.

This chapter begins with a description of the nuptiality model developed by Coale and McNeil (Coale 1971; Coale and McNeil 1972). It is followed by a description of the Coale–Trussell fertility model (Coale and Trussell 1974), which is in fact a combination of the Coale–McNeil nuptiality model and a model of marital fertility. The important papers cited above which describe the evolution of these models are fairly mathematical, but two quite readable introductions are the informal articles of Coale (1977) and Hill (1978).

The latter half of the chapter presents a short introduction to the Gompertz relational fertility model of Brass (1981). This is very similar in principle to the logit relational model life-table system described in the previous chapter.

The Coale–McNeil nuptiality model

The Coale–McNeil nuptiality model is an empirically determined mathematical equation describing the age pattern of first marriage amongst females. An example of the type of curve it produces is shown in Figure 14.1

By restricting its scope to only first marriages the model avoids the complications of divorce, widowhood and remarriage. The actual form of the equation is fairly complex, involving two parameters, a_0 and k, and a double exponential:

$$r(a) = (0.174/k) \cdot e^{-4.411 \cdot e^{-(0.309/k)(a - a_0)}}$$

In this model a represents age. $r(a)$ is the risk of first marriage at age a (i.e. the number of first marriages per woman aged a during the year), a_0 is the earliest age at which there are a significant number of first marriages. And, lastly, k is a parameter which alters the shape of the curve, essentially by making

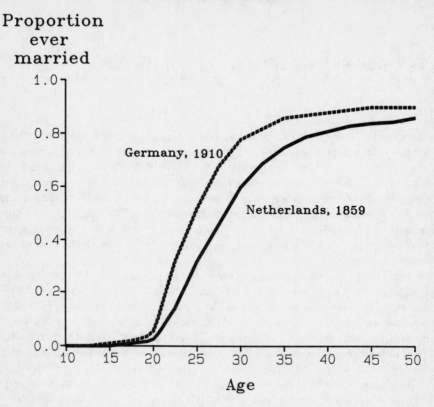

Figure 14.1 Proportions ever married, Netherlands, 1859, and Germany, 1910
Source: Coale and McNeil (1972)

it rise more or less steeply during the years shortly after a_0.

The range of a_0 is from about 12 in, for example, India in the past, up to perhaps 18 years in developed societies or where there is a legally defined minimum age at marriage. In England and Wales this minimum is 16. The purpose of this parameter is just to locate the origin of the curve, allowing the nuptiality schedule to be moved up or down the age scale.

Normal values for k range from roughly 0.2, indicating a very rapid rate of marriage after a_0, up to about 1.7, indicating very slow marriage, In fact, k expresses the rate of marriage in terms of the number of years of nuptiality in the population being modelled that is equivalent to one year in a standard population. The standard used happens to be that of Swedish women 1865–9. The value of k in the standard is, of course, 1.0; a value of 0.5 indicates a rate of marriage that is double that in the standard so that instead of, say, 50 per cent marrying during, say, the ten years after a_0, the 50 per cent would marry within five years. This information on the background of k is not in any way relevant for the application of the model, but it is perhaps useful for understanding its interpretation.

There is also a third parameter in the model, known as C, which has not been included in the equation above. It is simply a 'level' or 'scale' parameter and is the proportion of women who ultimately marry. It ranges from perhaps 0.7 in populations such as nineteenth-century Ireland, up to almost 1.0 in India or Bangladesh, where nearly all women eventually marry. Because it simply scales the model, whereas the main interest is normally in the shape of the model, it can generally be ignored.

Coale (1971) and Coale and McNeil (1972) go to considerable lengths to try to identify a plausible behavioural explanation of the marriage process which is consistent with the double exponential form of the model. They conclude that such a form is probably a consequence of first marriage consisting of a series of stages, the first being arrival at an age of marriageability, an age which has an approximately Normal (Gaussian) distribution, the second being perhaps first meeting one's future husband, then getting engaged, and finally marrying. These latter stages will each have approximately exponential distributions. This rationalisation is, however, unimportant for practical purposes. One is generally only concerned with the model's ability to fit a wide range of experience, not with its ability to reflect the underlying processes involved.

And, indeed, the model does fit a wide range of nuptiality patterns extremely well. It was, however, designed to model the behaviour of real cohorts and, although it can fit period, synthetic-cohort data, it only does this well when nuptiality has not been changing rapidly. If, say, nuptiality has been falling in earlier years, then a set of cross-sectional data will, in extreme cases, show decreasing proportions married with age. This could never occur in a real cohort and the Coale–McNeil model cannot fit such data at all well.

Apart from this limitation, the model can be applied in a wide range of circumstances for any of the purposes outlined in Chapter 10 (see pp. 118–19), including smoothing, interpolation, the estimation of future patterns, and the investigation of the impact of changing marriage patterns on other demographic phenomena.

Lesthaeghe (1971) provides an excellent example of the last of these. He used the model to simulate the impact of raising or lowering the average age at marriage on fertility and population growth. His important conclusion was that simply lowering fertility through such measures as the encouragement of family planning programmes would not in itself be sufficient to achieve a reduction in the population growth to desired target levels in most developing countries. There would also have to be a rise in the age at marriage.

The procedure for fitting the model or finding values of a_0, k, and C from a set of observed proportions ever married is given by Coale (1971: 214). It is straightforward, but very laborious since it involves interpolation within several tables (unless one has access to a suitable computer program). A concise illustration is thus not possible here. Moreover, it is in fact rarely used on its own; its primary importance has instead been its use as part of the Coale–Trussell model of fertility.

The Coale–Trussell Fertility Model

This model is a combination of the Coale–McNeil nuptiality model with a model of marital fertility also developed by Coale and Trussell in their 1974 paper.

The model of marital fertility starts from the concept of 'natural' fertility introduced by Henry (1961). Natural fertility refers to the fertility of populations in which no parity-specific birth control is practised. The classic example is the Hutterites (see p. 45). Henry showed that although the level of natural fertility varies between populations, mainly because of varying patterns of marriage, its shape is relatively unvarying. The pattern is roughly as in Figure 14.2.

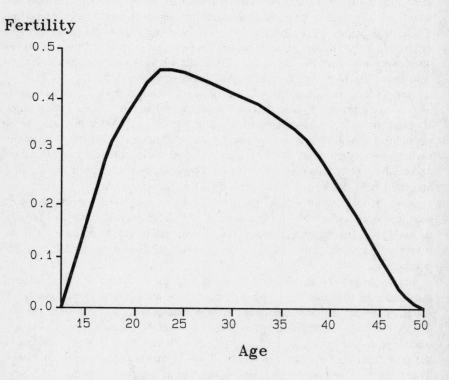

Figure 14.2 A typical schedule of natural fertility

Further, as fertility comes under increasing control, the pattern of marital fertility changes in a regular, predictable way: the decline is greatest at high ages. Therefore the shape of the marital fertility schedule depends essentially on the degree of departure of marital fertility from the fixed, natural or uncontrolled schedule. Consequently, a one-parameter model should be sufficiently flexible to fit a wide variety of marital fertility schedules well (plus a second for level).

The model constructed by Coale and Trussell is:

$$r(a) = n(a) \cdot e^{m \cdot v(a)}$$

where a is age and $r(a)$ is the proportion of marital fertility occurring at age a. $n(a)$ is a fixed schedule of natural marital fertility as shown in Table 14.1. $v(a)$ is also a fixed schedule. It expresses the typical departure from natural fertility. Again, it is given in Table 14.1.

The model has two parameters. One, m indicates the extent of fertility control. In normal populations it ranges from 0.0 up to about 2.5. If it is 0.0 then there is no fertility control (i.e. it is natural), while a value above 2.0 indicates extremely strong control. The second parameter, M, scales the model, like C does in the nuptiality model described above. It is not included in the equation above since it is only the shape of the schedule which is normally of interest. If needed it just multiplies the entire right-hand side of the equation to achieve the desired total marital fertility.

Only five-year values of $n(a)$ and $v(a)$ are shown in Table 14.1, though single-year figures are available. The $n(a)$ is the average of the natural fertility schedules collected by Henry (1961), while the $v(a)$ was calculated by Coale and Trussell as an average of forty-three schedules of marital fertility found in the 1965 *United Nations Demographic Yearbook*.

Table 14.1 Five-year $n(a)$ and $v(a)$ for Coale–Trussell fertility model

Age group (a)	$n(a)$	$v(a)$
20–24	0.460	0.000
25–29	0.431	−0.316
30–34	0.396	−0.814
35–39	0.321	−1.048
40–44	0.167	−1.424
45–49	0.024	−1.667

Source: Coale and Trussell (1974: 188)

The marital fertility model thus has just two parameters, m which controls the shape of the distribution, and M which alters its level. It can now be combined with the Coale–McNeil nuptiality model to produce a model of overall fertility.

Table 14.2 Sample Coale–Trussell fertility models

MEAN	24.0	24.0	24.0	24.0	24.0	24.0	24.0	24.0	24.0	24.0	24.0	24.0	24.0	24.0	24.0
STDEV	4.0	4.0	4.0	4.0	4.0	4.0	4.0	4.0	4.0	4.5	4.5	4.5	4.5	4.5	4.5
R1	0.2221	0.2299	0.2388	0.2462	0.2541	0.2599	0.2665	0.2768	0.2805	0.3553	0.3607	0.3662	0.3711	0.3891	0.3922
MED	23.17	23.22	23.26	23.29	23.32	23.35	23.37	23.38	23.40	23.09	23.12	23.16	23.19	23.20	23.22
SKEW	1.139	1.100	1.061	1.024	0.989	0.957	0.928	0.920	0.890	1.061	1.035	1.009	0.984	0.989	0.958
PAR1	0.0583	0.0635	0.0687	0.0734	0.0779	0.0816	0.0854	0.0853	0.0889	0.1024	0.1073	0.1120	0.1162	0.1147	0.1199
PAR2	0.5086	0.5051	0.5027	0.5004	0.4988	0.4969	0.4960	0.4968	0.4954	0.5442	0.5416	0.5393	0.5369	0.5390	0.5370
A0	17.23	16.85	16.48	16.14	15.81	15.52	15.24	14.94	14.71	16.46	16.03	15.62	15.23	14.78	14.46
K	0.200	0.250	0.300	0.350	0.400	0.450	0.500	0.550	0.600	0.200	0.250	0.300	0.350	0.400	0.450
M	3.461	3.516	3.576	3.639	3.706	3.773	3.842	3.888	3.960	2.907	2.942	2.981	3.024	3.039	3.091
12	0	0	0	0	0	0	0	0	0	0	0	0	0	0	0
13	0	0	0	0	0	0	0	0	0	0	0	0	0	0	0
14	0	0	0	0	0	0	0	1	19	0	0	0	0	11	91
10–14	0	0	0	0	0	0	0	0	4	0	0	0	0	2	18
15	95	166	265	380	515	649	804	653	1 015	1 263	1 610	1 980	2 345	1 321	2 204
16	1 976	2 707	3 529	4 325	5 128	5 832	6 571	5 337	6 255	9 239	10 492	11 679	12 738	9 873	11 589
17	10 496	12 370	14 217	15 798	17 258	18 418	19 585	19 174	20 087	25 750	27 279	28 617	29 720	30 373	31 209
18	32 600	34 565	36 379	37 759	38 968	39 790	40 669	43 808	43 792	51 066	51 578	51 964	52 198	58 174	57 222
19	76 668	74 977	73 793	72 718	71 874	70 978	70 390	72 869	71 758	85 356	83 160	81 259	79 598	82 753	80 792
15–19	24 367	24 957	25 637	26 195	26 749	27 133	27 604	28 168	28 581	34 535	34 824	35 100	35 320	36 499	36 603
20	120 304	115 163	110 990	107 530	104 696	102 220	100 235	98 540	96 999	110 386	107 100	104 146	101 563	99 050	97 228
21	124 073	121 536	118 989	116 663	114 571	112 692	111 049	109 310	108 066	108 322	106 991	105 537	104 118	102 020	100 933
22	116 261	116 021	115 355	114 586	113 738	112 933	112 116	110 901	110 311	100 684	100 681	100 452	100 115	98 746	98 445
23	102 189	103 115	103 620	103 946	104 074	104 165	104 099	103 524	103 543	89 584	90 208	90 672	91 024	90 321	90 578
24	85 739	86 968	87 919	88 737	89 360	89 939	90 317	90 228	90 615	76 957	77 737	78 454	79 107	78 866	79 400
20–24	109 713	108 501	107 374	106 292	105 288	104 390	103 563	102 500	101 907	97 186	96 544	95 852	95 185	93 801	93 317
25	71 580	72 738	73 746	74 691	75 488	76 265	76 850	77 064	77 635	65 939	66 674	67 418	68 147	68 178	68 812
26	47 618	48 283	48 927	49 591	50 200	50 839	51 352	51 718	52 231	46 572	47 019	47 526	48 068	48 277	48 783
27	47 618	48 283	48 927	49 591	50 200	50 839	51 352	51 718	52 231	46 572	47 019	47 526	48 068	48 277	48 783
28	38 087	38 519	38 947	39 408	39 840	40 313	40 692	41 010	41 399	38 503	38 807	39 170	39 571	39 774	40 154
29	29 415	29 645	29 875	30 136	30 382	30 672	30 894	31 121	31 357	30 909	31 084	31 307	31 562	31 728	31 966
25–29	49 240	49 926	50 565	51 206	51 779	52 372	52 838	53 135	53 600	47 646	48 101	48 601	49 123	49 279	49 755

Age															
30	21 886	21 964	22 040	22 139	22 231	22 362	22 446	22 577	22 677	24 038	24 109	24 214	24 343	24 461	24 572
31	16 198	16 186	16 169	16 169	16 165	16 194	16 191	16 254	16 265	16 596	18 600	18 627	18 669	18 748	18 771
32	11 982	11 920	11 853	11 797	11 739	11 708	11 655	11 673	11 634	14 378	14 341	14 319	14 306	14 354	14 321
33	8 834	8 750	8 661	8 578	8 494	8 432	8 355	8 346	8 281	11 081	11 022	10 971	10 926	10 952	10 886
34	6 684	6 595	6 501	6 411	6 320	6 248	6 166	6 144	6 072	8 715	8 648	8 585	8 525	8 538	8 458
30–34	13 117	13 083	13 045	13 019	12 990	12 989	12 962	12 999	12 986	15 362	15 344	15 343	15 354	15 411	15 402
35	5 036	4 950	4 859	4 771	4 683	4 609	4 529	4 501	4 430	6 826	6 757	6 690	6 623	6 627	6 543
36	3 766	3 687	3 604	3 524	3 443	3 374	3 300	3 271	3 205	5 306	5 239	5 173	5 107	5 105	5 022
37	2 801	2 732	2 659	2 588	2 517	2 456	2 391	2 363	2 305	4 102	4 040	3 979	3 916	3 910	3 833
38	2 063	2 004	1 943	1 883	1 823	1 770	1 715	1 691	1 641	3 141	3 086	3 031	2 974	2 967	2 898
39	1 486	1 439	1 389	1 340	1 291	1 248	1 204	1 183	1 143	2 352	2 306	2 258	2 209	2 202	2 143
35–39	3 031	2 962	2 891	2 821	2 751	2 691	2 628	2 602	2 545	4 345	4 286	4 226	4 166	4 162	4 086
40	1 029	992	954	916	879	845	812	795	765	1 693	1 655	1 617	1 577	1 570	1 523
41	677	650	622	595	568	544	520	508	486	1 158	1 129	1 100	1 070	1 064	1 028
42	429	410	391	372	354	337	321	312	297	762	741	720	698	694	668
43	254	242	230	218	206	195	185	179	170	469	455	441	426	423	406
44	138	131	123	116	110	104	98	94	89	264	256	247	238	236	226
40–44	505	485	464	441	423	405	387	378	361	869	847	825	802	797	770
45	71	67	63	59	55	52	49	47	44	140	136	131	126	124	119
46	38	36	34	31	29	28	26	25	23	77	74	72	69	68	65
47	20	19	18	18	16	15	14	13	12	42	41	39	38	37	35
48	10	9	9	8	8	7	7	6	6	21	20	19	19	18	17
49	3	2	2	2	2	2	2	2	2	6	5	5	5	5	5
45–49	28	27	25	24	22	21	19	19	17	57	55	53	51	51	48

Source: Coale and Trusserll (1974: 205)

The process of combining the two models is straightforward. Because the primary concern is with modelling the shape of the fertility distribution, its actual level being relatively unimportant, the two level parameters, C from the nuptiality model, and M from the marital fertility model, can simply be dropped. The combined Coale–Trussell fertility model thus has three parameters: a_0 giving the age of onset of marriage, k indicating the rate of marriage, and m giving the extent of fertility control.

This model can be expressed algebraically as:

$$f(a) = G(a) \cdot n(a) \cdot e^{m \cdot v(a)}$$

where $f(a)$ is the age specific fertility rate at age a, and $G(a)$, the only other unfamiliar element, is the proportion ever married at age a as determined from the a_0 and k parameters of the nuptiality model. Fortunately, it is not necessary to understand how $G(a)$ is computed from a_0 and k (but for details see Coale and Trussell 1974: 187). Since there is no scale parameter the $f(a)$s are relative so they add to 1.00 exactly. To inflate them to conventional ASFRs which sum to the Total Fertility Rate only requires that they are each multiplied by the TFR.

Fitting a model to a set of observed ASFRs can be achieved most easily by means of a pre-existing computer program. However, if that is not available it is possible to select one of the nearly 800 models given in Appendix B of Coale and Trussell (1974: 204–57). Selection is done using three measures: the mean of the fertility schedule, its standard deviation and the ratio of the fertility rates for the age groups 15–19 and 20–4. There are models for all plausible combinations of these three variables. A group is shown in Table 14.2. Each column of the table is a model and the fertility rates sum to 1,000,000 to avoid decimal points. For the model in the first column the mean of the distribution is 24 years, its standard deviation is 4.0 and R_1 is 0.2221. The parameters of the model are $a_0 = 17.23$, $k = 0.200$, and $m = 3.461$. If greater precision in fitting is required than is possible simply by selecting the best of the printed models, then it is possible to interpolate between them using weighted averages (Coale and Trussell 1974: 194–5).

These fertility models can be used in many ways such as for smoothing, for correcting, for producing single-year ASFRs from five-year data or for completing censored fertility schedules of young cohorts who have not yet completed childbearing.

The main drawback of the system arises from the fact that the Coale–McNeil nuptiality model which it incorporates can only model well either real cohorts or well-behaved synthetic cohorts where nuptiality has not been changing rapidly. If nuptiality has been changing the model is likely to fit poorly and the interpretation of the parameters also becomes very difficult. Another drawback is that because it is a three-parameter system, and these normally have to be found from only six or seven ASFRs, the model is quite sensitive to small differences or errors in the data. Thus a minor change in the observed pattern of fertility can produce quite different parameter values. Or, conversely, quite different combinations of the parameters can produce rather similar fertility schedules. Such sensitivity is an advantage when working with accurate data, but when working with data from developing countries which are likely to contain errors and biases, it is a positive disadvantage. These problems are to some extent, though far from entirely, overcome in the Gompertz relational model system.

Gompertz Relational Fertility Models

This system bears many similarities to the logit relational system of model life tables in that the model is expressed as a linear transformation of a set of standard rates and has two parameters, known as α and β. (It is assumed that the logit system, described in the previous chapter (pp. 151–9), is familiar to the reader.) But whereas the logit model life table system uses as raw data l_xs, the proportions surviving to age x, the Gompertz model uses ASFRs expressed as proportions (i.e. divided by the TFR) and cumulated. Such figures are given for Bangladesh, 1974 in Table 14.3 and are plotted in Figure 14.3. And, instead of using the logit transformation to linearise the data, a Gompertz transformation is used instead. Unfortunately there is no generally accepted name for a Gompertz-transformed value, but here 'Gompit' will be used. The transformation is then:

$$\text{Gompit } (p) = -\text{Log}_e(-\text{Log}_e p)$$

and its inverse (anti-Gompit?) is:

$$p = \exp(-\exp(-\text{Gompit})).$$

As with the logit, it can only be used for transforming proportions. Hence the use of p in the equations.

The key to the model is that plotting the Gompits of one set of cumulative proportional ASFRs against another, such as a predefined standard, produces an approximately straight line. Expressing this algebraically, if the Gompit of the cumulative relative fertility at age x is called $Y(x)$, and a standard is denoted by the subscript s, then:

$$Y(x) = \alpha + \beta \, Y_s(x).$$

The standard fertility schedule was generated by Booth (1984) and is given, together with their relative cumulative form and Gompits in Table 14.4. The standard was designed to represent the typical pattern of fertility in high-fertility

Table 14.3 Cumulative proportional ASFRs: Bangladesh, 1974

Age group	ASFR	Proportional ASFR	Exact age	Cumulative proportional ASFR
			15	0.0000
15–19	0.2004	0.1415	20	0.1415
20–24	0.3373	0.2382	25	0.3797
25–29	0.3109	0.2196	30	0.5993
30–34	0.2615	0.1847	35	0.7840
35–39	0.1970	0.1391	40	0.9231
40–44	0.0954	0.0674	45	0.9905
45–49	0.0135	0.0095	50	1.0000
TFR =	7.0800	1.0000		

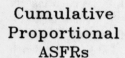

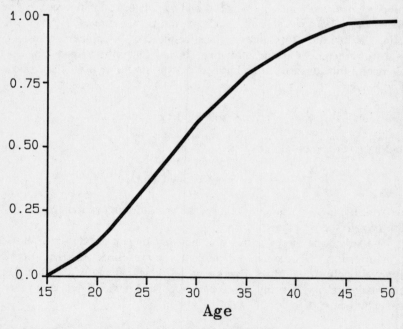

Figure 14.3 Cumulative proportional ASFRs: Bangladesh, 1974

Table 14.4 Standard cumulative ASFRs and their Gompits

Age x $Y_s(x)$	Gompits $F_s(x)$	Cumulative fertility
10	$-\infty$	0.00000
11	-3.17091	0.00000
12	-2.74255	0.00000
13	-2.36854	0.00002
14	-2.04079	0.00045
15	-1.75210	0.00313
16	-1.49286	0.01168
17	-1.25061	0.03043
18	-1.04479	0.05826
19	-0.85927	0.09428
20	-0.69130	0.13584
21	-0.53325	0.18187
22	-0.38524	0.22993
23	-0.24423	0.27897
24	-0.10783	0.32829
25	0.02564	0.37731
26	0.15853	0.42597
27	0.29147	0.47371
28	0.42515	0.52013
29	0.56101	0.56517
30	0.70000	0.60861
31	0.84272	0.65016
32	0.99014	0.68968
33	1.14407	0.72722
34	1.30627	0.76275
35	1.47872	0.79618
36	1.66426	0.82751
37	1.86597	0.85663
38	2.08894	0.88354
39	2.33992	0.90816
40	2.62602	0.93019
41	2.95500	0.94925
42	3.32873	0.96480
43	3.75984	0.97698
44	4.25499	0.98591
45	4.80970	0.99188
46	5.41311	0.99555
47	6.12864	0.99782
48	7.07022	0.99915
49	8.64839	0.99982
50	$+\infty$	1.00000

Source: Zaba (1981)

populations. For use in low-fertility populations a different standard would be better.

The parameters α and β have, as in the logit life table system, distinct interpretations. α changes the age-location of the model. If α is 0.0, the neutral value, then the location is the same as in the standard, indicating that about half the total childbearing occurs by age 27. If α is negative, then fertility starts later (not earlier), and the mean age of fertility is higher. A value as low as -0.5 indicates a very old pattern of fertility such as was experienced in Ireland during the nineteenth century. Positive values of α on the other hand, indicate earlier fertility than in the standard. A value of $+0.5$ describes an extremely young pattern of childbearing such as occurs in some parts of the Caribbean where families are started young and there is a very high rate of break-up of unions.

β may be interpreted as determining the spread, or degree of concentration, of the schedule. The neutral value is 1.00. Low values, down to perhaps 0.65, indicate a wider spread than in the standard, as might occur in natural fertility populations where marriage is also early. At the other extreme, a value of β above 1.5 would indicate a narrow spread, with a late start and early finish as is found in some contemporary European populations.

It should be remembered that α and β only have meaning relative to the standard. If a different standard is used, then the values of α and β will change.

The advantages of the Gompertz fertility model over the Coale–Trussell fertility model are first that it uses just two rather than three parameters. This is useful not only because it is simpler but also because it makes models less sensitive to errors and biases in data. Indeed, one of the most useful applications of the models is in the evaluation of data quality. Second, application is easy and can be done without a computer or large numbers of tables. Third, because it is based upon a relational principle rather than empirical regularities concerning the behaviour of cohorts, it might well fit cross-sectional data rather better, especially where nuptiality is changing rapidly.

One particularly useful application of the model has been for the estimation of total fertility from average parities since it has been found that the Gompertz relationship holds with such data as well as with information on current fertility as described above, and that α and β can be estimated even when total fertility is unknown. For details of this and other applications, see Zaba (1981) or Brass (1981).

The modelling of fertility using the Gompertz transformation has a long history (see Booth 1984: 495–6), but earlier models were not relational. Instead, they tried always to express fertility as a function of age alone. The descriptions of the relational Gompertz model by Brass (1981) and Booth (1984) both, somewhat confusingly, approach it from this angle, explaining the use of a standard fertility schedule as a replacement or transformation of the conventional age scale, thereby enhancing pre-existing models.

Other Models of Fertility

Finally one other model of fertility, which should be mentioned because it is used extensively in indirect estimation procedures, is the Brass 'Fertility

Polynomial'. This is :

$$f(x) = c(x - s)(s + 33 - x)^2$$

where x is age, $f(x)$ is cumulative fertility, c is a level parameter and s is the age at which fertility begins. $s + 13.2$ is always the mean age of childbearing. The reason for the 33 is that it is roughly the length of the reproductive period.

This model is not nearly as good as the two previously described. Its usefulness arises from its simplicity and its ability to model fertility within specific age intervals rather than over the whole age range (see Brass 1975: Ch. 4).

Exercise

1. The 1980 census of Barbados asked women for the number of births they had had during the previous year. Dividing the total reported births by the total number of women produced the ASFRs presented in Table 14E.1.

Fit a Gompertz relational fertility model to these data. What do the results tell you about the likely accuracy of the reported ASFRs?

Table 14E.1 ASFRs derived from 1980 census of Barbados

Age group	ASFRs (per 000)
15–19	61.2
20–24	117.0
25–29	103.8
30–34	75.9
35–39	35.0
40–44	18.1

15 Population projections and forecasts

Population projections vary enormously in complexity. At one extreme they may comprise little more than extending by hand a line of a graph showing how the total population changes over time. At the other extreme they may consist of a complex computer program which projects the population by age, sex, marital status and perhaps other characteristics using varying assumptions for different periods about the future courses of mortality, fertility, migration, marriage etc.

This chapter begins with a brief discussion of the purposes and uses of projections. Then, after briefly covering mathematical methods of projection, a simple component projection is described using India as an example.

The Uses of Projections

Demographers frequently use projections for what may be termed theoretical or research purposes in order to try to answer questions such as what would happen if a cure for some important cancers were to be discovered, or the likely impact on fertility of, say, a rise in the age of marriage, or the implementation of a family planning programme. One of the best-known applications of projections of this type is by Frejka (1973), who estimated the size to which various populations would ultimately grow if fertility were to fall to an NRR of 1.0 either very rapidly or more slowly.

But the most obvious and frequent use of population projections is for planning purposes. National, regional and local planners all need, for various purposes, to have some idea of likely future changes in the size, composition and distribution of the population in their particular areas. At the national level most central government departments require population projections as an input into their estimates of future income and expenditure, the level of demand for their services, and so on. The demand for pensions and health services, for example, is largely determined by the size and composition of the population.

At the regional level, the likely growth of towns and cities, caused by either rural-to-urban migration or differential natural increase, needs to be known so that housing, transport and other services and amenities can be provided. And, more locally, planners need to estimate likely demand for public utilities, schools, hospitals, recreation facilities, housing and many other things.

The above discussion implicitly regards population change as a phenomenon which essentially has to be reacted to and which cannot itself be affected by policy and planning. But population change can equally be regarded as being to some extent a dependent rather than an independent variable in the planning process. And so projections can be used to estimate the likely demographic impact of planning decisions and policy changes, as well as the planning and policy implications of demographic change.

Clearly, the importance of population size and composition for the various planning applications outlined above varies greatly. For some planning decisions, political and economic considerations dominate, but for such things as pensions, schools and hospitals in particular, demographic reality, and thus population projections, are crucial.

The level of detail required in projections also varies greatly. For a few purposes a simple population total is sufficient, but almost always some compositional detail is needed; and often it is much more than just a breakdown by age and sex that is necessary. For example, labour force projections require a breakdown by employment status and perhaps occupation, while for housing planning it is essential to produce projections of households by size and type rather than just population. The ultimate in respect of detail are the school planners who really require projections of school children by single years of age for each school catchment area.

What all planners, without exception, would ideally like are firm, accurate predictions about the future. Of course, however, demographers are no better at foretelling the future than anyone else. Moreover, as stated above, the actions of the planners themselves, to some extent influenced by existing projections, are almost certain to have some demographic consequences in the future. The best demographers can do in such circumstances is to use the available data together with realistic assumptions in their projections and, most importantly, they must present their results in such a way that the inherent uncertainties and interactions involved are obvious. This can often be done very simply. For example, if one is presenting a set of alternative projections using different sets of assumptions, then it is better to produce, say, two or four alternatives rather than three. In this way the user is forced to explicitly consider the alternatives before making a conscious choice. But if there were three (or five) alternatives, almost all users would automatically choose the middle one. With two or four there is no middle one.

Projections made using realistic assumptions are called 'forecasts'. It is important to remember that forecasts are usually no more than educated guesses dressed up in sophisticated ways. If the guesses ('assumptions') are wrong, then the forecast will be wrong. Moreover, the further one forecasts into the future, the more the assumptions are likely to be wrong. Thus forecasts usually tend to be reasonable for a few years ahead but then become progressively worse — the margin of error increases.

Techniques of Projection

It should be pointed out here that, although the following discussion only considers the projection of populations, the comments made apply equally to the projection of many other phenomena such as total numbers of births, marriages, migrants, deaths or hospital admissions.

The very simplest techniques of all just project the population according to some mathematical formula so that the population at time $t + 1$ is simply a function of the population at time t. Algebraically:

$$P_{t+1} = f(P_t)$$

Very little information on the population prior to time t is used. The best example of this is the exponential projection:

$$P_{t+1} = P_t \cdot e^r$$

where r is the growth rate. Being an exponential model, the resulting curve of the projected population will inevitably look like that in Figure 15.1.

The projection may be reasonable for a few years into the future, but the assumption of an indefinitely continuing constant rate of growth clearly eventually produces ridiculous figures. A more realistic approach would be to use a function which produces an upper-limit, such as the logistic, shown in Figure 15.2.

Two basic flaws of deterministic models such as these are firstly that they assume population growth follows simple mathematical rules and, secondly, that they use very little historical information. Yet, normally, populations do not grow in such regular ways and much historical information on the size of the population before time t is frequently both available and a useful guide to likely future trends.

It may, therefore, be better first to fit a simple descriptive model to the existing data and then to use the model to extrapolate into the future. This may involve fitting a curve to the time series of population totals using regression or similar statistical procedures, and then using the resulting equation of the fitted curve to extend the curve into the future. A picture of this type of projection is shown in Figure 15.3.

Simple curve fitting such as this can sometimes produce very reasonable results but it has the drawback that it gives equal weight to each data point used. But, clearly, more recent figures will normally give a better idea of future patterns than earlier figures. A technique which allows this to be taken into account is that of the weighted moving average. This also has the additional advantage over simple curve fitting in that each projected figure is taken into account when projecting the next.

Population

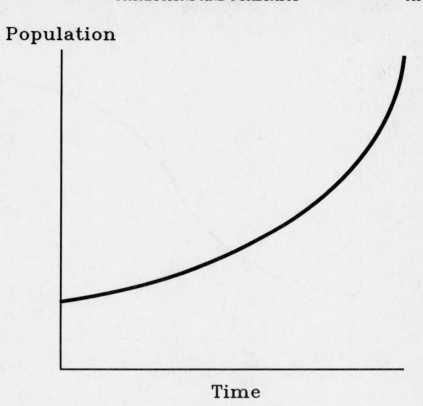

Time

Figure 15.1 Exponential population growth

Although the techniques mentioned so far are often useful for theoretical purposes, and are consequently used extensively by demographers and other researchers, they are not very useful for producing 'real' forecasts to be used by planners and others. This is, first, because they do not use information on the structure of the current population and, second, because they cannot easily be used to produce breakdowns of the composition of the projected population. There may be, for example, a large number of women just entering the childbearing years as a result of a baby boom twenty years earlier. This will produce an increase in the number of births in the near future, yet such information cannot be taken into account in a straightforward way using any of the techniques discussed so far. Instead, therefore, a different technique is normally used, known as the 'component method'.

Population

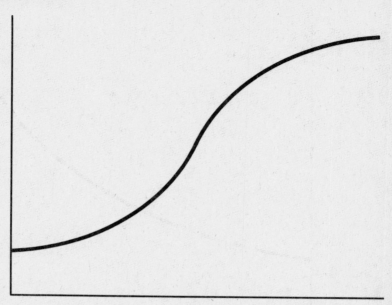

Time

Figure 15.2 Logistic population growth

The Component Method of Projection

This technique has the potential to become quite extraordinarily complex, but the basic idea is very simple. The whole method can be thought of as an extension of the Basic Demographic Equation (see p. 8). At its very simplest the equation states that:

$$\text{Population change} = \text{Natural increase} + \text{Net migration}$$

and this can be expanded to

$$P_{t+1} = P_t + \text{Births} - \text{Deaths} + \text{Immigrants} - \text{Emigrants}$$

which just breaks population change down into its individual components. Now, this equation can be applied not only to the whole population but also to its component parts. Thus it is straightforward to split the population by

Population

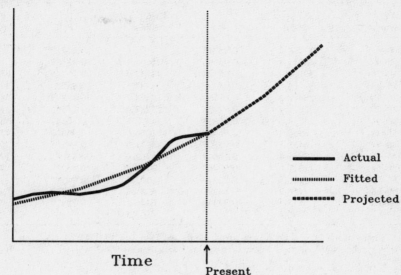

Figure 15.3 Projection by curve fitting

age, sex, marital status and whatever else is necessary and then, essentially, to apply the Basic Demographic Equation to each and every sub-group. But while this is theoretically and conceptually very simple, in practice it becomes very complex, mainly because it is necessary to ensure consistency between the sub-groups being projected. For example, if a marital status breakdown is being used, then the number of widows 'created' at any time must equal the number of married men dying in the same period.

To carry out any component population projection requires three things. These are, first, a base population from which the projection starts; second, a set of assumptions about the course of events during the period covered by the projection; and third, a method by which the assumptions are applied to the base population. The basic principles are best explained by means of a simple example.

Here the 1981 female population of India will be projected, initially for five years. Five years is very convenient because the base population is divided into five-year age groups. It is assumed that the net migration is zero in every age group and can thus be ignored entirely. Ways of taking account of migration will, however, be mentioned later. The base population to be used is from the 1981 census and is shown as the first column of Table 15.1.

It is normally best to start a projection from the most recent census rather than from the most recent estimates for two reasons. First, the estimates are in many

Table 15.1 Component projection: Indian females, 1981, mortality

Age group	1981 popn (000s)	$_5P_x{}^*$	1986 popn (000s)	$_5P_x{}^\dagger$	1991 popn (000s)
0–4	47498.2	0.96015	51900.9	0.96722	
5–9	44715.1	0.98696	45605.4	0.98899	50199.6
10–14	39465.4	0.98523	44132.0	0.98743	45103.3
15–19	33163.6	0.97995	38882.5	0.98281	43577.3
20–24	28482.3	0.97562	32498.7	0.97899	38214.1
25–29	25072.7	0.97226	27787.9	0.97595	31815.9
30–34	21734.6	0.96853	24377.2	0.97247	36879.1
35–39	18950.9	0.96417	21050.6	0.96820	23706.1
40–44	16452.8	0.95807	18271.9	0.96205	20381.2
45–49	13960.4	0.94649	15762.9	0.95081	17578.5
50–54	11321.4	0.92763	13213.4	0.93277	14987.5
55–59	9200.8	0.89713	10502.1	0.90359	12325.1
60–64	7466.9	0.84991	8254.3	0.85787	9489.6
65–69	5612.8	0.77968	6346.2	0.78879	7081.1
70+	7676.8		8563.3 4376.2		9460.9

* West, Level 15, $e_0 = 55.0$ years (from Coale and Demeny 1983: 49).
† West, Level 16, $e_0 = 57.5$ years (from Coale and Demeny 1983: 49).

respects projections themselves since they are almost certainly calculated by starting with the census figures, and adding or subtracting subsequent births, deaths and migration. Second, one can project to the present and compare the projected figures with the estimates. This provides a crude check on the accuracy of the projection for the first few years.

The assumptions about fertility and mortality that need to be made may be quite simple or very detailed, depending essentially on the level of detail required in the final projection results. For fertility, one can frame the assumptions in terms of the total numbers of births, the Crude Birth Rate, Age-Specific Fertility Rates or any other measures of period or cohort fertility, including fertility-model parameters. Breakdowns by parity, legitimacy and other factors are also possible. However, it is essential to use at least age-specific measures since component projections always involve an age breakdown of the population. Here the estimated 1981 ASFRs for India are used and it is assumed that these will remain constant throughout the period of projection. The figures are given in the first column of Table 15.2.

For mortality assumptions one could derive a life table from 1981 data for India. Model life tables are, however, particularly convenient as changes in mortality can be specified in terms of changes in model parameters or levels. Here the West Region model, Level 15 from the Princeton set is used (see Ch. 12, pp. 134–9). This choice is simply an educated guess. The Level 15 model for females has an expectation at life of 55.0 years. The particular life-table function used is the Survivorship Ratio, P (see p. 78), which gives the probability of surviving from one age group to another, and is just the ratio of two adjacent $_nL_x$ values. That is:

$$P = \frac{_5L_{x+5}}{_5L_x}$$

The figures, copied from Coale and Demeny (1983: 49), are given in the third column of Table 15.1. To obtain the population in 1986 one simply multiplies the 1981 base population by the Survivorship Ratios, remembering also to move the result one row down. Thus, in the first row of the Table, 0.96015 of the 0–4 age group survive to become 5–9. Thus 47,498,200 × 0.96015 = 45,605,397 survive, and this figure is inserted in the 5–9 row. This process is repeated for each age group to produce the 1986 population.

The process can then be repeated by surviving the new projected population to 1991. Here it is assumed that mortality has improved by one Coale–Demeny Level to an e_0 of 57.5. For example, the 45,605,397 females aged 5–9 are multiplied by the Survivorship Ratio, 0.98899, to give 45,103,281 10–14 year olds.

One detail which deserves pointing out is that for the 70+ age group the Coale–Demeny tables do not give a Survivorship Ratio. Instead, this has to be calculated using T_xs rather than $_5L_x$s, and is just T_{75}/T_{70}. For the Level 15 model, this ratio is 0.54543. The 1986 population aged 70+ then comprises the survivors of both the 1981 65–9 year olds (5,612,800 × 0.77968 = 4,376,188) and the 1981 70+s (7,676,800 × 0.54543 = 4,187,157). Second, and much more importantly, there are no figures yet for the 0–4 year olds in 1986, or 0–9 year olds in 1991. For these it is necessary, first, to use the fertility assumptions to estimate the number of births there will be between 1981 and 1986 and then to survive these since some will die before 1986. The estimation of the births is done in Table 15.2.

First, the average number of females aged 15–49 during 1981–6 is calculated simply by taking the average of the 1981 base population figures and the new 1986 figures calculated in Table 15.1. The female ASFRs, which constitute the fertility assumptions being used, are then applied to the average population to give the projected female births in one year. These figures then have to be multiplied by five because five years of births are required (1981–6). They are then summed to give a total of 58,429,300 births occurring during 1981–6. As stated above, some of these births will now have to be killed off as not all will survive until 1986. Very conveniently, the Coale–Demeny life tables provide a Survivorship Ratio giving the probability of five years of births surviving from birth to become the 0–4 age group (see p. 138). For West, Level 15 the figure is 0.88827. Thus the projected female population aged 0–4 in 1986 is 58,429,300 × 0.88827 = 51,900,990, and this figure can then be inserted in Table 15.1 to complete the projected 1986 population. These 0–4 year olds can then be projected to 1991. The Survivorship Ratio, given in Table 15.1, is

Table 15.2 Component projection: Indian females, 1981, fertility

Age group	Female ASFRs	1981 females (000s)	1986 females (000s)	Average 1981–6	Projected female births (000s)
15–19	0.0436	33163.6	38882.5	36023.1	7853.0
20–24	0.1242	28482.3	32498.7	30490.5	18934.6
25–29	0.1127	25072.7	27787.9	26430.3	14893.5
30–34	0.0795	21734.6	24377.2	23055.9	9164.7
35–39	0.0468	18950.9	21050.6	20000.8	4680.2
40–44	0.0236	16452.8	18271.9	17362.4	2048.8
45–49	0.0115	13960.4	15762.9	14861.7	854.5
					59429.3

0.96722, so there will be $51,900,990 \times 0.96722 = 50,199,676$ females aged 5–9 in 1981. The whole process could also be repeated to find the 0–4 year olds in 1991, using, perhaps, different fertility assumptions.

Discussion

Although the projection carried out here is very simplified, it does serve to illustrate the basic principles, and it allows several important points to be made. First, it is clear that projecting age groups born before the base year only requires assumptions to be made about their mortality, whereas age groups born after the base year require fertility as well as mortality assumptions. Further, mortality can generally be forecast with reasonable accuracy, since, unlike fertility, it is not really a matter of free will, and the trend over time is less variable. Thus one could probably forecast with considerable accuracy the number of Indian women aged 40–44 in 2011 because they would already have been born in 1981, but the forecast of the number of women aged 15 to 19 in the year 2011 would be less accurate as they would only be born during 1981–6, thus involving assumptions about fertility as well as mortality.

Second, the projection could be made much more complex, either by breaking the population down by factors such as marital or employment status, or urban/rural residence, or by making the assumptions more complex, notably by including migration. The importance of migration in demographic projections is only seldom reflected in the amount of attention paid to it.

Migration is extremely difficult to forecast accurately as it is affected greatly by inherently unpredictable events such as war, famine, economic conditions and, in particular, changes in administrative restrictions on immigration. Yet migration is often more important than either fertility or mortality in determining population change, especially in small countries. It is particularly important when making sub-national projections because then there is the additional problem of internal migration which is likely to occur on a very much greater scale than international migration. Yet it is even less predictable, and it is often extremely difficult even to obtain good data on current movements on which to base future estimates. Normally, migration assumptions are expressed in terms of net rather than gross migration rates by age. Net migration is normally easier to estimate and the great variability in migration by age makes it necessary to use an age breakdown at the very least. If migration were to be taken into account in the India projection example above, the projected 1986 or 1991 populations in Table 15.1 would just be adjusted up or down to take account of the assumed migration during the previous five years.

Although demographers tend normally to consider countries as a whole, forecasts for planning purposes nearly always require a sub-national breakdown. This adds an extra level of complexity. There are two basic approaches. Either separate assumptions and projections can be made for each region or district and these aggregated to produce the national estimates, or a national projection can be made and then disaggregated. The latter disaggregation approach is more frequently used because it requires fewer assumptions to be made. It also ensures that a realistic national-level forecast is made, and the national-level data are usually better and more detailed than the sub-national data. One can often disaggregate simply by making an assumption that, within each category into which the population is split, each sub-national population remains the same proportion of the national population. This technique is known as the 'Ratio Method' of projection.

The repetitive but essentially simple nature of the component method of projection makes it ideally suited for computers. Indeed, without computer programs the method would be extremely tedious for all but the simplest breakdown and shortest projection period. Many programs exist, each with their own particular features. The best known are by Shorter and Pasta (1974), but the program used by the United Nations Population Division for its 'official' projections is also widely used. Another, of particular interest here, is a program which requires the specification of the fertility and mortality assumptions to be in terms of relational models and changes in their parameters.

The basic simplicity of the method also makes it especially amenable to expression in matrix form. Leslie (1945, 1948) showed that the calculations involved can be elegantly described by considering the base population to be a vector (column matrix) and multiplying it by another matrix which is empty (i.e. contains zeros) except for the diagonal below the leading one which contains the Survivorship Ratios, and the top row which contains the fertility rates to be used (reduced by a factor to account for mortality at young ages). For an introduction to this approach to the algebra of component projection see Woods (1979: 221–4).

Exercises

1. Table 4.1 in Chapter 4 (p. 37), and Table 15E.1 are extracted from ODM (1977). The expectation of life at birth was estimated from the results of the survey to be 45.8 years for males and 46.6 for females. For a suitable model life table see Table 12.2 (pp. 136–7)

The 1979 estimate of the total population of Bangladesh, published by the Population Council, was 87.1 million. In the light of the results of the survey, do you consider this figure to be reasonable?

Table 15E.1 Estimated ASFRs: Bangladesh, 1974

Age group	ASFRs
10–14	0.002
15–19	0.198
20–24	0.337
25–29	0.311
30–34	0.262
35–39	0.197
40–44	0.095
45–49	0.014
Total × 5	7.080

2. Table 15E.2 shows the numbers of males by age group recorded in the Barbados censuses of 1970 and 1980. Also given are the estimated $_5L_x$ values of the life table for the inter-censal period. Estimate the extent of net migration during 1970–80 of men aged 20–50 in 1980. Under what circumstances might the figure be a poor estimate of the true figure.

Table 15E.2 Male population and life-table survivorship by age: Barbados, 1970 and 1980

Age group	Male population 1970	Male population 1980	Life table survivorship x	Life table survivorship $_5L_x*$
10–14	14 996	12 859	10	479 193
15–19	12 829	13 642	15	477 275
20–24	9 875	12 382	20	474 287
25–29	5 724	10 001	25	470 794
30–34	4 808	7 724	30	467 100
35–39	4 295	5 019	35	462 661
40–44	4 540	4 379	40	456 544
45–49	4 300	3 862	45	447 177

*Coale and Demeny (1983) West, Level 22

Exercise Answers

Chapter 3

1. Dominica age pyramid (Fig. A.1).

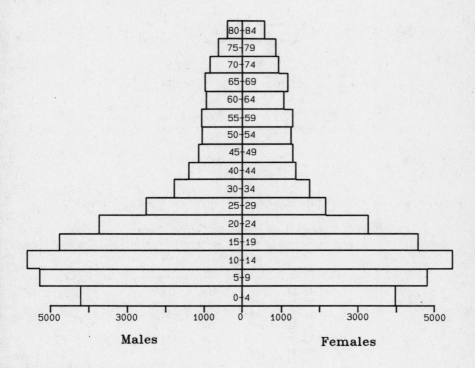

Figure A.1 Dominica pyramid

2. Rhodesian age pyramid: The census was taken on 1 April, exactly one-quarter of the way through the year. Thus, assuming births are evenly spread throughout the year, it is possible to estimate the numbers aged 0, 1, and so on by splitting the birth cohorts in the proportions 0.25 and 0.75. Thus, for females, the number aged 0 is 36,750 + (0.75 × 111,150) = 120,383; the number aged 1 is (0.25 × 111,510) + (0.75 × 94,870) and so on.

Table A.1. Population by age, Rhodesia 1969

Age	Females	Males
0	120 383	120 475
1	99 030	94 098
2	89 545	84 820
3	84 920	83 123

Chapter 4

1. Seychelles fertility rates:

(a) Child/Woman Ratio $= \dfrac{\text{Children aged 0–4}}{\text{Women aged 15–44}} = \dfrac{8,460}{10,600} = 0.7981.$

(b) CBR $= \dfrac{\text{Births in year}}{\text{Population at mid-year}} \times 1,000 = \dfrac{1,806}{58,014} = 31.1.$

(c) $GFR_{15-44} = \dfrac{\text{Births in year}}{\text{Women aged 15–44}} \times 1,000 = 170.4.$

$GFR_{15-49} = \dfrac{\text{Births in year}}{\text{Women aged 15–49}} \times 1,000 = 153.3.$

(d) Age-Specific Fertility Rates, Seychelles, 1975 (Table A.2).

Table A.2. Age-Specific Fertility Rates

Age group	Women	Births	ASFR
15–19	3090	414	133.9
20–24	1886	493	261.4
25–29	1480	341	230.4
30–34	1315	277	210.6
35–39	1394	194	139.2
40–44	1435	75	52.3
45–49	1179	10	8.5

(e) TFR $= \dfrac{\text{Sum of ASFRs} \times 5}{1000} = \dfrac{1036.3 \times 5}{1000} = 5.18.$

2. Bangladesh Coale's Indices: Table A.3 shows expected births to females, derived from Table 4E.3.

Table A.3. Expected births to females by age group: Bangladesh, 1974

Age group of women (1)	Hutterite Standard (2)	Estimated population (000s) All females (3)	Married females (4)	Expected births To all females (2)×(3)	To married females (2)×(4)
15–19	0.300	3 777	2 432	1 133 100	729 600
20–24	0.550	3 101	2 828	1 705 550	1 555 400
25–29	0.502	2 636	2 494	1 323 272	1 251 988
30–34	0.447	2 161	2 012	965 967	899 364
35–39	0.406	1 793	1 606	727 958	652 036
40–44	0.222	1 484	1 211	329 448	268 842
45–49	0.061	1 222	892	74 542	54 412
				6 259 837	5 411 642

Coale's indices can then be calculated as follows:

$$I_f = \frac{\text{Total observed births}}{\text{Expected births to all females}} = \frac{3,689,000}{6,259,837} = 0.59.$$

$$I_g = \frac{\text{Observed legitimate births}}{\text{Expected births to married females}} = \frac{3,689,000}{5,411,642} = 0.68.$$

$$I_m = \frac{\text{Expected births to married females}}{\text{Expected births to all females}} = \frac{5,411,642}{6,259,837} = 0.86.$$

3. South German village fertility: From Table A.4, Coale's I_g = Obs./Exp. = 208/202 = 1.03. This indicates that marital fertility was extremely high, higher even than that of the Hutterites. The data here is in fact invented, but marital fertility was probably higher than Hutterite levels in parts of Bavaria in the eighteenth century.

Table A.4. Expected births to females by age group: South German village

Age group	Hutterite rates	Women	Expected births
20–24	0.550	109	60
25–29	0.502	110	55
30–34	0.447	87	39
35–39	0.406	77	31
40–44	0.222	64	14
45–49	0.061	49	3
			202

Chapter 5

1. 1960 US Parity Progression Ratios: From Table 5E.2 764 women had *at least* one birth, 557 had at least two, and so on; that is:

CEB	0	1	2	3	4	5	6	7
Number with								
at least CEB	1,000	764	557	352	224	144	96	63

Note that the information that there were 115 births of order eight and above cannot be used because it isn't known how many of these occurred to the same women. The PPR a_n is calculated as the number of women with at least $n + 1$ births divided by the number with at least n. Table A.5 shows the calculations.

Table A.5. Parity Progression Ratios, United States, 1960

1901–5 cohort	1906–10 cohort
$a_0 = 764/1000 = 0.764$	$a_0 = 773/1000 = 0.773$
$a_1 = 557/764\ \ = 0.729$	$a_1 = 561/773\ \ = 0.726$
$a_2 = 352/557\ \ = 0.632$	$a_2 = 335/561\ \ = 0.597$
$a_3 = 224/352\ \ = 0.636$	$a_3 = 200/335\ \ = 0.597$
$a_4 = 144/224\ \ = 0.643$	$a_4 = 122/200\ \ = 0.610$
$a_5 = \ \ 96/144\ \ = 0.667$	$a_5 = \ \ 78/122\ \ = 0.639$
$a_6 = \ \ 63/96\ \ \ = 0.656$	$a_6 = \ \ 50/78\ \ \ = 0.640$

A comparison of the earlier figures with those for the 1931–5 cohort reveals much lower PPRs at high orders. This is not necessarily due to a decline in fertility or the popularity of large families, but simply due to the fact that the 1931–5 cohort were only aged 25–29 at the time of the 1960 census. They had not yet completed their fertility and thus their PPRs had not risen to their final, higher levels.

2. England and Wales cohort fertility, 1967–8: The mean family size is the mean number of first births plus mean number of second births, and so on, that is $a_0 + a_1 \cdot a_2 + a_0 \cdot a_2 \cdot a_2 + \ldots$ Assuming none has more than five children, non-manual mean family size is:

$$0.887 +$$
$$(0.887 \times 0.735\ ) +$$
$$(0.887 \times 0.735 \times 0.405) +$$
$$(0.887 \times 0.735 \times 0.405 \times 0.424) +$$
$$(0.887 \times 0.735 \times 0.405 \times 0.424 \times 0.357)$$
$$= (0.887 + 0.652 + 0.264 + 0.112 + 0.040) = 1.995.$$

Table A.6. PPR of women marrying, 1951–60, by. husbands' occupational status

PPR 1951–60	Non-manual	Manual
a_0	0.895	0.895
a_1	0.821	0.806
a_2	0.469	0.500
a_3	0.244	0.467
a_4	0.500	0.375

Chapter 6

1. England and Wales females, 1982 $_nq_x$s.

Table A.7. Female $_nq_x$s, England and Wales, 1982

Age group x	n	Mid-year population P_x	Regd deaths D_x	ASDRs $_nM_x$	$_na_x$	$_nq_x$
0	1	300 800	2 861	0.00951	0.1	0.00943
1–4	4	1 190 600	485	0.00041	0.4	0.00163
5–9	5	1 473 800	253	0.00017	0.5	0.00085
10–14	5	1 847 000	353	0.00019	0.5	0.00095
15–19	5	2 014 500	588	0.00029	0.5	0.00146
20–24	5	1 893 200	672	0.00035	0.5	0.00178
25–29	5	1 683 800	702	0.00042	0.5	0.00209
30–34	5	1 749 100	1 079	0.00062	0.5	0.00308
35–39	5	1 709 800	1 576	0.00092	0.5	0.00461
40–44	5	1 396 800	2 132	0.00153	0.5	0.00764
45–49	5	1 351 900	3 639	0.00269	0.5	0.01339
50–54	5	1 398 300	6 351	0.00454	0.5	0.02247
55–59	5	1 445 500	10 854	0.00751	0.5	0.03690
60–64	5	1 429 100	16 897	0.01182	0.5	0.05753
65–69	5	1 323 100	24 598	0.01859	0.5	0.08908
70–74	5	1 233 300	37 623	0.03051	0.5	0.14230
75–79	5	972 500	49 866	0.05128	0.5	0.22899
80–84	5	620 300	54 879	0.08847	0.5	0.36366
85+	—	428 000	76 287	0.17824	—	1.00000
Total		25 461 400	291 695			

Where

$$_nM_x = \frac{D_x}{P_x}$$

and

$$_nq_x = \frac{n \cdot {}_nM_x}{1 + n(1 - {}_na_x) \cdot {}_nM_x}.$$

2. Breast-feeding in Lagos:

(a) $_6d_{12}$ is the proportion who stop breast-feeding between twelve and eighteen months after the birth:

$$_6d_{12} = l_{12} - l_{18} = 0.485 - 0.169 = 0.316.$$

(b) p_{20} is the probability of continuing to breast-feed from twenty to twenty-one months after the birth:

$$p_{20} = l_{21}/l_{20} = 0.101/0.105 = 0.962.$$

(c) l_{12} is the proportion of mothers still breast-feeding twelve months after the birth:

$$l_{12} = 0.485.$$

(d) $_3L_{20}$ is the number of person-months spent breast-feeding between twenty and twenty-three months after the birth. It is most accurately calculated as:

$$L_{20} + L_{21} + L_{22} = 0.2885.$$

(e) $_6q_6$ is the probability of stopping breast-feeding between six and twelve months after the birth:

$$_6q_6 = {_6d_6}/l_6 = (l_6 - l_{12})/l_6 = 0.449.$$

(f) This is the calculation of a Survivorship Ratio, P.

$$P = {_3L_6}/{_3L_3} \times 100 = 2.4465/2.7625 \times 100 = 88.6 \text{ women.}$$

3. Graunt's 1662 London life table (Table A.8).

Table A.8. Graunt's life table for Londoners, 1662

x	n	l_x	$_na_x^*$	$_nL_x$	T_x
0	6	100	0.2	427.2*	1707
6	10	64	0.5	520.0	1280
16	10	40	0.5	325.0	760
26	10	25	0.5	205.0	435
36	10	16	0.5	130.0	230
46	10	10	0.5	80.0	150
56	10	6	0.5	45.0	70
66	10	3	0.5	20.0	25
76	10	1	0.5	5.0†	5

* $_6L_0 = (64 \times 6) + (36 \times 0.2 \times 6)$
† Assuming the one person alive at age 76 lives for five more years.

(a) $_{26}q_0 = 1 - (l_{26}/l_0) = 0.75.$
(b) $_{20}p_{26} = l_{46}/l_{26} = 0.4.$
(c) $e_0 = T_0/l_0 = 17.1$ years.
(d) See the very end of Chapter 6 (p. 78) or, for more details on Stationary populations, the start of Chapter 11 (p. 120).

Chapter 8

1. England and Wales, female nuptiality, 1981:

(a) Calculate the weighted mean where the values are the mid-points of the age groups and the weights are the numbers marrying. The sum of mid-points x Nos marrying is $(16.5 \times 2,685) + (17.5 \times 7,852) + \ldots + (60.0 \times 10,420) = 9,428,170.5$. Nos marrying $= (2,685 + 7,852 + \ldots + 10,420) = 351,973$. So mean age at marriage is $9,428,170.5/351,973 = 26.8$ years.

(b) Calculate the cumulative distribution of the numbers of marrying by exact ages 16, 17, 18 . . . Then find the age by which 50 per cent are married. 50 per cent is 175,987 women, so the median lies somewhere between ages 23 and 24. Interpolation produces a median of about 23.4 years.

(c) Calculate the proportions single (Table A.9). Since figures are available by single years, they should be used in preference to five-year groups, at least up to age 30.

Table A.9. Proportions single, England and Wales females, 1981

Age	% single
15	100.0
16	99.5
17	98.0
18	93.7
19	85.8
20	75.3
21	63.6
22	52.5
23	41.6
24	33.4
25	27.1
26	22.1
27	18.3
28	15.5
29	13.2
30–34	8.7
35–39	6.0
40–44	5.4
45–49	5.7
50–54	6.4

The years of singleness by 100 girls to age 15 is $100 \times 15 = 1,500$. The years of singleness from 15 to 50 (not 55) is $100.0 + \ldots + 13.2 + 5 (8.7 + \ldots + 5.7) = 968.6$. So the total years of singleness to age 50 is $1,500 + 968.6 = 2,468.6$.

The percentage still single at age 50 is $(5.7 + 6.4)/2 = 6.05$. The years of singleness to age 50 by those not marrying is $50 \times 6.05 = 302.5$.

Thus $100 - 6.05 = 93.95$ girls who experienced $2,468.6 - 302.5 = 2,166.1$ years of singleness. The SMAM is therefore $2,166.1/93.95 = 23.1$ years.

The difference between the SMAM and the mean age at marriage is essentially that whereas the mean age at marriage relates only to marriages in 1971, the SMAM is determined partly by marriages which may have taken place thirty or more years ago. The median is a better measure than the mean here because the distribution is markedly skewed.

2. Net Nuptiality Table, England and Wales males, 1980 (Table A.10): This can be done in several ways. They differ in the assumption made about whether, in any interval, those who died single would also have married and whether those who married would have died single. The correct way of taking into account the competing risks of marriage and death is slightly complicated. Here a simpler, close approximation is used.

For age 17 the proportion who died single is $0.979 \times 0.00052 = 0.0005$. The proportion ever married is $0.979 \times 0.00059 = 0.0006$. So the loss from death and marriage is $0.0005 + 0.0006 = 0.0011$, and thus the proportion still single at exact age 17 is $0.979 - 0.0011 = 0.978$.

For age 18 the proportion who died single is $0.978 \times 0.001100 = 0.0011$. The proportion who married is $0.978 \times 0.00360 = 0.0035$. So the loss from death and marriage is $0.0011 + 0.0035 = 0.0046$, and thus the proportion still single at exact age 18 is 0.973.

Table A.10. Net Nuptiality Table, males, England and Wales, 1980

| Exact age x | Proportion who had at age x | | |
	Died single	Ever married	Never married
16	0.0210	0.0000	0.979
17	0.0005	0.0006	0.978
18	0.0011	0.0035	0.973
19	0.0011	0.0156	0.956
20	0.0010	0.0330	0.922
21	0.0009	0.0560	0.865
22	0.0008	0.0785	0.786
23	0.0007	0.0871	0.698
24	0.0006	0.0888	0.609
25	0.0006	0.0803	0.528
26	0.0006	0.0707	0.456
27	0.0006	0.0543	0.401
28	0.0005	0.0478	0.353
29	0.0006	0.0422	0.310

3. Swedish SMAMs:

(a) In 1940 marriage occurs earlier than in 1935, though still 22 per cent never marry. Between 1940 and 1945 this trend continues, but marriage also appears to be becoming more common.

(b) SMAMs

	1935	1940	1945
Years of singleness to age 15:	1500.0	1500.0	1500.0
Years of singleness 15–50:	1667.5	1532.0	1359.0
Total:	3167.5	3032.0	2859.0
Per cent unmarried at 50:	22.6	22.2	21.0
Singleness experienced by the unmarried:	1130.0	1110.0	1050.0
Singleness experienced by those who marry:	2037.5	1922.0	1809.0
Per cent marrying by age 50:	77.4	77.8	79.0
SMAMs:	26.3	24.7	22.9

The SMAM is slower to react to changing trends than the ordinary mean since it reflects nuptiality over twenty or so years. It will thus be higher, unless age structure is extremely odd since the SMAM is age-standardised while the ordinary mean is not.

(c) One can calculate proportions married for a synthetic cohort and then calculate a SMAM for that. For example, the first cohort, 10–14 in 1935 are 15–19 in 1940 and 100 - 98.1 + 1.9 per cent marry in the interval. The second figure is 98.8 − 71.6 = 17.2 per cent. These percentages can then be chained to generate the percentage unmarried from which the SMAM can be produced in the usual way. The first value is 98.1, the second 98.1 × (100 − 17.2), and so on.

Chapter 9

1. Hong Kong reproductivity 1973.

Table A.11. Net Reproduction Rate: female ASFRs and Net Maternity Distribution: Hong Kong, 1973

Age group	Female ASFRs*	Age x	l_x	$_5L_x$	Net Maternity Distribution (FASFR × $_5L_x$)
15–19	0.008	15	0.97518	4.8694	0.0390
20–24	0.063	20	0.97258	4.8544	0.3058
25–29	0.119	25	0.96196	4.8360	0.5755
30–34	0.068	30	0.96524	4.8133	0.3273
35–39	0.035	35	0.96006	4.7803	0.1673
40–44	0.011	40	0.95205	4.7324	0.0521
45–49	0.002	45	0.94091	4.6632	0.0093
		50	0.92435		

* Assuming a Sex Ratio at Birth of 105 : 100

$$\text{GRR} = \Sigma \text{ Female ASFRs} \times 5 = 1.53$$

$$\text{NRR} = \Sigma \text{ Net Maternity Distribution} = 1.48$$

The NRR is only slightly less than the GRR, indicating that mortality is very low in Hong Kong, a feature also apparent from the l_x column. Thus Hong Kong women would produce, on average, about 1.5 daughters if they were to experience the 1973 Hong Kong levels of fertility and mortality.

Chapter 11

1. USA Stable population 1920.

Table A.12. Female ASFRs and Net Maternity Distribution: United States, 1920

Age group $x - x+5$	Female ASFRs	$l_{x + 2.5}$	$_5L_x$	Net Maternity Distribution
10–14	0.00009	0.88567	4.42835	0.00040
15–19	0.02202	0.87438	4.37190	0.09627
20–24	0.07310	0.85509	4.27545	0.31254
25–29	0.07481	0.82960	4.14800	0.31031
30–34	0.05780	0.80181	4.00905	0.23172
35–39	0.03898	0.77417	3.87085	0.15089
40–44	0.01552	0.74664	3.73320	0.05794
45–49	0.00172	0.71610	3.58050	0.00616
50–54	0.00005	0.62937	3.14685	0.00016

Using the data calculated in Table A.12:

$$\text{NRR} = \text{Sum of Net Maternity Distribution} = 1.16639 = 1.17.$$

The Mean Length of Generation, T, is estimated as the Mean Age of Childbearing, μ (mu).

$$\mu = ((12.5 \times 0.00040) + (17.5 \times 0.09627) + \ldots + (52.5 \times 0.00016))/\text{NRR}$$

$$= 28.4709 = 28.5 \text{ years.}$$

So the Intrinsic Rate of Natural Increase is $\text{Log}_e\text{NRR}/T = 0.005406 = 0.54$ per cent per annum. The Intrinsic Doubling Time is $\text{Log}_e 2.0/0.005406 = 128$ years, and the Crude Doubling Time is $\text{Log}_e 2.0/0.0101 = 69$ years.

2. England and Wales halving time: This is the same as calculating the doubling time except 0.5 is used instead of 2.0. The Intrinsic Growth Rate, r, is given as -0.0057, so the halving time is $\text{Log}_e 0.5/-0.0057 = 21.6$ years.

3. Norwegian growth rates, 1984: Using the data in Table A.13, $\mu = 21.8722/0.79857 = 27.39$ years, which is approximately equal to T. For the Intrinsic Growth Rate, $r = (\text{Log}_e 0.79857)/27.39 = -0.0082 = -0.8$ per cent per annum.

Table A.13. Growth rates: Norway, 1984

Age x	l_x ($l_0 = 1.0$)	$_5L_x$	ASFRs per woman Both sexes	Females*	Net Maternity Distribution	Mid-. points	Product
15	0.9887	4.94275	0.0192	0.00937	0.04631	17.5	0.8104
20	0.9884	4.94125	0.0939	0.04580	0.22631	22.5	5.0920
25	0.9881	4.93975	0.1237	0.06034	0.29806	27.5	8.1967
30	0.9878	4.93775	0.0683	0.03332	0.16453	32.5	5.3472
35	0.9873	4.93500	0.0222	0.01083	0.05345	37.5	2.0044
40	0.9867	4.93050	0.0041	0.00200	0.00986	42.5	0.4191
45	0.9855	4.92225	0.0002	0.00001	0.00005	47.5	0.0024
50	0.9834				0.79857		21.8722

* Assuming a Sex Ratio at Birth of 105 : 100

4. England and Wales 1973 Stable Population: Because the NRR is exactly 1.0, the Intrinsic Growth Rate must be zero, so the Stable population is in fact Stationary and thus just the life table $_nL_x$ column, (Table A.14). The main differences between the actual and Stable distribution are due to past fluctuations in fertility, though the rapidly declining IMR may also be significant.

Table A.14. Stable population: Engand and Wales females, 1973

Age x	$_nL_x$	%
0	4 912*	6.5
5	4 908	6.5
10	4 903	6.5
15	4 895	6.5
20	4 885	6.5
25	4 873	6.4
30	4 858	6.4
35	4 835	6.4
40	4 798	6.3
45	4 733	6.3
50	4 630	6.1
55	4 480	5.9
60	4 260	5.6
65	3 933	5.2
70	3 440	4.6
75	2 720	3.6
80+	3 525	3.2
Total	75 788	100.0

*$_5a_0$ assumed to be 0.1

Chapter 12

1. Childhood mortality, Keneba, Gambia: The raw data can be rewritten, excluding the one week and one month figures, as shown in Table A.15. To fit a Coale–Demeny model, first use the figures for l_1 to l_5 given in Table 12E.2. Inspection of only l_1 and l_5 for each family shows South to be clearly the best fitting family and Level 3 or 4 to be closest to the observed level of mortality.

Table A.15. Childhood mortality: Keneba, Gambia

Age x	l_x
0	100 000
1	76 100
2	64 300
3	56 500
4	52 300
5	50 100

Determining the best fitting South model poses two problems. First, the raw data combines both sexes, while the tables split males and females. One solution is to amalgamate the models in proportion to the Sex Ratio at Birth (e.g. 105 : 100), but this is time-consuming and not really necessary. Instead, just use the best model, irrespective of its sex. Second, the phrase 'best fit' is vague. Algebraically, it can be defined in many ways, such as the model giving the smallest maximum difference between the observed and model values, the smallest average difference or, most commonly, as the smallest sum of squared differences. Here the last is used, and the process is simply to calculate d^2 for likely candidates. The differences are calculated in the following Table A.16.

Table A.16. Calculating the differences between observed and model values

x	Obs. l_x	South, M, 3 l_x	Diff.	South, M, 4 l_x	Diff.	South, F, 3 l_x	Diff.
1	76 100	71 056	−5 044	73 058	−3 042	73 567	−2 533
2	64 300	59 951	−4 349	62 645	−1 655	61 479	−2 821
3	56 500	54 829	−1 671	57 842	+1 342	55 913	− 587
4	52 300	52 083	− 217	55 267	+2 967	52 974	+ 674
5	50 100	50 567	+ 467	53 846	+3 746	51 304	+1 204

Squaring and summing the differences gives:

South, males, Level 3   47,413,156
South, males, Level 4   36,629,358
South, females, Level 3 16,622,591

d^2 is smallest for South, females, Level 3, so that is the best-fitting model life table. The whole life table is shown in the first panel of Table 12E.3 (p. 146). The expectation of life at birth is 25.00 years and at age 5 it is 42.58 years. The probability of surviving from 0–4 to 5–9 is the second number in the $P(x)$ column; that is 0.77965.

This example is contrived for several reasons. In particular, it is not a good idea in reality to fit a model only to data on child mortality as is done here, unless only child mortality is of interest. Some estimate of adult mortality should also be used because the relationship between adult and child mortality in Keneba may be very different from any of the model life-table patterns. This may also be true even within the young ages. In Keneba the data suggest that child mortality is higher, relative to infant mortality, than in any of the Coale–Demeny models.

2. Icelandic mortality: Comparisons of the differences between the observed and model figures clearly shows the East model to be the best fitting. This is perhaps surprising since Icelandic life tables were used in the construction of the North family. The òther models fail badly to fit the extremely high observed infant mortality rate. This suggests that infant mortality was unusually high (around 170 per 1,000) in mid-nineteenth century Iceland. A less plausible explanation is over-reporting of infant deaths.

Chapter 13

1. Malawi 1970–2.

Table A.17. Fitting logit relational model life table: Malawi, 1970–2

Age	Obs.				Fitted	
x	l_x	$Y_{Obs}(x)$	$Y_s(x)$	$Y_{Fit}(x)$	l_x	l_x
0	1.000				1.0000	1 000
1	0.858	−0.8994	−0.8670	−0.4256	0.7008	701
5	0.653	−0.3161	−0.6016	−0.2515	0.6232	623
10	0.603	−0.2090	−0.5498	−0.2176	0.6071	607
15	0.592	−0.1861	−0.5131	−0.1935	0.5956	596
20	0.559	−0.1186	−0.4551	−0.1555	0.5771	577
25	0.548	−0.0963	−0.3829	−0.1081	0.5538	554
30	0.528	−0.0561	−0.3150	−0.0636	0.5318	532
35	0.511	−0.0220	−0.2496	0.0207	0.4897	490
40	0.492	0.0160	−0.1817	0.0238	0.4881	488
45	0.460	0.0802	−0.1073	0.0726	0.4638	464
50	0.435	0.1307	−0.0212	0.1291	0.4358	436
55	0.404	0.1944	0.0832	0.1976	0.4025	403
60	0.381	0.2427	0.2100	0.2807	0.3632	363

First plot observed against standard logits, $Y_{obs}(x)$ and $Y_s(x)$. To fit the line use the Group Average Method. Because the points for ages 1 and 60 look very out of line, exclude them from the fitting process (Fig. A.2). Split the other points roughly in half, 5–25 (five points) and 30–55 (six points), and find the average of each group.

The first, for example, is calculated as:

$$(-0.3161 + -0.2090 + -0.1861 + -0.1186 + -0.0963)/5$$

The average $Y_{Obs}(x)$ points are: −0.185 and +0.057 and the average $Y_s(x)$ points are: −0.501 and −0.132.

The value of β is:

$$\frac{-0.185 - 0.057}{-0.501 - -0.132} = \frac{-0.242}{-0.369} = 0.6558$$

and, using for convenience one of the group average points:

$$\alpha = -0.185 - (0.6558 \times -0.501) = 0.143.$$

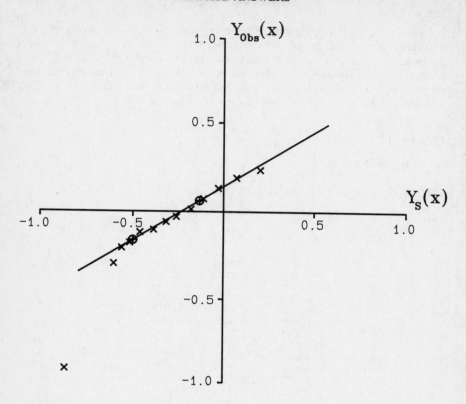

Figure A.2 Malawi logits

The fitted logits, $Y_{Fit}(x)$ are then obtained using the formula $Y_{Fit}(x) = \alpha + \beta\, Y_s(x)$ and the fitted l_xs are found using the inverse of the logit transformation (see p. 162).

Comparison of the fitted and observed values suggests that the model fits the data very badly. In particular, the figures for infant and child mortality are very different. This may be due either to the omission of infant deaths or to their deaths being reported as occurring after rather than before age 1. If it is the former, then there are serious problems because then all the l_x values are wrong.

Overall, the process of fitting the model only enables one to say that the reported pattern of infant and child mortality in Malawi is very odd. Child mortality seems to be extremely high relative to infant mortality. This may actually be true, or it may be due to misreporting and omissions. Without further data it is impossible to go further. Using the African Standard might improve matters, but only marginally, and to fit a four-parameter model would imply that one accepted, more or less, that child mortality is in reality extremely high relative to infant mortality in Malawi.

2. Farr's English Life Table for 1841: The fitting of the line in Figure A.3 can be done by the Group Average Method, but the points form such a straight line that fitting by eye is equally good. α is about 0.04, β about 0.92. These imply that mortality is

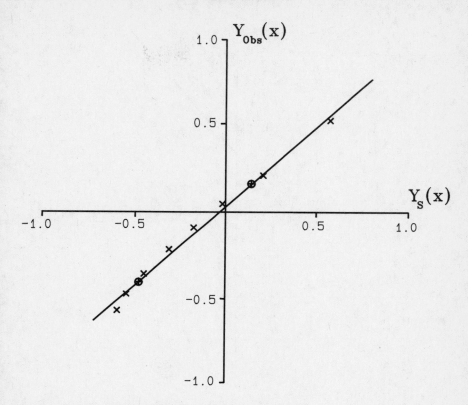

Figure A.3 Farr's England and Wales 1841 logits

slightly higher than in the General Standard and the ratio of child to adult mortality is slightly lower. The differences are, however, small. The fitted l_{15} is about 0.7050, derived from a $Y_{Fit}(15)$ of -0.4357.

The more parameters, the more flexible the model. Flexibility is a good thing if the data are trustworthy since it allows the supposedly real features of the data to show through. If, however, the data are poor, a more rigid model is better as it will smooth out the supposedly erroneous irregular features of the data.

3. Halley's Breslau life table: The observed IMR is $l_0 - l_1 = 145$ per 1,000. The plot of observed and standard logits below reveals a curved line of points, a common result, normally caused by the omission of infant deaths and exaggeration of age by the elderly. This indicates that when fitting the line the points for ages 1 and 80 should be ignored (perhaps also 5 and 70). Fitting the line by eye is quite suitable as more sophisticated methods would only give slightly different answers. $Y_{Fit}(1)$ can then be read directly from the graph (Fig. A.4). There is no need to find α and β. The figure is about -0.67, which converts to a fitted l_1 of 0.793. This implies an IMR of 207. This estimate is probably more accurate than the old, observed figure of 145 since there is evidence of

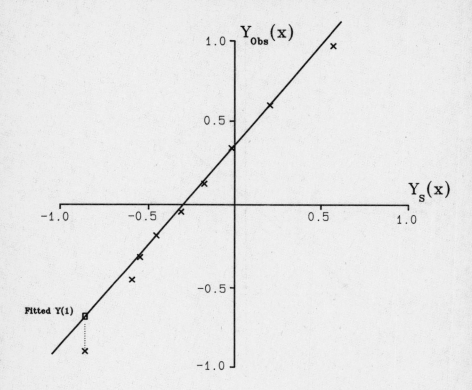

Figure A.4 Halley's Breslau logits

omission of infant deaths. However, it may be that the pattern of mortality in Breslau in 1690 was far removed from that of the General (or African) Standard. Another possibility is the reporting of infant deaths as occurring after age 1.

If the new estimate of the IMR is accepted, then, because subsequent l_xs are calculated by chaining down from l_0, the other observed l_xs become inconsistent with it. One must either fit and accept the whole of a fitted model, or none of it. Replacing just one or two observed values with fitted ones does not work.

Chapter 14

1. Modelling Barbados fertility.

Table A.18. Modelling Barbados fertility — basic data

Age group	ASFR (per 1)	Propn	Age x	Cumul. propn	$Y_{Obs}(x)$	$Y_s(x)$
15–19	0.0612	0.1489	20	0.1489	−0.6442	−0.6913
20–24	0.1170	0.2847	25	0.4336	+0.1796	+0.0256
25–29	0.1038	0.2526	30	0.6862	+0.9766	+0.7000
30–34	0.0759	0.1847	35	0.8709	+1.9788	+1.4787
35–39	0.0350	0.0852	40	0.9561	+3.1035	+2.6260
40–44	0.0181	0.0440	45	1.0000		
Total:	0.4110	1.0000				

$(x5 = \text{TFR} = 2.0550)$

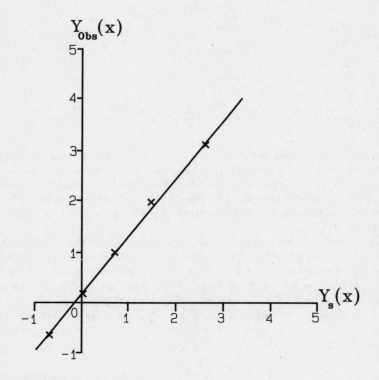

Figure A.5 Barbados Gompertz

Table A19. Modelling Barbados fertility — calculations

Age x	$Y_s(x)$	$Y_{Fit}(x)$ ($\alpha = .11$, $\beta = 1.18$)	Fitted Cumul. ASFRs	Age group	Fitted propn ASFSs
20	−0.6913	−0.7057	0.1319	15–19	0.1319
25	+0.0256	+0.1402	0.4193	20–24	0.2874
30	+0.7000	+0.9360	0.6756	25–29	0.2563
35	−1.4787	+1.8549	0.8552	30–34	0.1796
40	+2.6260	+3.2087	0.9604	35–39	0.1052
				40–44	0.0396*
					1.0000

* Obtained by subtraction

Table A.20. Modelling Barbados fertility — fitted and observed values

Age group	Fitted ASFRs (using Obs. TFR)	Observed ASFRs
15–19	0.0542	0.0612
20–24	0.1181	0.1170
25–29	0.1053	0.1038
30–34	0.0738	0.0759
35–39	0.0432	0.0350
40–44	0.0163	0.0181
	TFR = 2.0550	TFR = 2.0550

This example is simplified in two important ways. First, because the observed ASFRs are calculated from reports on births during the previous year, the women will have been, on average, half a year younger at the time of the birth than at the time of the census. Thus the ASFRs really refer to the exact age groups 14.5–19.5, 19.5–24.5 . . . The standard Gompits used to fit the model should therefore really be for ages 14.5, 19.5 . . . rather than 15, 20 . . . .

Second it is assumed here that the observed TFR is accurate. All the model is doing, therefore, is smoothing the ASFRs. The assumption that the TFR is accurate is unlikely to hold in most parts of the world. Fortunately, there is a technique, called the Ratio Method (Zaba 1981), which uses the Gompertz model to estimate total fertility, though the procedure is too complex to be included in a simple example.

The results reveal that the fitted ASFRs are generally close to the observed ones, and there is thus no evidence from this of poor reporting of age or under reporting of births by some age groups.

Chapter 15

1. Bangladesh projection 1974 to 1979: Use a simple component projection. The base population is the 'corrected' age distribution produced from the results of the 1974 survey. The assumptions made are, first, that the level and pattern of fertility will remain

constant at 1974 estimates. Second, the level and pattern of mortality will be constant at Princeton West Region, Level 12, which gives an e_0 of 47.5 for females and 44.5 for males. This is reasonably close to the estimates from the survey. Third, there is zero net migration into or from any age/sex category.

Note that the base population figures are adjusted to take account of age misreporting and so on. They are also adjusted to correspond with the total population figure derived from the 1974 Bangladesh Census — 76.4 million — a figure which included an estimate of underenumeration of 5 million (subsequently revised). All this implies that these base population figures may be to some extent wrong.

Table A.21. Projecting Bangladesh population 1974–9 — mortality

Age group	1974 Popn	Males West, M, 12 $P(x)$	1979 Popn	1974 Popn	Females West, F, 12 $P(x)$	1979 Popn
0–4	7 457	0.93430	8 379*	7 192	0.93573	8 150*
5–9	5 820	0.98108	6 967	5 625	0.97994	6 730
10–14	4 730	0.97938	5 710	4 533	0.97794	5 512
15–19	4 017	0.97076	4 632	3 777	0.97122	4 433
20–24	3 362	0.96379	3 900	3 101	0.96561	3 668
25–29	2 891	0.95932	3 240	2 636	0.96110	2 994
30–34	2 391	0.95258	2 773	2 161	0.95627	2 533
35–39	1 983	0.94269	2 278	1 793	0.95136	2 066
40–44	1 635	0.92966	1 869	1 484	0.94523	1 706
45–49	1 343	0.91070	1 520	1 222	0.93247	1 403
50–54	1 066	0.88344	1 223	974	0.91091	1 139
55–59	858	0.84357	941	784	0.87608	887
60–64	658	0.78593	724	601	0.82407	687
65–69	487	0.70832	517	440	0.75034	495
70–74	339	0.59517	345	304	0.63844	330
75+	399	0.40000†	202‡	334	0.43000†	194‡
80+			160			144
			45 381			43 071

* Computed in Table A. 22
† Estimated in an arbitrary way
‡ Relates to the 75–79 age group

In Table A.21 the 1974 population is survived to 1979, separately for males and females, using the $P(x)$ column of the life tables. In Table A.22 the births occurring between 1974 and 1979 are calculated by applying the ASFRs to the average population of females. The 19,971 are split into male and female births using a Sex Ratio at Birth of 105.6 (i.e. proportion of females of 0.488), and are survived using the Survivorship Ratios which Coale and Demeny label P (Birth) (0.83896 for Females and 0.81679 for Males.) The resulting figures for the 0–4 age group are included in Table A.21.

The projected total population in 1979 is thus 45,381 + 43,071 = 88.4 million. This compares with the Population Council's estimate of 87.1 million. Given the fact that both the base population used, and the assumptions made, may be somewhat wrong, the difference is not large. If mortality has been falling the projected figures would be higher, while if fertility is falling, then they would be lower. Migration may also be significant.

Table A.22. Projecting Bangladesh population 1974–9 — fertility

Age group	ASFRs	Female population 1974	1979	Av. 1974–9	Estimated births
15–19	0.198	3 777	4 433	4 105	4 064
20–24	0.337	3 101	3 668	3 385	5 704
25–29	0.311	2 636	2 994	2 815	4 377
30–34	0.262	2 161	2 533	2 347	3 075
35–39	0.197	1 793	2 066	1 930	1 901
40–44	0.095	1 484	1 706	1 595	758
45–49	0.014	1 222	1 403	1 313	92
Total					19 971

2. Barbados migration 1970–80: The 1970 population aged 10–40 is projected for ten years using an assumption of no migration. The difference between the projected and actual totals is the estimate of net migration. The first Survivorship Ratio, 0.9898 is calculated as $_5L_{20}/_5L_{10}$. The projected 1980 20–24 year olds is then 14,996 × 0.9898 = 14,843. The projected population aged 20–50 is 51,696 which compares with an actual census count of 43,367. The estimated net migration is thus 8,329. This figure would be a poor estimate if completeness of coverage at the two censuses was different; if age-reporting in the two censuses was of different quality; or if the mortality schedule used (Coale–Demeny West Level 22) was wrong in respect of either level or pattern. One way of improving the estimate would be to do a back projection from 1980 to 1970 of the same cohort and take the average of the resulting estimate and the one above.

Table A.23. Actual (1970) and projected (1980) male population: Barbados

Age group	Male popn 1970	$_5L_x$	Ten-year Survivorship Ratios P_x	Projected 1980 popn
10–14	14 996	479 193	0.9898	—
15–19	12 829	477 275	0.9864	—
20–24	9 875	474 287	0.9848	14 843
25–29	5 724	470 794	0.9827	12 654
30–34	4 808	467 100	0.9774	9 725
35–39	4 295	462 661	0.9665	5 624
40–44	4 540	456 544	—	4 699
45–49	4 300	447 177	—	4 151

References

Armitage, P. (1971) *Statistical Methods in Medical Research*, Oxford: Blackwell.

Barclay, G.W. (1958) *Techniques of Population Analysis*, New York: Wiley.

Blacker, C.P. (1947) 'Stages in Population Growth', *Eugenics Review 39*: 88–101.

Bongaarts J. and Potter, R.G. (1983) *Fertility, Biology and Behaviour: An Analysis of the Proximate Determinants*, New York: Academic Press.

Booth, H. (1984) 'Transforming Gompertz's Function for Fertility Analysis: The Development of a Standard for the Relational Gompertz Function', *Population Studies 38*: 495–506.

Brass, W. (1971) 'On the Scale of Mortality', in W. Brass (ed.) *Biological Aspects of Demography*, London: Taylor & Francis.

Brass, W. (1975) *Methods For Estimating Fertility and Mortality from Limited and Defective Data*, Chapel Hill, NC: Poplab, University of North Carolina.

Brass, W. (1981) 'The Use of the Gompertz Relational Model to Estimate Fertility', *IUSSP Population Conference, Manilla*, vol. 3, pp. 345–61.

Bulusu, L. (1986) 'Recent Patterns of Migration to and from the United Kingdom', *Population Trends 46*: 35–9.

Campbell, A.A. (1983) *Manual of Fertility Analysis*, London: Livingstone/Longman.

Carrier, N.H. and Hobcraft, J. (1973) *Demographic Estimation for Developing Societies*, London: Population Investigation Committee, London School of Economics.

Cassen, R. and Dyson, T. (1976) 'New Population Projections for India', *Population and Development Review 2*: 101–36.

Chandrasekar, C. and Deming, W.E. (1949) 'On a Method for Estimating Birth and Death Rates and the Extent of Registration', *Journal of the American Statistical Association 44*: 101–15.

Chiang, C.L. (no date) *Life Table and Mortality Analysis*, Geneva: World Health Organisation.

Coale, A.J. (1955) 'The Calculation of Approximate Intrinsic Rates', *Population Index 21*: 94–7.

Coale, A.J. (1957) 'A New Method for Calculating Lotka's r: The Intrinsic Rate of Growth in a Stable Population', *Population Studies 11*: 92–4.

Coale, A.J. (1967) 'Factors Associated with the Development of Low Fertility: An Historic Summary', *Proceedings of the World Population Conference, 1965*, vol. 2, pp. 205–9.

Coale, A.J. (1971) 'Age Patterns at Marriage', *Population Studies 25*: 193–214.

Coale, A.J. (1973) 'The Demographic Transition', *Proceedings of the 1973 IUSSP Conference*, Liege, vol. 1 pp. 53–72.

Coale, A.J. (1977) 'The Development of New Models of Nuptiality and Fertility', *Population 32, (Numero Spéciale)*: 131–50.

Coale, A.J. and Demeny, P. (1966) *Regional Model Life Tables and Stable Populations*, Princeton, NJ: Princeton University Press.

Coale, A.J. and Demeny, P. (1983) *Regional Model Life Tables and Stable Populations*, 2nd ed, New York, Academic Press.

Coale, A.J. and McNeil, D.R. (1972) 'The Distribution by Age of the Frequency of First

Marriage in a Female Cohort', *Journal of the American Statistical Association* 67: 743–9.

Coale, A.J. and Trussell, T.J. (1974) 'Model Fertility Schedules: Variations in the Age Structure of Childbearing in Human Populations', *Population Index* 40: 185–258.

Cochran, W.G. (1977) *Sampling Techniques*, 3rd ed., New York: Wiley.

Cox, P.R. *Demography* 5th ed., Cambridge: Cambridge University Press.

Dublin, L.I. and Lotka, A.J. (1925) 'On the True Rate of Natural Increase, as Exemplified by the Population of the United States 1920', *Journal of the American Statistical Association* 20: 305–39.

Dublin, L.I. and Lotka, A.J. (1936) *Length of Life: A Study of the Life Table*, New York: Ronald.

Euler, L. (1760) 'A General Investigation into the Mortality and Multiplication of the Human Species' (English translation), *Theoretical Population Biology 1 (1970)*: 307–14. Also reprinted in Smith and Keyfitz (1977).

Ewbank, D.C., Gomez de Leon, J.C. and Stoto, M.A. (1983) 'A Reducible Four-Parameter System of Model Life Tables', *Population Studies* 37: 105–27.

Frejka, T. (1973) *The Future of Population Growth: Alternative Paths to Equilibrium*, New York: Wiley.

Glass, D.V. (1940) *Population Policies and Movements in Europe*, Oxford: Oxford University Press.

Glass, D.V. (1950) 'Graunt's Life Tables', *Journal of the Institute of Actuaries* 76: 60–4.

Hajnal, J. (1953) 'Age at Marriage and Proportions Marrying', *Population Studies*, 7: 115–36.

Hajnal, J. (1965) 'European Marriage Patterns in Perspective', in D.V. Glass and D.E.C. Eversley (eds) *Population in History*, London: Arnold.

Halley, E. (1693) 'An Estimate of the Degree of the Mortality of Mankind Drawn from Curious Tables of the Births and Funerals at the City of Breslau', *Philosophical Transactions of the Royal Society of London* 17: 596–610.

Henry, L. (1961) 'Some Data on Natural Fertility', *Eugenics Quarterly* 8: 81–91.

Henry, L. (1972a) *On the Measurement of Human Fertility: Selected Writings of Louis Henry*, Amsterdam: Elsevier.

Henry, L. (1972b) 'Nuptiality', *Theoretical Population Biology* 3: 135–52.

Hill, A.B. (1978) 'Model Fertility Schedules and Their Uses', in United Nations Economic Commission for Western Asia (ed.) *The Population Framework*, Beirut: United Nations.

Keyfitz, N. (1968) *Introduction to the Mathematics of Population*, Reading, Mass: Addison-Wesley.

Keyfitz, N. and Flieger, W. (1971) *Population: Facts and Methods of Demography*, San Francisco: Freeman.

Kosinski, L. A. (1975) 'Data and Measures in Migration Research', in L.A. Kosinski and A.M. Prothero (eds) *People on the Move: Studies in Internal Migration*, London: Methuen.

Kuczynski, R.R. (1935) *The Measurement of Population Growth; Methods and Results*, London: Sidgwick and Jackson.

Langford, C.M. (1976) *Birth Control Practice and Marital Fertility in Great Britain: A Report on a Survey Carried Out in 1967–68*, London: Population Investigation Committee, London School of Economics.

Ledermann, S. and Breas, J. (1959) 'Les dimensions de la mortalité', *Population* 14, 637–82.

Leslie, P.H. (1945) 'On the Use of Matrices in Population Mathematics', *Biometrika* 33, 183–212.

Leslie, P.H. (1948) 'Some Further Notes on the Use of Matrices in Population Mathematics', *Biometrika* 35: 213–45.

Lesthaeghe, R. (1971) 'Nuptiality and Population Growth', *Population Studies* 25: 415–32.

Lotka, A.J. (1907) 'Relation Between Birth Rates and Death Rates', *Science* N.S., 26: 21–2.

Lotka, A.J. (1922) 'The Stability of the Normal Age Distribution', *Proceedings of the National Academy of Sciences* 8: 339–45.

Malthus, T.R. (1798) *An Essay on the Principle of Population*, ed. A. Flew, London: Penguin, 1970.

Menken, J.A. (1978) 'Current Status of Demographic Models', *Population Bulletin of the United Nations*, No. 9, 22–34.

Milne, J. (1815) *A Treatise on the Valuation of Annuities and Assurances on Lives and Survivors*, London: Longman.

Moser, C.A. and Kalton, G. (1971) *Survey Methods in Social Investigation*, 2nd ed., London: Heinemann.

Norges Offisielle Statistikk (1985) *Folkemengdens Bevegelse 1984*, Oslo: Government of Norway.

Notestein, F.W. (1945) 'Population: The Long View', in T.W. Schultz (ed.) *Food for the World*, Chicago: Chicago University Press.

ODM (1977) *Report of the 1974 Bangladesh Retrospective Survey of Fertility and Mortality*, Population Bureau, UK Ministry of Overseas Development, London, with the Census Commission, Statistics Division, Ministry of Planning, Dacca.

OPCS (1975) *International Migration*, UK Office of Population Censuses and Surveys, series MN, no. 2, London: HMSO.

OPCS (1983) 'Population Definitions', *Population Trends* 33: 21–5.

OPCS (1984) *Death Statistics 1982*, UK Office of Population Census and Surveys, series DH, no. 13, London: HMSO.

Page, H.J. and Lesthaeghe, R. (eds) (1980) *Childspacing in Tropical Africa: Traditions and Change*, New York: Academic Press.

Pollard, A.H., Yusuf, F. and Pollard, G.N. (1981) *Demographic Techniques*, 2nd ed., Oxford: Pergamon.

Pressat, R. (1972) *Demographic Analysis*, London: Arnold.

Pressat, R. (1974) *A Workbook in Demography*, London: Methuen.

Rogers, A. (1975) *Introduction to Multiregional Mathematical Demography*, New York: Wiley.

Ryder, N. (1968) 'Cohort Analysis', in D.E. Sills, (ed.) *International Encyclopaedia of the Social Sciences*, vol. 2, New York: Macmillan.

Ryder, N. (1980) 'Components of Temporal Variation in American Fertility', in R.W. Hiorns (ed.) *Demographic Patterns in Developed Societies*, London: Taylor & Francis.

Ryder, N. (1982) 'Fertility Trends', *International Encyclopaedia of Population*, vol. 1, London and Glencoe, Ill.: Macmillan/Free Press.

Sharpe, F.R. and Lotka, A.j. (1911) 'A Problem in Age Distribution', *Philosophical Magazine*, Series 6, 21: 435–8.

Shorter, F. and Pasta, D. (1974) *Computational Methods for Population Projection*, New York: Population Council.

Shryock, H.S. and Seigel, J.S. (1976) *The Methods and Materials of Demography*, abridged ed., New York: Academic Press.

Smith, D.P. and Keyfitz, N. (eds) (1977) *Mathematical Demography; Selected Papers*, Berlin: Springer-Verlag.

Spiegelman, M. (1968) *Introduction to Demography* 2nd edn. Cambridge, Mass.: Harvard University Press.

United Nations (1955) 'Age and Sex Patterns of Mortality: Model Life Tables for Underdeveloped Countries', *Department of Social and Economic Affairs, Population Studies*, no 22.

United Nations (1956) 'Methods for Population Projections by Sex and Age', *Department of Social and Economic Affairs, Population Studies* no. 25.

United Nations (1982) 'Model Life Tables for Developing Countries', *Department of International Social and Economic Affairs, Population Studies*, no. 77.

United Nations (1983) 'Indirect Techniques for Demographic Estimation', *Department of International Social and Economic Affairs, Population Studies*, no. 81.

US Bureau of the Census (1986) *Current Population Reports*, series P-25, no. 985.

van de Walle, E. (1982) *Multilingual Demographic Dictionary, English Section*, Liege: IUSSP Ordina.

Whelpton, P.K. (1954) *Cohort Fertility: Native White Women in the United States*, Princeton, N.J.: Princeton University Press.

White, P. and Woods, R.I. (eds) (1980) *The Geographical Impact of Migration*, London: Longman.

Woods, R. (1979) *Population Analysis in Geography*, London: Longman.

Woods, R. (1982) *Theoretical Population Geography*, London: Longman.

Wunsch, G.J. and Termote, M.G. (1978) *Introduction to Demographic Analysis: Principles and Methods*, New York: Plenum.

Zaba, B. (1979) 'The Four-Parameter Logit Life Table System', *Population Studies* 33: 79–100.

Zaba, B. (1981) 'Use of the Relational Gompertz Model in Analysing Data Collected in Retrospective Surveys', *Centre for Population Studies Working Paper 81–2*, London: London School of Hygiene and Tropical Medicine.

Zelinsky, W. (1971) 'The Hypothesis of the Mobility Transition', *Geographical Review* 61: 219–49.

Zelinsky, W. (1979) 'The Demographic Transition: Changing Patterns of Migration', in IUSSP, *Population Science in the Service of Mankind*, Liege: Ordina.

Index